THE BELT BOY

KEVIN LUESHING

THE BELT BOY

As told to
MIKE DUNN

AUSTIN MACAULEY
PUBLISHERS LTD.

A CIP catalogue record for this title is available from the British Library.

ISBN: 978-1-78612-909-3

www.austinmacauley.com

First Published (2016)

Austin Macauley Publishers Ltd.
25 Canada Square
Canary Wharf
London
E14 5LQ

Printed and bound in Great Britain

DEDICATION

I am dedicating this autobiography to the NSPCC – and also to my own children, Louie and April; to the only woman I have ever been faithful to, Zoe Floyd; to Morgan Blake – and to the memory of my unlikely saviour, Stella. She helped save my life – in the same way the NSPCC can save a child and the adult that child will become.

ACKNOWLEDGEMENTS

Kevin would like to thank Zoe for putting up with all his highs and lows and for being so supportive during the past year as he has written this book.

He would also like to extend a special thank you to Maria Pedro, who introduced him to the NSPCC and, in so doing, helped change his life.

Further, he would like to add: "I wish to acknowledge Mike Dunn's patience and persistence with me in times when I wanted to throw in the towel. A true friend in need, is a friend indeed!"

Mike would like to thank his daughter Eleanor, son Luke and wife Sally for being ferocious critics. They were right just about every time. And special thanks to a remarkable author, Wallace Peters; front cover photographer Mark Robinson; design advisor Michael Maurer; and friends David and Norma Savery. They all helped in their unique ways.

Finally, Mike would like to offer 'respect' to Kevin Lueshing for having the courage and strength to dare to bare his soul. Once a champion, always a champion.

Both Kevin and Mike would like to thank their friend Mike Gruber, who believed in this project from the start and helped make it a reality.

CONTENTS

INTRODUCTION

THIS IS THE WORST BEATING I EVER TOOK.

Bang -- a vicious blow explodes straight into my solar plexus and the pain is blasting across every part of my body, letting me know it's there and ripping to shreds any scraps of resistance I may have left.

Bang – this time straight into the liver and that's a pain like no other. *Bang* – to the top of my head; *bang* – on the arms – one, two, three in succession and each strike hits a fresh point of pain that instantly feels worse than the previous ones.

I raise my inadequate hands for a shield but there is no escape from this onslaught.

My opponent knows what he's doing: he's stronger, he's bigger, he's more ruthless and he's hurting me badly. He is towering over me in every way, crushing me with his raw, brutal and utterly remorseless power.

I want to crawl away, I want to run but I'm hemmed in, there's no escape from this barrage. I can't dodge, can't summon the strength to duck and dive. I can't run, I'm paralysed, totally static as the blows come cascading towards me.

My body erupts into bruises, ugly red scars polluting my skin, and – as the physical damage disfigures me – I realise my mental strength is evaporating, too. It feels like I'm being beaten into a pulp, like carrots and parsnips in a blender, smashed and pulverised and reduced to a vegetative state so there is no strength, no ability to think, no courage left.

No dignity.

And through this infinite onslaught, I am felled by an icy coldness. I want to scream: "Please, please, end this coldness."

And then I'm on the floor and my arms are around my head. I'm trying to comfort myself, I'm trying to protect the top of my head,

I'm in a pathetic foetal position, nakedly exposed and completely vulnerable. My defences are shot, I am degraded; I am a wreck, a shambles, a disgrace, there is nothing left of me.

Tears are burning my eyes, pride and courage are turning to water. It should never end like this. Then, in the blind panic, I sense my opponent is closing in on me: I turn and see a wild, raging, tormented monster. Instinctively, I look for the eyes of the deranged beast who is doing this to me, because that's the only mental reaction I have left. Look into the eyes of your opponent to see where the next blow is coming from.

So I lie there, utterly broken, utterly crumpled, utterly battered and bruised, barely daring to look up.

Our stares lock and I shiver with fear and dread and loathing and hatred and rage and anger and agony as I look directly into the eyes of…

My father.

PART ONE:
MY CHILDHOOD

Chapter One

BLOOD IN THE SNOW

MY FATHER WAS A MAN I COULD NEVER LOVINGLY CALL 'Dad', no matter how much I wanted to. And I really wanted to, in the natural, happy way any son should call his father.

I could only call him by his Christian name, George, because – by the time I was five years old – he had already beaten emotion and love out of my tiny body and soul.

I would only call him Dad if I was begging for mercy.

Beatings were a cruel, callous and regular way of life in my childhood. I genuinely can't recall happiness, laughter, Christmas, birthdays, a harmonious family growing together in a loving environment.

We were the opposite: totally dysfunctional. I had three brothers and two sisters; we grew up in wretched poverty. Christmas presents would be necessities – socks, pants, jumpers. Where most children enjoyed laughter and love in equal measure I endured pain, hatred, fear, racism and physical abuse. In equal measures.

Beatings were the only constant but the crimes never justified the punishments. Ever.

I took many but the one I have just referred to was by far the worst. In fact it became legendary among my brothers and sisters. Nothing that ever happened to me as I went on to become a champion boxer, and fight for a world title, compared to that beating.

I have to admit the beatings were never gratuitous – they were always for a reason, even if that reason was spurious. On this occasion, I had been bad at school, fighting, and the school suspended me – two days before term was due to end for the Christmas holidays.

One of my teachers said: "Don't bother coming in for the last couple of days, Lueshing. We don't want to see your face again until next term." I said: "Fine."

I thought I was being smart and had got off lightly. Until I remembered George was at home.

My father worked on oil rigs and would get called all across the world to do jobs as and when they came up. The trouble was, he hadn't received any calls for some time, so he was spending his time at home, getting edgy, drinking too much, smoking dope. It was coming up to Christmas, he'd got six kids and he had no work.

I could see all this, I could sense the tension around him, so, instead of explaining what had happened at school, I got up the next morning, shouted "See ya!" – and went off on my own like I was going to school in the normal way.

Instead, I headed to the park, where I stayed until 4 o'clock, on my own, killing time. And it was no barrel of laughs there – thick snow had been falling, it was freezing cold, real icy cold, and all I wanted to do was get back home into some warmth.

I did the same on the second day, counting down the minutes, shivering endlessly, trying to take shelter in an old bandstand but at the same time trying not to get noticed. It really was no fun but 4 o'clock slowly approached so I set off for a nearby BP petrol station, where my brother Edwin was working. I wanted to get some sweets off him.

But as soon as I walked in, he screamed: "Oh man... you're going to get a lickin' tonight."

I remember the fear of that moment and stammered: "Why, why, what do you mean?"

And Edwin explained that a social worker had phoned the house and told my mother about the school suspension. Edwin was the executioner and his words were my death sentence.

I asked Edwin what mood my father was in and he replied: "Kevin, he's been smoking." That gave me some hope. I actually thought: "Touch, I might be alright, that might calm him down a bit." So, I headed home.

Over the years, I've thought long and hard about that walk home and the feeling that consumed me as I walked the half mile.

It was a feeling I experienced again many years later when I walked towards a boxing ring to face world champion Felix Trinidad in Tennessee. It was stomach-churning fear, anxiety, a dread of what lay ahead – an anticipation of impending hell.

I was ten years old and I was terrified of going home: I knew deep, deep down what was about to happen. The feeling was so over-powering: raw, naked dread.

But I couldn't stop myself, I couldn't not go home; just like I couldn't turn round in front of thousands of fight fans and millions of TV watchers and not face Felix Trinidad.

So I went through the door and instantly the house felt like a morgue, like a graveyard. My brothers and sisters were all there, and they were looking at me like I was a lamb to the slaughter. *He's going to beat you, man.*

Their eyes were telling me to run but I was thinking: "Just stay calm." I remember my mum saying: "Kevin, yer dad wants to talk to you," and then I heard his voice.

"Kevin, where were you today, boy?"

And in the next breath he was yelling: "Don't bother lying to me, son. This is your last chance."

So I came clean and explained I was in the park. George demanded to know why I was there and not at school.

"Because they suspended me, but I was too scared to tell you. And I'm scared now, I'm scared of you, Dad."

And I said 'Dad' – not out of love or affection. Out of panic, out of fear and out for desperation. I was crying now because I knew I was done for.

"Don't bother cry, don't bother," he said, "because that is only going to make it worse." The word 'worse' was said with such ferocity it felt like a blow in itself.

"Get upstairs and get into your pyjamas." I trudged up and as I was climbing I could hear my mum pleading: "George, pleeeezze, George. Then screaming: "GEORGE, GEORGE. You can't beat him with that, don't beat him with that," at the top of her voice, pleading, hysterical.

Upstairs, my brothers were begging me to jump out of the window and run to my granma's house. So, I took Errol's shoes, which were two sizes too big for me, jumped out of the window – in my pyjamas – and I started running, fast as I could.

I was panicking now and headed for the BP garage again, knowing Edwin would still be there. I told him what had happened, he gave me 10 pence out of the cash till for a bus fare, and urged me to go to Granny's. And he gave me one of those black, fluffy jackets they used to sell at petrol stations in those days: he saw how I was shivering with the cold.

I jumped on a 54 bus, arrived at Granny's house, knocked on the door and yelled: "He's going to kill me." I didn't have to tell her who, she would instinctively know.

Bless her, I'm about four stone, very frail, very small, I didn't start growing until I was about 16, and she said: "Don't worry son, you'll be alright here."

The main reason I went to Granny's was because the tactic had worked before, for my brother Andrew. My dad was going to beat him, he ran to my granny's, my dad calmed down and he didn't get a beating.

I sat down with her; she gave me some food and some Horlicks and I slowly started to feel calmer when suddenly there was a crashing bang at the door

I shivered, colder than the cold outside and thought "Christ, help me now, he's here. George is here."

My gran opened the door and said: "You ain't taking him, George, I'll call the police."

And I remember him saying: "Call the fuckin' police' and he brushed right past her. Suddenly gran yelled: "Quick, Kevin, run upstairs, run upstairs to my bedroom and jump in the wardrobe."

I pelted upstairs, straight into her bedroom where there was one of those big old-fashioned wardrobes, like in the film *The Lion, the Witch and the Wardrobe*. Only I wasn't about to be jumping into some magic land full of bloody fairies and rosy gardens.

I climbed in and tried to hide behind some tatty old clothes hanging inside. All of a sudden I saw a light come on through the crack in the door.

Panic consumed me: I was mortified, real, deep terror, so suffocating I could barely breathe with it.

I knew what was coming, the expectation of pain, the knowing there was nowhere left to run to. It would be him and me; he's bigger, angrier, he has the weapons and I'm just a child. Knowing all this, seeing what was about to happen in my mind, picturing it, picturing the hell, the pain: how could a child rationalise or escape that?

A child in a wardrobe, shivering now with gut-wrenching dread, nowhere else to go other than hell.

And that moment would return to haunt me when I turned to boxing, when I walked towards the ring, knowing pain and hurt was waiting for me. But at least I was taking that walk because I wanted to, because maybe I could stop the pain and make my opponent suffer it instead. But it was no boxing match against George; it was no level playing field.

He's coming, he's coming. The terror pumped through me, the door flung open and he screeched Jamaican slang at me: "Where you there, where you there?"

The clothes I was desperately trying to hide behind were now being violently yanked apart as George moved in to grab my cowering body. I was hunched up, praying that somehow he would fail to see me. But his hands appeared through the swirling clothes, grasped my hair and dragged me out – not gently but violently and urgently. George was tugging at me like you might tug at an old suitcase jammed inside.

Silly, irrelevant details I remember so clearly. Maybe an analyst would say they're all significant, maybe it was just the sight of George's big status symbols that made him feel big and important in his own mind. It's just I remember he had his white sheepskin coat on, his cowboy boots on, his gold rings on, his Rolex watch – and I was still in my pyjamas.

He carried on dragging me down the stairs – bump, bump, bumping – and my gran was yelling: "George, George, don't take him."

Oh Christ, I'm scared.

It was the fear that was so suffocating. I'd never known fear like that. Was it the fear a condemned man feels as he walks towards the gallows? For a child, and I was a child, it felt even worse.

George pulled me to the car, barking "You come with me," and I was crying, I had no defiance or resilience left in me. I was like a floppy rag doll, nothing left inside, drained of everything. I know now that I was in deep trauma but I couldn't rationalise such things then. I was just sated by the fear.

There was no need to fight, no logic to it: the lion had his prey. All that's left is death. I remember my gran shouting somewhere in the distance, "I'm calling the police George," and then she'd gone and I was in the car alone with me captor.

A big black shiney BMW – it was spotless. We used to clean his wheels every Sunday; we had a toothbrush each and some stuff that kept the wheels silver. George kept the car immaculate. Spotless, clean, and I was in the front seat alongside him.

The silence between us was overwhelming and was only broken when he switched on the radio. It was Bob Marley, it was bloody 'No woman, no cry'. I remember this because I liked Bob Marley then, I still do now.

George stayed silent. There was only the music between us until he suddenly turned the volume down, leant slightly towards me – his evil eyes piercing into mine – and spoke in a menacing, poisonous whisper: "This is going to make it WORSE." And the word 'worse' echoed in my head and still echoes in it today. *Worse, worse, worse.*

I was a child.

And he banged his hand down ferociously on the arm rest, repeating the same seven words until they sounded like an hysterical chant:

"This is going to make it worse.

This is going to make it worse."

He didn't explain what was going to make it worse: I was too terrified to ask but I assumed he meant the fact he'd had to come to get me from Granma's.

Suddenly he pulled over and stopped the car. I shivered. *This is it.* But I looked outside and saw we were alongside Unwins, the bloody off licence. I knew what that meant: he was going to get some liquid, some fuel. He wanted to get tanked up before he started on me. That's what 'getting it worse' really meant.

He stepped out, in his fancy fuckin' coat and boots, said nothing and walked straight into the store as calm as could be. He was in there for what felt like an eternity.

As the seconds turned into minutes and the dread inside me boiled and boiled, I thought about making another run for it. It was though my whole being was saying: "Get out Kevin, get out, run, run for your life." It was clear thinking: I was alone, waiting for my executioner to return and there was clear daylight in front of me and the chance to run straight into it.

Then, just as quickly, I thought to myself: "Kevin… what are your options?" And I weighed it up very quickly: where would I run to? I couldn't go back to Granma's, he'd just come tearing back in a worse state.

My mind carried on dissecting my choices: *Is there anyone else? Who'd be willing to save your skin, Kev? Who, who? The police? No. They're white, you can't trust white men. I'm just a little Paki.*

So I stayed. The light went off as quickly as it had switched on: there was going to be no escape.

George got back in the car, he had his cans, and we drove home. I walked into the house and he instantly barked: "Take your clothes off and get outside into the back garden."

I was crying now: the moment had come and stripping me naked was the first part of the torture. Taking my clothes off, exposing me so I'd be open, vulnerable, defenceless, a pathetic, weedy and insignificant body with no resistance and no strength.

I stood outside in the freezing, biting cold in a shabby pair of Y-fronts, eleven years old, shivering violently and waiting for the horror to begin while George stood in front of me, still in his coat and boots.

I could hear my mum, stood by the back door, wailing and shouting "No George!" in between hysterical convulsions.

Her sobbing clearly rattled George; he turned from me and roughly pushed her back into the house – locking the door, so she couldn't get out. And I could see my brothers with their faces pressed against the window, squinting into the darkness to see what was going on. Waiting for my screaming to begin.

Then George suddenly had something in his hands, dangling down – jump leads. But not like the ordinary jump leads you get from a petrol station: these were for juggernauts and lorries, these were big, heavy duty, coated in thick rubber with copper inside.

I remember staring at them as George started to wind one of the connector ends round his hand so he could get a solid grip. The cables were dangling by his side: one black, one red – those colours screaming out at me against the white snow. And the open jaws of the other connector ends were swinging around his ankles, mouths open, ready to take bites out of me, laughing at me, mocking me.

I am a child and I am to be torn apart, cut to shreds, lacerated, split open.

George was close now and whispered menacingly: "Hold out your left hand." Seized with terror, I slowly pushed my trembling open palm towards him. As soon as it was close enough for his liking, he lashed the jump leads down on my feeble flesh, already blue from the freezing air. And before the pain and the shock even started its journey through my body, he ordered me to hold out the other hand, and he struck me again.

I can still see the look in his eyes. As he hit me, my eyes locked on to his, looking for tiny clues that might tell me where the next blow would be coming from. George had already taught me that survival tactic.

And he wasn't finished: "If you move your hand, I'm going to give you more," he snarled. My eyes stayed locked on his as more blows rained in. One, two – the pain was unbearable and I instinctively put my hands between my legs in the hope it would give them some temporary comfort. But George wasn't having that: "Hold your hand out again, boy, and don't move it." I offered him my left and right in quick succession, hoping to spread the pain evenly, but always keeping my open palm upwards, so George would be happy that I wasn't trying to stop him having easy targets.

But the pain was rapidly becoming unbearable: like a sharp chill blain, the sort you feel when it's freezing cold outside, you have no gloves and you suddenly trip unexpectedly and throw out your palms to try to break the fall. A bit like that but way more severe, way deeper.

I cried with the intensity but after a while I simply rolled with the pain, becoming increasingly braced for it as every blow rained in. Even George tired from the exertion and needed an interval: so, he took some swigs of beer before coming back for more. "Open your fuckin' hand"– bang – "open" – bang – "again" – bang. Then back for another little break until it was time to start up again.

And while he was hitting me, I became consumed with hatred. I wanted to fight back but more than anything I wanted to say: "You're bullying me, Dad, don't beat me like this, talk to me. Please don't hurt me any more – please, Dad. Dad, I love you; don't do this to me, Dad."

I wanted to call him Dad, only because I reasoned that word might connect with him and soften him. But I couldn't say it, I was too scared, he was hurting me and I just wanted it over and done with. I didn't want to say anything that might make him more angry and make the torment last even longer.

All I wanted was to be out of that garden and back in the house – 101 Clockhouse Road. Back in my room and back in my bed, back in my little sanctuary where I could suck my fingers and hug the pillow and will the pain to go away.

Then George barked: "Lie down." So I lay in the snow, in a foetal position, my inadequate hands and arms around my head, desperately trying to protect random parts of me. But my weedy body was open and prone in the snow; shivering, exposed. Then – whack – down came the jump leads against my shoulders and – whack – down again, against the small of my back just above the buttocks.

And I didn't know any more where the pain started, only that it never ended and it had taken over my being. It was on top of me, inside me, in my head, deep, deep inside: everywhere was raging with hurt and violence – an insufferable combination of throbbing, stinging and Arctic cold.

This was my breaking point: I couldn't take any more. So I thought 'fuck it', and somehow dragged myself up – my body heaving with sobbing and pain and desperation – and half-ran, half tumbled to the bottom of our garden, where I scrambled over a low-slung fence.

There was a train line on the other side and George knew it. So what did he do? The snow was falling heavily now, I was cowering and shivering on the other side of the fence and watched in disbelief as he fumbled in his pocket, pulled out one of his roll-ups, lit up and calmly started puffing a big one.

My head was throbbing wildly, torrents of tears were stinging my eyes, my body was blue with the cold and the icy snow was driving into me like body blows but George looked like he hadn't a care in the world. "Son, I can stand here nice and warm in this sheepskin for as long as you want. But how much more can you take?"

He could hear me shivering, he could see my breath gasping in the freezing air but he simply added: "You might as well come now, boy, because I promise I will wait here 'til morning if that's what you want. It's up to you."

That's when I gave in.

I jumped back over. I'd weighed up the options and I had none.

His approach changed, though, and he started talking. He'd had a few cans and I could smell foul beer as the cold air came pouring out of his mouth and drifted across me, freezing its staleness over my face and nostrils.

"Why did you do it?," he asked. So I told him: "Because I was scared of you, Dad. I didn't mean to, please don't beat me any more, I am so sorry." I called him Dad because I was begging now, there was no courage or dignity left in me, but maybe this was a chance to halt the onslaught.

But the words were wasted on him: as I cowered in front of him he whipped me again, still with the jump leads but now across my back.

I pleaded: "Dad, I'm cold, I'm cold." I'll never forget his reply because it revealed how he was justifying himself: "But boy, you must love the snow because you chose to go to the park and play in it for two days, rather than stay at home and tell us the truth."

"No, Dad, I didn't want the beating, that's why I went to the park. I wasn't going there to play; I didn't want the beating, I was scared." He wasn't having it, though: "No, I'm beating you in the snow because you must love it so much. I've taken your clothes off because you must love the snow."

Then, as if he needed to find a way of continuing my punishment, he opened the back door, took off his belt and ordered me back into the kitchen – hurling the jump leads on to the snow as though they'd finished their work.

My mum was hysterical, screaming: "No more, no more, he can't take it." But George wasn't finished: he wrapped the belt buckle round his hand and sorted his grip so he had the maximum hold to strike me again. I was stood in the middle of the kitchen, my mum by another door and George again ordered me to hold out a hand. The leather belt came lashing into me – smash, smash, smash.

The jump leads had left me with a bruising kind of throb: the belt was whip-like. It was a different kind of pain.

Inside the kitchen was pandemonium: tears, screams, hysteria. But amid all the carnage George remained disciplined, in control. He'd been drinking, he'd been smoking but he knew absolutely what he was doing. He was angry, he was furious, but he had not lost his temper. *How do you make sense of that?*

I've often wondered about the cans of beer. What was the alcohol all about? Was it to calm his nerves, was it to give him courage, was it to complete the night's entertainment, like having a lager while you're busy watching a movie on the TV?

The punishment was wild, but it wasn't executed in a wild way. There was always time for a pause and another drink. Then George would ramble on, in his Jamaican slang, about how he'd done this for me, that for me; how he'd sent me to school and this is how I repaid him, this is what I did to him.

And I'd try to form some words in my mouth but before a sound could be formed, he'd snap: "Don't answer me back," and then, bang, another one, another lashing.

He was justifying himself to me and lecturing me as if I was in some form of fit state to absorb a single word.

He knew he'd hurt me, broken me, shattered me and here he now was, Mr Big Man in his Big Coat with his Big BMW, trying to be the Big Philosopher while his naked son stood in front of him, sobbing uncontrollably, shivering, bruising, broken.

I was in a stupor by now, pain searing through me, my eyes incapable of vision through all the tears and I vaguely remembered hearing a distant voice say: "Kevin, Kevin, I tried to help you my son, I even went to the neighbours and begged them for help but they said they couldn't get involved, son."

Thanks Mum – but you didn't try hard enough.

Next, George ordered me upstairs, and told me not to make a sound. "Don't let me hear from you, don't let me see you come out the door over Christmas."

I scrambled up, falling over myself in the rush to escape the pain. My mum came in and started bathing me, probably with Dettol, or something to deal with the bruises and lacerations.

They were big bruises, too: the jump leads had made sure of that. And it was traumatic and hard for my brothers and sisters to witness as well. I remember as I went up the stairs they were whispering: "Are you alright, Kev; Kev does it hurt?" They would have been frightened to be heard talking to me. They would have been thinking: 'Is he going to start on us?'

Later on, they wanted the details: what happened at Granny's, where did he take you, where does it hurt? Then the compassion and the kindness: do you want my bed, can I get you anything, Kev; are you OK?

"Yep, I'm fine, I'm fine." They know I'm not. The marks are on me, outside and inside: the visible and invisible scars of my torture.

Chapter Two

A TORTURED CHILDHOOD

I STILL DON'T KNOW HOW TO RATIONALISE THAT beating in the snow and I absolutely don't know how to justify it. I try to think of the love I feel for my son today and I know George couldn't have loved me because there is no part of me that could dream of doing that to my boy.

And the scars won't heal, they really won't. Tears fill my eyes as I write this now.

I remember seeing those leads ten years later. One of my brothers had them and he said: "Go to the back of the garage and get me the jump leads, would you Kev?"

I went in there, not really making the connection and then I saw them and my body just froze to a standstill. I was transfixed and instantly went back into what had happened. I stared and stared at them and every single blow came roaring back to me as ferociously as they'd been delivered at the time. It was like I'd stored that beating up inside me and never, ever re-visited it until that moment.

I couldn't even pick them up – I had to go back to my brother and get him to do it. I'm not saying this was a therapeutic experience: it was simply what happened and it made me realise what happened to me can never be erased from my body, or soul.

Despite a career in boxing, that was the worst beating I ever took. There's no comparison: in boxing, I never bruised, I could be knocked down but I would get back up and fight another day. I lost about 12 amateur fights out of 80 but recovered from every one of those to go on and turn professional.

But I couldn't do anything about this beating; I couldn't dodge, I couldn't slip out of reach, I couldn't counter. It was like in the TV series about slavery, *Roots*: I had an empathy with the slave who took a ferocious beating. He just took it – like I had to.

If I concentrate, I can still feel the pain. And I can still see the look in George's eyes.

Evil.

No compassion, just coldness. It was a look I got familiar with when I turned to boxing and it was a look I saw in Felix Trinidad's eyes when I fought for the world title. I've seen it in Mike Tyson's eyes as well: that same stare, cold, impersonal, emotionless. The look of death.

When you see that look coming from the eyes of someone who's meant to be your protector, your mentor – your father – what chance do you have?

When boxers dish out a beating, they do so clinically. Years of training have taught them to be in control, to have no remorse or compassion. But a boxer is heroic. He puts his own life on the line – he is facing someone who could hurt him more, who can fight back and who can deliver pain themselves.

George was in control, like a boxer, and – like a boxer – he showed no compassion. He couldn't give a beating with compassion, that would have been a contradiction to him. A compassionate beating is not a beating, is it?

You have to be ruthless, commit to the kill and execute without sentiment, without holding back.

But unlike a boxer, George was a bully and a coward. I couldn't fight back; his size and strength, then, overwhelmed me. Boxing isn't like that, it's much, much fairer.

George's coldness undoubtedly prepared me for the brutal world of boxing: I'm not thanking or praising him for that, I'm simply saying the effect it ultimately had. I am incapable of emotion in the ring and that's how it should be. How it must be.

I certainly wouldn't have been a boxer if I'd been loved in a caring, family environment: I was used to the kind of coldness you need to be a top professional fighter.

I don't even believe George was getting any kind of thrill out of what he did to me, mental or sexual. He was doing it because that's how he'd been taught, those were the values drilled into him during his upbringing. Discipline equals beatings equals obedience equals good behaviour.

His parents beat him: there was no other way for him, he didn't know any better. I don't believe in that: love is love.

I called him George because he made me cold, he'd beaten the love out of me and using the word 'Dad' would have suggested affection, even weakness; worst of all, love. I couldn't love him, even though I had wanted to.

And please don't think I'm this screwed up because of one beating. We got beatings for anything and everything. Another time he had an audience.

Every summer, the fair would come but we were poor and had no money. This particular year, my brothers and I were arguing over who would ask George for some money so we could go: "You ask him, no you ask him." We were scared, it was like asking the messiah, but we needed the money.

Errol eventually cracked and summoned up the courage: "Dad, can we have some money for the fair tonight?"

To our astonishment, George took out a twenty pound note; my God, unbelievable. We were ecstatic, it felt like a fortune and probably was then.

Errol came running back to our room, screaming: "Dad's given us a twenty." And at that point, in sheer excitement, I instinctively yelled out a bad Jamaican expletive. It was just the sheer unexpected joy of the moment.

But, in Jamaica, that expression was a bit like saying the c-word here. My mum heard it and instantly shouted: "What did you say just then, Kevin?"

"Nothing Mum, nothing," and I was panicking and yelling: "Please don't tell him, please, please."

But she stormed downstairs and said: "George, guess what I just heard coming out of Kevin's mouth." As I look back on this, I can't help thinking: *Mum why did you do that, you knew how he'd react and what he'd do. You knew what he was like.*

George angrily ordered me outside, where he was having a smoke with one of his pals, Desmond.

But first he made me pick one of his belts from his wardrobe. I remember my brother saying he'd got a new one, PVC, and that might be less painful. So I picked that one.

Outside, Desmond was laughing and joking with my father and smirked: "Give him a few little whacks, he shouldn't have said that word at his age."

I wanted to explain to George: *"For Christ's sake, I only learnt that word from you, where else would I get it from, nobody round here knows what it even means. I didn't make it up, Mum doesn't say it. It's your fuckin' word George."*

But I had seen the look in his eyes. He ordered me to pull my pants down in front of Desmond, and whacked me across my naked buttocks, roaring: "Where did you get that word from, boy?" I was bursting to say: "You, you bastard." But I knew that would've made it worse so I just sobbed and begged for forgiveness.

Bang again: "I'm sorry Dad, I'll never say it again, I promise."

"You're damned right you won't", then all of a sudden Desmond interjected: "Alright George, that's enough now," and chuckled.

And that was like the red rag to the bull. My Dad started beating me more ferociously – bang, bang, bang. The pain seared across my buttocks and up into my back. Then George calmly asked: "Desmond, is this your son?"

Desmond replied "No," to which my father responded: "Fuck off then. Don't fuckin' tell me how to discipline my children."

I was ordered upstairs and wasn't allowed to go to the fair that night: everyone else did, but not me. They brought me back some candy though.

And we were like that as brothers. Sometimes we would take a beating for something we hadn't done, so the guilty brother would be spared. I remember Errol doing that once to spare me, and that was horrible. Seeing him go through that agony – George was whacking him hard on the open hand – but Errol stubbornly refused to cry.

He'd done absolutely nothing wrong, but George was getting more and more ferocious and inside I was begging Errol to cry. I could imagine him saying to himself: *I ain't cracking for you, you bastard.* I knew that was in his mind.

But George was getting angrier and undid the belt from his hand and struck Errol with the buckle instead. All of us were begging him to cry by now – "Cry Errol, cry." Then George tried to hit him again but missed and the buckle crashed against a table, smashing into pieces such was the force.

He stopped only because the buckle had broken, not because of what he was doing.

"Fuck off to your rooms, fuck off all of you," he screamed, furious that he'd lost his weapon. And I remember Errol running into the room and going straight to the corner where he burst out in floods of tears. And now it was my turn to say: "Are you all right?"

"Yeah, I'm alright."

I was five years old when I got my first beating. I found two pence in the backyard, went to a sweet shop and got some Bubblicious, 1p each.

I got home, walked around the house with the bubblegum in my mouth when George suddenly said: "What you eating there, son?"

"Bubblicious dad." To which he replied: "Where did you get that from, where did you get the money to get that from? Is it yours?"

I confessed and told him I'd found it in the backyard. He then ordered me to take my pants down, hauled me across his lap and smacked me with his hand about six times on the backside. I was only five and it was a shock to me but it put in my head that this was what he did.

I had already witnessed my brothers suffer beatings and now I was following them. But the punishment was never commensurate with the crime.

I adored it when George went away. I would bribe my brother with Marathon chocolate bars because he would know in advance. He'd eavesdrop on telephone conversations – he'd listen when Dad got a call saying there's a job for him in Saudi Arabia, or Scotland, or where ever.

And when he was gone: Freedom. Freedom at last, it was like Martin Luther King saying "Free at last!"

When my dad walked into the room, you'd try to find excuses to walk out. But you had to find a believable reason, which wasn't easy. I remember once mumbling that I needed to go to my room to do some school work but he just said: "Don't talk shit man, sit down and you watch the news."

It was horrible, it was intimidation, it was control. He didn't give a fuck if we wanted to be there, if we were happy: he just wanted to dominate the room. I'm king of the jungle and you are my servants.

When George beat me, I saw real rage and anger in his eyes.

Why was he so angry? I became infatuated, intrigued, about his childhood and whether the answer was there: had he been mistreated, was this the only way he understood how to raise children?

There were rare, rare moments when he tried to connect. A few days after one of my beatings, Mum ordered me to take his dinner tray up to his room. I pleaded with her not to make me but she wouldn't budge – so off I went up the stairs, fearing the worst.

I walked into the room, saw my dad lying on top of the bed, walked past him and put the tray on a table in a corner. As I walked back past him he lurched forward and tried to grab me in a sort of give-me-a-cuddle way.

I froze, my body went completely stiff and he just said: "Why did you let me beat you the other day, son?" I said: "'Cos I was naughty, Dad," and he just let me go.

It was the right answer and he would have been happy with that.

And that was one of the very few times he almost showed some emotion; there was another when he got me a Timex watch for Christmas and I went to kiss him but he pushed me away and said: "No, men don't kiss, they shake hands." So he shook my hand. I was eight.

Sometimes my family will say: "He wasn't that bad." Well, in an entire lifetime I can only recall those two moments of warmth. Are they really enough for me to forgive him, for me to say: "OK, he meant well, he loved me really"?

I'm sorry, it's too few to remember, too few to repair the damage.

There was a time when he was shot over a dodgy business deal in Jamaica; he'd imported cars, people weren't paying up, and a gang tried to get him killed. He was shot in the liver and lost a finger and although he was seriously ill in hospital, he survived.

But I wouldn't go and see him. My brothers asked me to, I wouldn't, I wasn't interested and in the end Andrew gave in.

And this is how cold George was. When my brother went all the way over there, and walked through the hospital ward door, the first thing my father said was: "Bloody hell, of all my sons, they had to send you." He wasn't trying to be funny.

After hospital, he was sent to prison in Jamaica for his part in the fraud.

I never loved my father: I wanted to, but I had to see some signs of it and I never saw that.

Yes, I was fed and I was clothed but there was never any love, it was just their duty to raise me. And my mum only gets off half-heartedly: she didn't know any different. The men ruled the house, the women followed orders and made the best of it.

She came from a tiny village on a Caribbean island, her life had been hard and, if anything, I pitied her. In fact, sometimes she showed compassion. I remember in the middle of another beating, she lay on top of me and took the blows herself.

George was whacking her as he tried to get to me and he actually said to her: "If you want to take the beating then you can take the beating, woman."

Nothing I did warranted the beatings, nothing; you'd think I'd murdered someone. But the beatings are all I have for childhood memories. I don't remember warm moments, gentleness, harmony, Christmas, birthdays, laughter. I just remember the beatings, fear and the overwhelming dread of walking towards my father knowing he was going to hit me and beat me rotten.

In his defence? He was probably never shown love as a child, either, just discipline as a means of keeping order. So my home life was purely about survival; it was like doing time in prison. How long have you got before you can escape? That was my childhood.

My car crash illustrates this coldness. Mum was going to the shops in an old Ford Anglia and I insisted on going with her, even though she told me not to. She hadn't passed her test – she'd failed at least five times by then – but I jumped on to the front seat and refused to budge.

We set off, she drove round a corner and ploughed straight into a big Granada, hard. I wasn't wearing a seatbelt and went hurtling straight through the windscreen.

It was bad: I broke my leg and my face was slashed to bits from the glass. I needed about 40 stitches in my face alone.

I was lying on an operating table in Bromley Hospital, barely able to see anything, when suddenly two figures appeared in front of me: my dad and one of his mates.

"Dad, Dad is that you,?" I asked feebly. His reply was cold, quick and utterly heartless: "Yes it is, and this serves you right for getting in the car when your mother told you not to."

And before I could reply or protest or say anything, he turned round and walked out.

He never came again to see me during the nine weeks I had to stay in that hospital – and nor did my mum, either.

My brother always said I wouldn't have been the fighter I became if Dad hadn't treated me any differently and, in a perverted sort of way, he's right. But I would have abandoned boxing in an instant to have felt the natural love of a father.

My dad would sometimes support me as I started to get into boxing but even then, it was done in a heartless, emotionless way.

He'd never show for my big fights; if I got to a semi-finals, he wouldn't turn up and I'd lose.

The following anecdote illustrates how George would try to 'help' me make it in boxing. My brother was a very good runner and I needed to do running to improve my fitness.

I wasn't as good as my brother, so my dad got him to run behind me with a stick and any time I slowed down or tired, he'd whip me with it across the back of my calves. It sounds funny but it wasn't – the backs of my legs would be red raw and my dad would come down in the mornings, chuck a cold flannel over them and order me to get back out again for another run.

Other times, George would watch me get on my bike – a tiny 20-inch thing – and cycle in the rain, the snow, the cold to get to the boxing gym. But he'd climb into his BMW, wait for me at the other end, watch me for 20 minutes maximum and then go – leaving me to cycle back after a fight or a tough training session.

Maybe he thought he was preparing me for the world. But discipline has to go hand in hand with love and when the love is removed, all that's left is cruelty.

We're talking about a man I wanted to love: even then I wanted to say to him: "Listen Dad, I'm going to be someone, back me, I'll take care of you as you get old."

I never got near him.

I used to be envious of Nigel Benn, who became a big part of my life later on. I'd see Nigel's dad get in the ring with him and I'd think: "Why didn't my dad do that, why wasn't he there as well?"

The truth is, he didn't deserve it. He beat me raw and never, ever showed remorse, or found time to explain himself to me. Even when I was old enough and strong enough to do without him, I still wanted him to be part of my boxing life, so he could feel proud of me, and be shoulder to shoulder with me at title fights.

Why did I crave that after all he'd done to me? And why did he throw that in my face as well? Why couldn't he even make that effort for me after all the vile things he'd done to me?

I don't know.

I guess the point of no return came the day I tried to have it out with him. I was about 21, out on the street, doing drugs, being Mr Big Time and feeling like nobody could lay a finger on me any more.

George and I were in his car going somewhere, my brother in the back seat, and I suddenly said: "Oi, Dad, remember that time when you beat me raw in the snow? What did you do that for, eh?" And I was giving it large, menacing: I was full of 'go-on-try-and-hit-me-now' attitude.

I hadn't pre-planned it, it just came flooding out. I was speaking to him like he was a bloke in the street; it was liberating and I felt empowered – so I carried on. "Come on – Dad – tell me, Dad, why did you beat me like that? I loved you, what was all that about, Dad?"

It was like he was a different person, someone who had no hold over me at last. He was just a Homeboy and I was demanding an explanation.

You're just one of us now, George, and I'm going to give it to you if you don't come up with the answers.

"What you talking about?" he snapped.

"You remember. Listen, do you think you could do that now, eh? I'd knock your fuckin' head off."

25

That was it. George stopped the car and got out. I got out, too: we were about to go for one another. Revenge, atonement, justice: the balance of power between father and son. All would be sorted in the next few brutal moments.

I could see that cold look in his eyes again, the one I saw during all those beatings. But I was giving it back now and I was ready and equipped and willing to lash back, to hit him hard, to flatten him, beat him to a pulp for all he'd done to me.

Left, right, straight to the head, sledgehammer to his gut, it'll be over in seconds, he won't see the punches coming – bang, bang, bang – this is for the jump leads you vicious bastard, wham, right in the kidneys for the first beating when I was five years old. You ain't getting up from this, you evil, evil shit.

And make no mistake my dad wanted to do it to me, as well: he was King Kong being challenged. *I'm your dad, you don't dare defy me.*

With the anger I felt in that moment, I would have destroyed him, maybe worse. I had violence in me, it was consuming me and I was bursting to unleash it on to his pathetic, ageing body.

But suddenly my brother leapt out of the car and snapped me out of it. "Kevin, Kevin, no, don't – go, go, get out of here – right now."

I looked at George, I looked at my brother and I turned away.

I didn't return for another seven years.

Chapter Three

A CHILD WITHOUT PARENTS

I TRIED TO KILL MYSELF WHEN I WAS NINE YEARS OLD. IT wouldn't the last time, either.

I'm not saying I was suicidal. I was nine, I doubt I'd even heard of the word suicide. What I did was impetuous; spur of the moment.

But how many nine year olds are driven to such insanity?

George caught me – red-handed – trying to steal from Mum's purse. He walked in the kitchen, I had the purse in my hand and I was physically lifting the coins out with my fingers.

He roared my name with such ferocity I dropped the purse, turned and fled straight out of the kitchen door. I can still hear him yelling: "Kevin, you little bastard, get back in here now and get me my belt."

Instead, I ran straight out into the road at the front of our house and crouched behind one of the parked vehicles.

And I was so terrified of George, my plan – in the madness of that moment – was to hurl myself in front of the next car that came down the road rather than face another beating.

I was terrified and in my tiny little nine-year-old brain, I was better off dead.

Suddenly a car emerged, going ever-so-slowly down the road. I watched it get nearer and nearer, then, just as it was almost level with my crouching body I lurched up – but sufficiently slowly for the driver to see me and swerve away.

"You little black bastard" and a prolonged blast of the horn was as close as I actually came to death.

I'd had the feeling a couple of times before: *I'm just going to race out into the road and get run down.*

I've no doubt I was trying to find a way of escaping the beatings and the violence of my home life. The sad moments far outnumbered the genuinely happy ones.

I never witnessed any true signs of warmth or emotion between my mother and father and I was convinced they definitely didn't love me. Now and then I'd see them talking, and she might laugh but I was never brought into conversations. There was no "Kevin, what did you do today or can we help with your homework?" None of that.

They both came from Jamaica, and both came over when the British government were happy to grant passports to cheap labour.

George's father was Chinese but emigrated to Jamaica where he and his wife raised their children with strict – and often brutal – discipline. In fact, George once told me it was his mother who dished out the worst beatings of his own childhood.

My father met Mum, Barbara, in England: both had left Jamaica independently of one another, driven by the dream of a new life, prosperity and employment in London.

George was about five foot nine inches tall; no more than 11 stone three pounds in weight; small hands really.

But he looked evil.

He looked dangerous. He looked psycho. He looked like the actor Charles Bronson. Intimidating, his eyes were piercing and cold. There was no warmth in those eyes; no compassion; no understanding; no re-assurance; no 'you can count on me'.

No love.

My dad could freeze you with fear from 100 yards away. If I saw my dad so much as lift a finger towards his belt, it would stop me dead. He didn't have to theatrically grab it: he could just look at you and lift a finger towards it.

I never heard the word 'love' in our house. I never heard: "I love you son." Or even "It'll be all right." I never heard any of my brothers say: "Dad, I love you." Or even: "Mum, I love you."

My dad would beat me, but my mum wouldn't be averse to giving us a slap, either, if we were trying to jump out of the bath or something. She'd hit us, just no-where near as badly.

You could run from my mum, laughing at her – but not with her. You couldn't do that with George: you had to stand to attention.

Compassion and love? Never from George.

My mother had endured an impoverished upbringing herself, spending her childhood in a Jamaican village where day-to-day life was about the basics of survival. There was no power or electricity; she knew nothing about life beyond that, although she trained to be a nurse before she came to England.

Barbara was a God-fearing, Seventh-Day Adventist, though. I never heard her swear – or rather she'd never say bad white-man words. But my God, she would say the black ones: hard, ugly, offensive Jamaican words. Never F-words. None of them.

She made us attend service every week, always on Saturdays – not Sundays. My dad would never go.

I was bored out of my brains. They used big words there and rattled on about psalms. I didn't understand a word of it.

And it would have been way too hard to believe in God given how we were suffering at home. I believed my mum believed in God: I believed the Seventh Day Adventists did, too –otherwise, why did they put so much money in a little basket each week?

But how could I really believe in God then? I was definitely praying – but only for the beatings to stop. I was praying Dad would get a job that would take him away. Or he'd just get up and go. Those prayers rarely got answered.

Sometimes I'd pray for the moment when I could climb into my bunk bed and find sanctuary there. I'd cower into a foetel position – like when I was in the snow – and cling onto a thin blanket and sheet, trying to calm a combination of shivering from fear and shivering from cold.

I'd will myself to sleep, praying, and dreaming of doing something heroic. I loved comic books and wanted to be Spiderman. But it always turned into a troubled, disturbed sleep and at some point in the night I'd wet the bed.

That became a habit which my father decided had to end. So he bought an electric blanket, which one of his pals had told him would solve the problem.

It had little strips of metal going through it; George would plug it in, put it under the top sheet and if I wet the bed during the night, it would set off a little shock and alarm that would jolt me out of my sleep. I was about ten years old – when I was getting the worst beatings off George – and now I was being punished in my sleep as well.

Beating, wet bed, electric shock; beating, wet bed, electric shock; beating, wet bed, electric shock.

My life.

Suddenly, every part of my night and day was a torture, physical and mental. I didn't want to wake up and now I didn't want to go to sleep. In the end, I cracked and ripped the blanket to shreds, hurling it out of the window in an explosion of anger and tears.

I was terrified I'd be in trouble for such defiance. Surprisingly nobody argued, George was away on a job, and nobody spoke of the matter again.

I never asked my parents questions, I never asked them to explain stuff to me, or to try to learn things from them. That might have even antagonised my dad, and I was desperate to avoid that.

I'd never say: "Dad, why this, why that; how does this work, what's the meaning of such and such?" I was too scared to do that. Too much fear went with it.

And I didn't bother to ask my mum simply because she wouldn't have known the answers in any case.

So, I never knew what love was until my own children were born and I felt for them a sensation, a warmth, a bond that I'd never, ever felt before for anyone. I needed to instantly do all the things for them that my mum and dad never did for me.

That's how I knew they couldn't have loved me. Love cares, love gives security, love re-assures. I like the expression: love is, what love does.

The only woman I loved during my childhood was my grandma Celina, my mum's mother. She was a Christian woman, endearing. I'd go round her house and she'd give me a bit of cake and I absolutely adored her fussing over me.

I'd always sit next to her in church and play with the veins in her hands because she was so old. The bond between us then was the nearest I think I ever got to feeling natural love between and adult and a child.

Chapter Four

MY HOUSE OF HORROR

MY FATHER WORKED ON OIL RIGS AND PIPELINES AND eventually Mum saved enough money to buy a terraced house in Beckenham – 101 Clockhouse Road.

My house of horror.

On the outside, 101 Clockhouse Road looked likely every other house in the street – pebble-dashed, crammed in shoulder to shoulder with a long line of identical-looking properties. You could only tell them apart by the colour of their front doors. Ours was yellow, with a red-tiled front step my mum was constantly polishing.

Technically 101 was a semi: there was an alley down the left-hand side. That was my escape route if I was trying to flee a belting. Or trying to kill myself.

Our lounge was too small for all of us, even though it had a bay window. The walls, mantelpiece and sills were covered with photo-graphs of my dad: big pictures of him on an oil rig, or by a pipeline in a desert somewhere, standing there with his ridiculous cowboy hat and cowboy boots on and a toothpick in his mouth.

The sofa and armchairs were covered in plastic to keep them clean. Dad, of course, had his seat, his throne, his power base. Nobody dared sit on that: a brown, reclining leather armchair.

Then there was *the cane*. Whenever my father got a call to work on the pipelines it would often be in places like Saudi Arabia, Libya, Abu Dhabi – always some way off.

After one of those jobs ended, he brought back a huge, giant cane that, in our minds, looked like a massive matchstick. And he put it in the middle of the lounge and left it there as a deterrent. A permanent reminder of what he would do to us, no matter where in the world he might be.

It did the job alright.

We'd instantly imagine George grabbing it in a demented rage, thrashing it through the air insanely like an orchestra conductor, and then laying into our open palms, or across our naked backs and legs and chests until all that was left was a frenzy of pain and blood and bruising and screams and torment.

Oh yes, that cane did that to us and George didn't even need to be in the house.

There weren't enough chairs to go round – if we all packed into the lounge, us kids would be on the floor, splayed across a threadbare carpet.

Mum would try to inject some brightness: she was for ever trying to paint stuff in what she thought were sunny Jamaican colours. But it always looked half finished, there'd be cans of paint and cloths and jam jars with white spirit abandoned all over the place. Her colours always clashed, everything was an explosive mis-match.

It was permanently freezing, too, and there was a constant battle between the Lueshings and the electricity meter. Sometimes we won: Errol worked out a way of slowing down the meter wheel by wedging an old film negative under it – the sort you got when you had your photos developed at Boots in the old days.

But mainly the meter won. We'd be watching TV – I was fascinated by Richard Attenborough's wildlife programmes – when, all of a sudden, the power would go off and everything would shut down. We'd sit there, looking at my dad in the dark – completely quiet but thinking the obvious: *put some money in the meter, Dad.* But never daring to say it. *Please, put some money in the meter:* you could hear those words echoing round the room even though they were never spoken.

But George would just stand up, get his coat and leave us all there in the dark, heading for the pub or a mate's house. That was it, entertainment over, night over; no options other than bed.

And because of the crushing, overbearing cold, I would often go to bed with a duffel coat on, plus socks and tracksuit trousers.

This was a house where there was never enough of what you needed, including food. Our kitchen was permanently greasy and grubby because Mum cooked bubbling West Indian dishes that splashed all over the oven and floor.

Her specialities would be rice 'n' peas and chicken; jerk chicken; cow's foot; stew, peas 'n' rice; swordfish. But her food never left you feeling full: there never seemed to be enough on the plate. I never had a roast dinner, ever, until I got invited to a friend's house. This is how poor we were: one day we ran out of powdered milk and Errol had hot water with Weetabix for his breakfast.

We never had brands: chocolate biscuits would never be 'McVitie's'; everything in a packet was the cheapest supermarket version. We had baked beans but rarely 'Heinz'.

Beyond the kitchen we had two back bedrooms – one of them in a cheaply-built extension with wafer-thin walls that left you hearing everything. George and Barbara let those out to students. We had students in the house for as long as I can remember.

There were three more bedrooms upstairs and a tiny bathroom. The toilet was always getting blocked up: we kept using newspaper because there was never enough toilet rolls. I swear, we had the daily news imprinted on our backsides.

Many times we'd have to go down to the man-trap outside and ram big, long sticks down the sewer pipes to unblock all the newspaper clogged down there. Because I was the smallest, it'd often be me who had to jump in. If I protested, Mum would say: "Son, it's only a dirty conscience that soap and water can't clean."

Even now, that saying has stayed with me. I still say it to my own son if he doesn't want to clean up his bedroom or something.

Errol, Andrew and I would sleep in one bedroom together in a single and bunk beds. But if we suddenly had extra student tenants, then we'd all have to sleep head to tail in one bed in another room.

To this day, I can remember the phone number at 101 Clockhouse: 0208 650 2080 – it was drilled into my brain in the highly-likely event of something bad happening to me; if I was attacked or in trouble with the police.

And there was a distinct pecking order inside 101 that depended on age. At the top was my eldest brother Edwin, then my sister Lorna, followed by Errol and Andrew. I was next – then came my youngest sister, Sharon.

And this was the law of that jungle: George was lord and master, free to distribute beatings as he saw fit. That culture of violence spread downwards: we would often squabble and fight among ourselves. The older you were, the more likely you'd have the final say. Needless to say I lost out the most because I was the youngest boy.

Edwin and I barely spoke to each other and rarely do even today. I reckon we've spoken to each other for no more than 120 minutes during our lives together. He was a lot older than me, seven years and we had little in common.

Andrew was a bit of a loner and would often stay in his bedroom but Errol was far more like me, always taking the piss, trying to have fun, even if we'd taken a beating. If I was being picked on, or teased by my brothers, Errol would often say: "Leave Stan alone."

And we have to talk about this word, Stan.

As in Paki-Stan.

Kids at school called me Paki, in their eyes I had that skin colour, so that became a nick-name. But I pleaded with my brothers not to call me that at home. So they said: "Alright, we'll just call you Stan."

And here's a strange thing: when it came to beatings from our dad, George, the bond between us children was unbreakable. In the face of his most ferocious rages we would be totally united – no army could have separated us in those moments.

But when it came to fighting each other, we could be cruel and vicious.

There used to be a huge suitcase in the house and one time Errol said to me: "Kevin, I bet you can't fit in that case."

We were bored and I stupidly rose to the challenge and climbed inside. I was only tiny then, about eight years old, and it wasn't too difficult to contort my small body. Suddenly, Errol – seizing a chance for some childish fun – slammed the lid down, physically sat on top of it and locked the case shut.

I was stuck inside, panicking and shrieking: "Errol, let me out, let me out, I can't breathe, please, please." I was overcome with anxiety inside: to this day I get panic attacks if I'm in a confined space. I can't stand lifts, even aeroplanes.

Then he manoeuvred the case to the top of our stairs, tilted it forward with me still inside and sent it crashing down to the bottom, where the lid burst open.

I clambered out, gasping for breath and ran out of the house as fast as I could. That's what we could be like to each other.

Then there was the time when my brother Andrew slit the top of my left wrist with a knife.

He was playing Tarzan, he was sharpening the knife on a stone and I was next to him.

He wanted to see how sharp it was, so he ran it across the top of my wrist – where you'd have a watch. It was a childish, not malicious – but the cut instantly started bleeding, heavily. Again, it was childish rather than malicious: I know deep down he didn't genuinely set out to harm me.

"Oh my God, Kev, I didn't mean to do that" and all of a sudden my dad came through the door. "What the hell is happening here?"

And for a split second I had to decide whether to hang my brother, whether to grass, because this wasn't my fault.

Dad didn't have a job then, he was angry and frustrated and he was in the mood to punish. I looked at my brother's eyes and they were clearly begging: "Kev, don't do it, bruv."

So I took the blame: "It was me, Dad, I was just playing and cut my wrist, Dad."

"You stupid fucking idiot, I haven't got time to stand in a queue at the white people's hospital." And George whacked me right across the top of my head: hard, deliberately, so I was unbalanced with the force of the strike.

"Get upstairs, get upstairs, and get a towel round it", he barked. And that's what happened: we never went to the 'white people's hospital' even though the cut was really bad. I still have the scar to this day.

Later that night, when we were in our bedroom, Andrew whispered to me: "Thanks Stan." And that was really important among us, moments like that. Even though we could be cruel to one another, we were united when it came to being attacked by our father.

That's how I look upon my childhood and my home, 101 Clockhouse Road. It was like doing time, like being in prison and having to get through a sentence.

I remember taking beatings and looking at a calendar on the wall, trying to work out when I'd be 16, when I could walk out of the house. I was counting the days to be able to do that.

And it wasn't just us boys who would get the beatings.

I remember one wild night when my dad was belting us all so badly that Mum rushed to the phone to ring 999. It was in the days when phone numbers had to be dialled and each number took an eternity to get round the dial. She got the first nine done, the second nine was half way through its cycle and we were willing her to get on to the third, when George spotted what she was doing.

He charged over to that phone, yanked the wire clean away and hurled it straight against the front door, smashing it to bits. We all ran to our bedrooms in terror.

Sometimes I would hear my dad say to her: "Put them in a home, I don't fuckin' want them." He'd say this in front of us, and we'd be thinking "Mum, don't listen to him, please don't put us in a home."

We'd all go upstairs and spend the night fretting: "What do you think, will he put us in a home, who'll go first?" Even though our own home life was wretched, the fear of 'going into a home' repre-sented something, in our tender minds, that must be far, far worse.

I remember overhearing conversations in the lounge, as we sat on the stairs trying to eavesdrop: "Mrs Lueshing, we can take them all away, we can find other homes for them, we can help you." And I remember my mum yelling: "NO: you're not taking my kids." I can hear her crying and convulsing: "You can't take my children, you're not taking them, you can't."

There were other times when Mum would pull me aside me and say: "They're coming around Kevin, and they're going to take you away unless you tell them everything's OK."

So these strangers would arrive at the house, and ask me whether I was alright, and I'd be saying: "Yes, I love it here, I really do."

I'm still only nine, maybe ten years old, having conversations like that with people I'd never seen before but who, I was told, could take me away if they so wanted.

I remember going round mates' houses, and their families would be kind and ask after me and offer me the sort of food we never had at home. It all felt completely alien but also how things should be in a normal family.

Even now my brothers and sisters say: "Kevin, it wasn't really that bad." It'll make me sad if I offend any of them now but my honest reply is: "I'm sorry but you must have had a different life from me. You must have lived at 102 Clockhouse Road, not 101.

"Because I saw no love at 101 Clockhouse Road, I saw no compassion, I saw no sympathy, I saw no loyalty – I saw none of those instincts that should come from parents in that house."

PART TWO:
TEENAGE YEARS

Chapter Five

TAUGHT TO BULLY

MY PRIMARY SCHOOL WAS BALGOWAN IN BECKENHAM. I was probably the only black kid there, although my skin complexion was more Asian than Caribbean. And even though it was only a Primary School in 1975, I was called names like 'Paki', 'nig-nog', 'nigga', 'golliwog', 'blackie'.

But mainly 'Paki'.

Maybe inevitably, I became a bully, even at this tender age. I would intimidate classmates, give them the eye – eye contact was something I associated with power and brutality.

"What you looking at, who you looking at, you looking at me...?" I could gauge fear this way: who was going to fight back, who wasn't. Easy.

I'd fight with kids just for the sake of it. I'd walk the street looking for trouble: "Did you look at me just then?" If I felt they had, I'd hit them.

Fighting for me when I was eight, nine and ten was completely normal: I was the hardest in my year. *Get out of my way.*

I was absolutely tiny, too, but I could throw punches and hurt. I've no doubt now that I was looking for fights to get rid of all the aggression I wouldn't dare unleash against George or my older, bigger, brothers. I bullied other kids like George bullied me.

I was looking for any lame reason to fight, I enjoyed it, enjoyed the adrenalin rush. I'd snatch kids' sweets, intimidate them, give them loads of threats. And loads of eye.

If a new kid arrived, I'd want to fight him straight away to prove I was the hardest in that year. Even at this age, I never lost a street fight. There was too much anger and aggression inside me.

But it wasn't all one-way traffic. If I wasn't getting hit at home, I'd be getting hit at school.

In those days, headmasters were allowed to strike you on the backside: Balgowan's head was a big, fat Welshman – Mr Davis – and he'd literally pick me up with one hand and swipe away at me, almost rhythmically.

"Kev-in, you nor-tee boy; Kev-in you nor-tee boy… " It had a real jingle to it.

After three or four whacks, I'd start sobbing: "I'm sorry Mr Davis, I won't do it again, please don't hit me." But a violent pattern was emerging: the only contact I was having with adults in authority – my father and my head teacher – was to be their victim. To be hit, to experience pain, to feel brutality and to link all that with authority and control.

I was eight years old and learning how hitting causes fear, panic and dread. All that did was teach me how to use it to my own advantage against kids more my size.

I realise now that I haven't mentioned the name Mr Davis to anybody for 35 years and yet now I see him like I'm eight all over and he's striking me again.

He always kept my shorts on, there was no cane; he just struck me with his palm. It was how he did it that remains planted in my head:

"Kev-in, you nor-tee boy, Kev-in you nor-tee boy."

There was no real pain, just the mental shock of being struck. The sight and thought and sound of it. After all, the pain was nothing to the onslaught I endured at home.

I wanted to learn, I really did, but from an early age I sensed everyone thought I was a trouble-maker, disruptive. Put Lueshing at the back and keep him out of the way of the cleverer kids.

And I was very, very slow – which wasn't surprising really. Nobody realised, nobody identified or spotted it, but I was dyslexic. All I heard was: "You're thick, Lueshing, what's wrong with you?"

I couldn't even pronounce certain words properly. The dyslexia left me with a slight speech impediment, and I really struggled to say basic childhood words like sausages, or even chicken. But instead of seeking help and advice, my mother would laugh it off and let me carry on mis-pronouncing words as if it didn't really matter.

When we reached our final year at primary school, the ten and eleven year-olds could go to summer camp in Somerset as a fare-well treat before leaving for big school.

It was legendary: there'd be photographs of previous summer camps all over the corridor walls, with kids laughing and waving next to their tents and sleeping bags. It was a five-day adventure and I wanted to go, badly. Anything to get away from home.

But the teachers knew what I was like, so they gave me the big lecture. "Kevin, we want to take you, but you're so destructive. Other parents have complained about you and said they're worried about their children being bullied if you go on the trip."

I begged and pleaded and promised to be good and was granted one last chance. If I could behave for one whole term, I could go.

There were three weeks left when a kid gave me some back-chat, I think he called me 'golliwog' or something like that. I erupted and slapped him. He started crying, Mr Davis appeared from nowhere: there was big drama. "Kevin, you nor-tee boy" – smack – "Kev-in, you nor-tee boy… "

And for a fleeting second I thought the matter was over. But a couple of days later my parents got a letter from the school saying I couldn't go on the trip.

I was in floods of tears, stormed straight outside the house and immediately killed three of my stag beetles, which I used to collect in a jar.

Chapter Six

THE GROOMING

I WAS TEN AND A HALF YEARS OLD.

I first noticed Derek at weekends when my brothers or pals would hang round Beckenham Park, playing football. He'd be there walking his dog and sometimes he'd pass and casually say: "Hi lads, how's it going, who's winning?" That sort of stuff. Eventually we got to know his Christian name and it was all very innocent and normal.

I remember he walked with a limp and I noticed one of his shoes had an abnormally high heel, probably because one leg was shorter than the other. I didn't really care.

But I became more involved with Derek at our local newsagents. I'd got a job as a newspaper delivery boy, £2.50 a week.

The shop was run by an old man who used to smoke a pipe and could barely see or hear anything.

His shop was chaos: papers everywhere, magazines, comics, *Reader's Digests*, everything scattered and thrown randomly and in all the wrong places. Lots of sweets. Lots and lots of cigarettes: Benson and Hedges, Players, Embassy, every cigarette you could think of, plus an old display cabinet full of cigars and pipes.

It was a real old-fashioned newsagents: the main window was packed with everything a ten year-old doesn't want while inside was an oasis of everything a ten year-old really needs.

My eyes always went straight to the comics: *Beano*, Spiderman, Batman, Superman. Newspapers seemed to be everywhere – and glossy magazines for just about everyone, young and old. I remember noticing something called *Playboy* high up on the shelf – but I never saw inside it.

To my surprise Derek was there when I turned up on my first morning. He was in charge of organising all the paperboys and telling them which roads they would be delivering in that day.

"Hallo, Kevin, what you doing here, my friend?"

"Hi Derek. I've got a delivery job."

"That's great, little buddy, I sort all the rounds out. Tell you what, you do Cromwell Road today, that's a nice easy one for starters. There you go, Kev, take care – see you later."

Now, for the first time proper, I started to look at Derek more closely.

He had a limp, everything about him looked seedy, dishevelled, dirty and shabby. His face was thin and there were lots of veins round his cheekbones and neck that looked uncomfortably close to bursting out of his skin at any moment. His clothes seemed too big for him: they hung, they didn't fit.

He was about six foot tall and I noticed a thin silver chain round his neck with a small cross of Jesus inside a circle dangling on the end. He was Catholic.

He also had tattoos: one of a bulldog, another of a heart with a dagger ripping through it in a blaze of bright red blood. Both were on his right arm; he was right-handed.

I noticed, also, that Derek had rotten teeth: he chain-smoked roll-ups – Golden Virginia from a green tin. His fingers were sickly yellow from all the smoking.

He wasn't completely bald, but he certainly had receding hair that revealed so much forehead that his face looked out of proportion with itself. And he wore glasses with lenses that bulged out of thick black frames: they looked more like magnifying glasses than normal lenses.

But the sad thing about it was, his eyes looked kind.

Reassuring, don't-worry eyes.

I'd guess he was about 55, I never found out. He was just a man and his name was Derek.

And yes, we had warnings about not talking to strangers, although we didn't know exactly why. But the reality was, if anybody came up to me and said, "Hello, how are you?" I'd automatically think: *he's nice*. I wasn't getting that sort of attention or interest off anyone back home. Nobody at 101 Clockhouse Road was inquisitive about Kevin. Nobody said: "Are you OK, what've you done today?"

But this guy would be interested, or so I thought, in whatever I was up to. In particular, he was happy to talk to me about my love for superhero comics.

Then, over the next few days and eventually weeks, he might say: "What's your mum and dad do, Kev?" or "You got a girlfriend, Kev"?

And he noticed I had a roaming eye for sweets. Especially Black Jacks and Fruit Salads. The shop did 25 Black Jacks and 25 Fruit Salads, mixed, for 50 pence. Derek would crouch down, whispering in a conspiratorial way, his arm round my shoulder, all friendly with a let's-do-something-naughty-smirk across his face. "Go on, you take 'em, son. Don't tell anyone, go on, off you go, you enjoy them, buddy."

It all seemed normal and friendly and I enjoyed chatting along with him and sharing stuff with him. Absolutely nothing felt wrong. In fact I was looking up to him and enjoying his interest in me and his friendliness – only because I was getting none of that at home, or at school.

Derek's attention was better than no attention.

About five weeks later, there was only the two of us in the shop and Derek was getting my bag ready.

"What's your favourite comics then, Kev?"

"Oh, I love the *Beano* and Spiderman."

"That's incredible – so do I, Kev. Whereabouts do you live then, my buddy?"

"Clockhouse Road."

"Clockhouse Road! That's really near me. Tell you what, Kev, I've got bundles of comics back in my house. You'll have to come over one day and see them."

Then one weekend, I saw Derek at the park while I was waiting to meet up with some mates and he came over for a chat. "Hi, Kevin, how's it going, buddy? You on your own then, where is everyone?"

I explained I was waiting for my pals to show. He went off to walk his dog round the park, returning once the pair of them had done the full circle. "Your mates still not here, Kev?"

"Nah, don't think they're coming by the looks of it."

"Not coming!? What time you got to be home then, Kev?"

"About five o'clock."

"Plenty of time! How do you fancy coming back to mine? – I've got something you'd really like."

"What?"

"Spiderman!" And he said "Spiderman" triumphantly, as though it was the Crown Jewels, like he'd nicked them and he desperately wanted me in on his little secret. "Spiderman". The very name played havoc with my ten year-old imagination. Come to think of it, Spiderman actually was the Crown Jewels then: it was about 60 pence, out of my reach.

"Are you thirsty, Kev? How would you like to come back to my house, have a drink, and see my Spiderman comic?"

I was hooked. We walked side by side in broad daylight, Derek, me and his dog – a shabby, small bull terrier, just like Bull's Eye – the one that gets killed in *Oliver Twist*.

It was a sunny, summer's afternoon, and we walked down roads that I recognised because they were on my paper rounds. We chatted about superheroes and comics and what I was doing at school – the things that interested Kevin.

I was happy, I was walking with Derek, he was asking nice questions; he was like a mate, taking an interest.

Spiderman and lemonade.

"You're a good-looking boy, aren't you Kev. Tell me, where's your parents from?"

We arrived at his house and it was just like Derek: run-down, shabby, unattractive – seedy. It was semi-detached, small, with a very pale yellow front door that had two glass panels at the top with flowers engraved on them. The walls were coated in a heavy, disfiguring grey pebbledash. There was a small drive but no car.

The house is still there today. Just past the cemetery.

Derek was leaning over me to get his key in the front door. It opened and there was absolutely no foreboding in my mind, no sense of danger, no premonition of walking into something dark and menacing. But before he let me in, he said: "Hang on a sec, Kev, I just need to check my landlady is alright before you come in."

And I heard this old, female, disembodied voice coming from a distant place: "Who's that? Derek, that you, Derek? Everything OK?"

"Yes… it's just me, Val, I'm fine, I'm just coming in with the dog."

And he ushered me inside, half-pushing, half-directing me to go straight up the stairs that were right in front of me. I must be very quiet and not make a sound. He whispered: "Up you go, top of the stairs, first door, go on my little pal."

The house smelt instantly of old people and urine; it was suffocatingly warm, too, like the heating was permanently on full blast – even though it was hot and sunny outside. I reached upstairs and opened a white door into Derek's room.

Straight away I noticed a single bed on the right-hand side, under the window. Two dirty-looking pillows, a stained and discoloured wooden headboard and metal frame, with a burgundy blanket.

And in a flash, I was scanning that room for things to steal. It was like an automatic, natural impulse: what could I nick? If not today, then maybe next time.

I noticed ripped-open envelopes, old unwashed cups of tea, scattered newspapers on the floor. There was a radio on a white bedside cabinet next to his bed, switched on, even though Derek was not yet in the room with me. I could hear the jingle: "Oh, oh… Afternoon Delight!" To this day, I am convinced that was a section in Tony Blackburn's Radio One Show.

Later on in my life, when I was looking after former boxer Nigel Benn, we met Tony in Australia for the reality television show *I'm a Celebrity – Get Me Out of Here*. I went straight up to him and said: "I remember you, Tony Blackburn, I used to listen to you!"

I remember, too, noticing the bedside cabinet was open; inside it was heaving with what looked like prescription pills and medicine jars, cough tablets, torn-apart silver packets, all squashed in and wedged on top of one another ready to spill out on to the floor.

I spotted a Parker pen. The sort the newsagent sold in his shop, but kept in a padlocked display cabinet because they were so expensive.

There was a dull grey carpet and the room was overwhelmingly dusty. On one wall was a picture: the face of a little boy crying, with a circus in the background. It hung, haphazardly, above the bed, directly opposite you if you put your head on the pillows.

That picture has stuck with me ever since.

Then Derek came in, sat down on the bed and said: "You alright, son, come on, sit here – sit next to me. Let's look at the comic."

There is one over-riding memory of that moment, side by side on the bed, that still haunts me today. The smell. Derek didn't smell of drink – I'd noticed a bottle of Bell's on a table – or stale fag ends.

Derek smelt of Old Spice.

I have carried that heavily-scented, overly-perfumed odour with me all these years until all that's left is a retched, foul, nauseating assault that I recognise the moment it walks into any room, anywhere.

I am ten and a half.

And suddenly there it was in his hands: the Spiderman comic.

He had it. And we sat, side by side on his bed, pouring through the comic, pointing and laughing at the illustrations and discussing superheroes and who was the mightiest and the best. I even had a glass of lemonade as we talked.

Eventually, I announced: "I'd better be going now." And Derek was cool with that. "Of course, Kevin, it's been lovely to have you here, you must come again when I get some new comics." And he let me keep the Spiderman.

But he added: "Listen!

"This is between me and you, buddy. I like you, Kevin, you're a good boy and don't let anyone tell you different."

"Thanks Derek."

As I left, he reminded me to go quietly down the stairs because there was an old lady in the house who didn't like to be disturbed. I was laughing inside: I've got my Spiderman, I've clocked, I'm coming back and when I do, I'll nick that Parker pen.

Derek didn't have to tell me not to tell anyone. There was no way I would tell my brothers I'd found an old bloke who gives me comics, lemonade and lives in a house where it'll be easy to nick a few bits and pieces.

I'm keeping this secret, no problem. I'm not sharing this with anyone.

I saw Derek the next morning at the newsagents. "Alright, Kev, did you have a nice time yesterday? "

"Yeah, great." It's got to the stage now where I'm swiping handfuls of sweets – even packets of cigarettes that I can sell on – right in front of him, and he doesn't care. He lets me get on with it; the owner's far too old and confused to spot anything.

Increasingly, I'm the last paperboy left in the shop so there's just me and Derek chatting before I go off on my round. Just the two of us and the deaf old owner.

"Everything all right at home, Kev?"

"What about school?"

"Is your dad away at the moment, Kev?"

"You know what, buddy, I've got the latest *Beano*, I wasn't going to mention it, but you fancy coming over again next Sunday? I'll get some cakes and stuff. Come over Sunday, about five o'clock. OK?"

"Yeah, that'd be great Derek."

So I went back, and it was the same routine, and then again a third time – and then a fourth.

The fourth was different.

On the fourth visit, I walked into his room just like before and noticed something different straight away on the floor in front of his bed: glossy magazines like I'd seen on the top shelf at the shop – *Playboys*. I remember the vague outline of a woman's naked flesh on the front cover, nothing specific, just white woman flesh.

Derek saw me looking at them, sat next to me on the bed as usual, and said: "Kev, come and have a look at these."

But he wasn't holding *Playboy*. He had a different magazine open and he was showing me pictures I'd never seen before.

Men and women, naked, explicit; men aroused; women's faces, legs apart; flesh exposed, so closely it might be medical. Mouths dripping. Pubic hair. Men's faces.

Derek said it was called sex. Intercourse.

He continued slowly turning the pages over, one by one, letting me stare at them. Then vile whispering: "Do you like that, Kevin, how does that make you feel then, son? Hang on a second… What's this, Kevin?"

And he touched my crotch.

"Are you getting excited? You are, aren't you Kevin? Don't worry, son, that's natural, that's good, don't worry about it, we've all done that."

Everything was reassuring, like going into an operation and hearing a room of soothing voices as they prepare to inject you to sleep.

But Derek's trousers had now sunk to his ankles and his voice was getting more and more urgent: a deranged but softly-spoken torrent of perverted encouragement – "We like this, don't we, Kevin" – the word "we", his left hand on me, his right on his own groin. He was sounding more and more hurried and desperate and frenzied and rambling until –

Until his sickly voice checked to see whether he'd got away with it. "That was nice, wasn't it Kevin? You enjoyed that, didn't you, Kevin? You've been good, haven't you, Kevin?"

That was the first time I ever saw semen: it was horrible, grey. Grey like Derek, grey like his underpants, grey like the pebbledash on the outside of the house. That was the first time I had ever been touched like that. I didn't know if it was good or evil but I think something inside felt dirty. But not dirty enough to worry me or scare me.

Tissues. Then I was being ushered down the stairs, Derek whispering – "hush, hush" – front door opening quietly and I'm outside.

Grey clouds, grey pebbledash.

Grey. Everything about that house, grey.

I walked hurriedly home, my mind re-living the exposures: the magazine, the flesh, the bare legs, the bare groins; Derek's left hand, Derek's right hand.

Old Spice.

And while I had no understanding, no analytical concept of what had happened, and no idea of its illegality, its depravity, its sickness, its vileness, its corruption, I did have a moment of revelation.

I understood that I was more in control of this situation than Derek.

What can I get out of this? What can I steal? What can I earn?

I thought about the mysterious old woman, Val; she was my get-me-out-of-here safety net. If I raised my voice, if I shouted out, she'd want to know what all the fuss was about. I was protected.

So I went back the next weekend, and this time Derek said: "You know what, Kevin, let's look at those magazines again – but this time, I'm going to give you £2.50. You're such a good boy, Kevin."

Result.

"You can't tell anyone, though, Kevin. This is between me and you. This is our secret, isn't it?"

I am a little boy called Kevin.

Outside, I could hear birds singing. Derek hadn't drawn the curtains, it was still daylight and I was suddenly aware of birds chirping and flapping their wings.

I become increasingly aware of everything else in the room that wasn't Derek or even Kevin: the boy crying in the picture; a fly climbing the wall opposite; an unwashed enamel cup of tea that looked old and battered and maybe came from the army. Was Derek in the army once?

I heard the birds again. They could be my witnesses, like the old woman downstairs – the birds would protect me, just like Val.

I looked out of the window and the illusion was shattered. They were just bloody birds and, just like Derek, they were *grey*.

This time my left hand was on his left hand and my right hand on his right, moving, up and down. And I was getting £2.50. Nobody would believe me, even if I told them. In any case, there was no way I would be sharing this situation with anyone. *Don't worry, Derek, your secret is safe.*

I'm so fucked up at home, and at school, this wasn't going to make any difference. I won't tell anyone. If I told my brothers, they might take my £2.50. I don't want that.

Chapter Seven

INNOCENCE RAPED

MY MIND ONLY LETS ME RECALL TWO OR THREE MORE visits: a mechanism within me is refusing to let me remember the others. But there must have been more because I worked out a way of short-cutting to Derek's house. All I had to do was cross the train line at the back of Clockhouse Road, squeeze through a fence into a big wood yard, through an alley and I was there – 10 minutes instead of 45.

I became more aware of Val with each visit, although I never saw her. I noticed a wheelchair, and occasionally her forlorn cry: "Who's with you, Derek? You know you're not allowed anyone in your room. No lady friends."

There was definitely a second time, and a third, and I was earning. Sometimes Derek used his mouth instead of his hand. "Go on, look at these pictures, Kevin. Look what's happening there, that's nice isn't it. You'll love that."

£2.50. Sitting on the bed, leaning back, elbows pressed into the eiderdown.

Boy in the picture; birds; Val. My protectors.

And although I was determined to keep it secret, every time I went home I'd scrub myself clean: my hands, my face, the parts Derek had abused. I wanted that smell off me. The Old Spice. Then I'd get into my bed, suck my fingers and play with my pillow.

Sometimes Mum would see I'd got some money and say: "Where you get this from Kevin?"

"Oh, just washing cars." She wasn't interested.

She wouldn't have noticed me twitching or scrubbing my hands, my fingers, playing with the pillow, going off to bed on my own. She wasn't aware. She should have been but she had too much violence and chaos at 101 Clockhouse to notice something was wrong with Kevin.

Then, one morning, I walked into the newsagents and there was no sign of Derek. "He doesn't work here anymore."

I felt instant panic. I felt the loss of £2.50. *What shall I do?*

So I took a chance. The following Sunday, I crossed the train line, squeezed through the fence, out of the wood yard and knocked on Derek's door. He answered, mouth wide open in complete disbelief that I was stood in front of him.

He looked furtively behind him to check no-one was in the hallway and whispered: "What you doing here, son? Get away, go." His eyes darted anxiously up and down the street, then back over his shoulder again, then back to the street. Nervous, agitated Derek.

And that's when I did the one thing that repulses me now more than anything else.

I touched him.

On the front of his grey trousers. On the doorstep.

I am a little boy called Stan.

"I've come for you. It'll only take 10 minutes. Come on."

"OK, OK: come back in an hour, son."

So I hung round the park, killing time. And when it started getting dark, I went back.

I walked into his room: the electric heater was on. He must have spilt something on it because there was a strong, burning smell, like something frying on the elements. Smelt like burning coffee.

This time, Derek had a different magazine in his hand which he wanted to show me. But before he does, he says in an excitable voice: "Guess what I've got for you, Kevin. I've got… £10! Ten pounds for you, Kevin. £10 – if we do this…"

And The Predator showed me the magazine. This time, the pictures were different. There were no women. Just men. Men on top of one another. Naked men leaning over. Naked men leaning into each other. Contorted faces. Pain there, maybe.

"This is what we'll do, Kev."

I didn't understand. I couldn't quite tell from the pictures what these bare men were doing to each other, or how. I'd never seen these sorts of pictures before. But I thought I registered pain in some of the faces.

"It won't hurt, honest, it won't Kev. Trust me, son. Don't worry, I've got some Vaseline."

I've seen Mum use Vaseline on her hands.

Then Derek told me I had to go into another bedroom this time, on the opposite side of the landing. "We don't want to disturb my landlady, do we, Kevin?

"Remember, Kevin, you're going to get £10." And he showed me the giant brown note, holding it aloft as though it's the world's wealth in the palms of his hand. And I'd inherit it all. Cinema, jam doughnuts, comics; Black Jacks and Fruit Salad sweets.

My only fear was not what I'd have to do to earn that £10. It was how I would hide the note back home.

And a tiny little voice, so tiny inside me I could barely hear it, said: "No, Kevin. Get out."

But it just wasn't quite loud enough. I looked at the pictures, looked closely again at what I suspected was pain – but I wasn't still sure. Derek could see what I was puzzling over and said: "Look how much fun they're having. Look, that man is laughing. Don't worry, Kevin, it doesn't hurt. You just go into that room, take your clothes off and I'll be with you in a minute."

I need that £10. I want that £10.

So I went into the room but it was too dark inside. There was a faint red light from somewhere, I couldn't tell where because the curtains were drawn. It wasn't like Derek's room at all.

I saw the outline of a small single bed: focussd on it and saw it was messy, untidy, nylon sheets screwed up, no headboard.

Then Derek walked in. "Take your clothes off, son, that's a good boy." So I stripped but kept my underpants on. "Take them off, son. It's alright, nothing's going to hurt. Don't worry, you'll really like it. And you'll get your £10."

Derek undressing, Derek exposed now.

Derek with Vaseline in his hand: Derek pushing me face first into the bed; Derek starting to press against the back of me; Derek spreading grease over me.

Derek's arms around my neck; Derek cuddling me but tight enough so he can manoeuvre my naked body. Derek's stale cigarette breath on my neck; Derek kissing my neck; Derek's coarse stubble on my skin. Derek snuggling into me with his beard and his crusty arms, covered with eczema.

Derek's got moles and a big, ugly purple birthmark stain high on his right leg.

And he's caveman hairy.

He stinks, too: and this time it's not Old Spice. It's a suffocating, squalid, filthy, dirty, repulsive odour. The worst kind of male BO. Naked Derek smells…

Soiled.

Like unclean toilets.

And his hands are on my back, he's cuddling me and I can feel the greasy Vaseline on his hands as he paws me.

And it's like being in that suitcase again; I'm claustrophobic. I have to get out, Derek is holding me too tight, I'm wriggling, my breath is rapidly panicking, his tongue is on my neck, his lewd leather lips licking the surface of my skin. I can feel the hairs on his arms: he's like a python, manoeuvring his prey, getting him into position, squeezing until all that's left is surrender.

What am I? Who am I?

Am I Kevin?

Am I Stan?

I am scared. Mother-of-God terrified. Save me God. Save Kevin or save Stan, save one of them.

Save me Mum.

"Mum, Mum, where are you, I need you. Mum."

It's kicking in. It's not right, I don't like this. Mum – I want Mum. I yell: "No."

I scream: "Stop."

"NO."

Hysterical now: "No, Derek, no. I don't like it, Derek, no." And I'm starting to cry.

"I want Mum. I want my mum."

Then I hear the landlady: "Derek, what's going on? Have you got someone with you up there, Derek?"

My safety net.

Now Derek's panicking. "No, no, everything's alright, Val."

And he's frantically whispering to me, but in a sort of menacing, teacher-disciplines-child kind of way: "Listen, be quiet, nothing's happened to you. Everything's alright. Now calm down and stop crying, I'm going to sort out Val, stay here, I'll be back."

Derek went downstairs and I realised that was my moment to get out. *I'm never coming back to this hell again. This is worse than being at home, so I might as well be at home, back to the shithole I come from. That's safer.*

I grabbed my clothes, yanked on pants and trousers and plimsolls in a wild frenzy of arms and limbs and panic. But I'd still got my nerve: on the floor was the £10 note; I stooped, picked it up and stuffed it in my pocket. I'm having that. I'd earned it.

But I wanted more, so I ran into Derek's room, looking for stuff to steal. I looked round – there, something silver, what's that? His bloody chain with the medallion of Jesus inside a circle. I'll take that.

What else? A Parker pen – I'm nicking that, too, that's mine now.

I raced down the stairs, out through the kitchen and I tore down the road. And here's a thing: I was crying but I was laughing.

Laughing at Kevin getting out of that, getting the £10, the bit of silver, the Parker pen.

Laughing because I know Kevin was free, he would never be going back, he'd got away with it.

But crying because I was terrified, too; crying because I almost lost control. Crying because I could still smell him on my skin.

Crying because I hated being Kevin.

Chapter Eight

TEACHER CRUELTY

PRIMARY SCHOOL HAD BEEN BAD ENOUGH: BUT TAME compared to what lay ahead. All the Lueshing brothers went to Kelsey Park Comprehensive, where we were despised by the teachers and feared by classmates. On day one, I was greeted with: "Oh no, not another Lueshing."

To be fair, I was wasted before I even got to the school gates. I'd hooked up with a pal, Dean, and we'd meet up at around 8am each morning by the nearby railway tracks and sniff Evo-Stick.

I'd seen some skinheads doing it in the park; it looked tough and cool and I wanted to copy them.

There was an element of excitement and danger about it and I loved that. That was the turn on for me. We'd get the glue, tip it into a bag, stick the bag to our mouths and inhale the fumes. This was definitely what got me hooked on drugs in later life; it would send me places, it would block my mind from just about anything and everything.

Glue-sniffing was a weird kind of buzz; Dean and I would both be hallucinating but somehow manage to drag ourselves up and walk like zombies into school.

We were getting so hooked, we'd want more during the day. It even got to a point where we'd be sticking ink cartridges into the pin holes on our blazer lapels and sucking up the fumes as hard as we could.

The teachers eventually cottoned on: on one occasion, during a drama class, a teacher came up to me and told me to take off my blazer. I handed it to him, he immediately smelt the lapel and ordered me straight to the headmaster.

Another thing we used to do was gas. We used to put our mouths over cigarette lighters and suck up the gas: it would totally screw our heads. We were doing this in the playground. There were areas where you could go where you'd always see discarded lighters on the floor and you knew kids had been gas-sniffing.

On my fifth day at Kelsey Park, I was suspended.

A big kid tried his luck with a Lueshing and started to push me about in the playground. Errol – who was a vicious fighter himself – beat him so ferociously, he knocked him flat out and was suspended on the spot.

And even though I was the victim, I was the one who had been bullied, I was suspended as well because I was a Lueshing. They really didn't want us at that school and I knew from the very beginning I would have no sympathy or help from the teachers.

They could be brutal and racist in equal measure. "Oi, Lueshing, come here, where've you been, you waste of space, you little wog."

There were around 1,000 pupils at Kelsey but maybe only 20 black kids and teachers would regularly call us 'golliwogs', or 'wogs', or 'blackie' – that was a favourite. Sometimes they'd say it as though we were some worthless sub-class, some piece of filth on their shoes. Other times, they'd say it because they had a white audience, and they wanted to get a laugh.

All the black kids wanted to play football at Kelsey Park but we were never picked for the school first teams, no matter how good we might be. I was in the second team, that was allowed, but I could never get into the top team, never. I was good, I was fast, I could control a ball. In fact, I would often hear the teachers on the sideline shouting: "Get the black bastard, get Lueshing."

I even got assaulted by one of the teachers. I'd been mucking around in class and annoyed the master. His punishment was to make me hold a heavy book in each hand and stretch my arms out as far as they would go, holding the books straight without dropping them in front of the whole class.

If you dropped one, you'd get the slipper: inevitably, I did. The master made me stand outside the classroom, and when the lesson was over he called me back in and started lecturing me: "You little black bastard, I've had problems with you all year, I can't wait to get rid of you."

He was spewing out these words, with genuine force and anger. Then he grabbed me round my throat – I was still only small and started gasping and squirming – and ranted: "We can't wait to get rid of you, you bastard. And your bastard brothers."

Then he let go but he was still pumped up and heaving with hatred and roared: "Get outside, you're getting the cane."

I stood in the corridor, gasping and sobbing. Then, one of my brothers, Errol, approached. "What the hell's going on, Kev?"

I told him I was about to be caned but he insisted: "Kevin, they're not allowed to. They'd have to phone home and get Mum's permission to do that. Tell them you can't remember the phone number or just get the number wrong."

And he ran off, promising to tell my dad what was going on. I wasn't sure that was such a good idea but he was gone.

I was eventually called into the headmaster's office. He explained I was to be caned, but it would only be one strike. "Yes, sir, but sir, could you please ring my mother first to see if she gives permission for this to happen, sir."

That completely disarmed him: he started mumbling about what the phone number was, then maybe this could be a final warning if I promised to behave. In the end, I escaped the cane.

But by then Errol had got back home and explained to my father what had happened: that a master had me up by the throat against a wall.

Next, I spotted my dad hurtling up the school driveway in his BMW, leaping out of the car and tearing into the main reception area where the headmaster's office was. I was petrified, I had no idea which way this would go but I feared the worst.

But my dad's philosophy was: I can beat the shit out of my boys but nobody else can lay a finger on them. Everyone could see my dad was in a rage and staff were trying to reason with him: "Mr Lueshing, do you realise it's a criminal offence to come barging into this school?"

His reply? "Fuck off, fuck off, where's that fuckin' bastard teacher?"

And then George spotted him, trying to creep into the headmaster's office.

My dad had those bloody cowboy boots on again; he tore straight up to the master, pushed him violently against a wall that almost collapsed with the impact and wrapped his hands around his throat.

That was the only moment in my life when I felt proud of my dad. My father had my back for me: the same man who intimidated and bullied me and who stole my childhood and who turned me into the violent, angry, disturbed child I was.

Here he was, suddenly standing in my corner. Now it was the teacher's turn to gasp for breath, his terrified body wriggling and twisting and trying to break free. But with each limp movement my dad was getting more and more ferocious: "If you ever lay a finger again on my son – or any one of my sons – I will fuckin' do life for you, you bastard."

I will never forget those words.

I will fuckin' do life for you.

And I could see the same look in George's eyes at that moment – wild, vicious anger – that I saw when he was beating the life out of me and my brothers. In fact, this time, it was wilder and more violent, if that were possible.

The master whimpered and grovelled and my dad just suddenly let go, turned round and walked straight out, past all the other teachers and staff who had rushed to see what all the commotion was about, who were hysterical, but who hadn't dared lay a finger on him.

I just stood there, in awe, mouth wide open, and watched my dad climb back in to his BMW and drive out of the gates.

Everyone was looking at me, and I was looking back at them, into their eyes and their eyes were saying: "Wow, man, I ain't touching you again."

I was 12 and a half.

I got my own back on another teacher, who I despised more than any of the others.

Ironically, he had a gentle, feminine face and his voice was equally at odds with his nature: quiet and soft, almost as though it had never properly broken. Talk about appearances being deceptive.

He was on my case all the time: once, he ordered me to do litter duty outside while everyone else was packed inside the main hall for morning assembly. It was humiliating: it felt completely demeaning, everyone looking at me, giggling and pointing as I picked up scraps of paper and rubbish.

Maybe he was justified, maybe he was simply doing his job, but it seemed to me he was on my case all the time. His mantra was: date, time, offence, culprit. I can hear him now: "The fifth of the fourth, Kevin Lueshing swears at teacher."

Another time: "You know where you're going to end up, Lueshing? I know where you're going to end up: borstal. You can't help it, can you Lueshing? You have to be just like your brothers, don't you Lueshing?"

Or: "There's not a talent in you Lueshing, you're worthless, no good to anybody. What you going do with your life, eh?"

"Don't know, sir."

"Well I'll tell you. You're going to do nothing, Lueshing, because you're a nobody, a worthless, useless piece of nothing."

But my moment for revenge came when I was waiting outside his classroom one day. A secretary came along the corridor with a cup of tea, saw I was waiting and asked me to take it in for the teacher.

"Yes, Miss, will do."

There was nobody around in that moment and the temptation was overwhelming. I leaned my head over the cup and gobbed right into the tea – a really great big, fat frothy gob of saliva and spit. I then picked up the spoon and stirred it all in as quickly as I could.

You have no idea how proud I was of myself at that moment. I had real balls and I couldn't wait, couldn't wait, to tell all my mates and brothers what I'd done.

Almost straight away, the teacher called me into his room. I walked in confidently and said: "Cup of tea for you, sir." I didn't care what I'd done, or what he was going to do or say, he was sipping the tea in between telling me off for something and I was completely alive inside. My adrenalin was pumping, I was triumphant, top of the world: the undisputed champion.

Got you, you bastard.

Inevitably, I carried on being a bully and even started running my own protection racket, just like something out of a Mafia movie.

I would observe kids and see who was getting bullied, who was vulnerable and who was doing it to them. There were even times when I felt sorry for some of them. When I made it as a boxer, old classmates I barely remembered would get in touch with me out of the blue and thank me for having stood up for them over something.

I'd pick a vulnerable kid, go up to them, and say: "Right, you give me your dinner tickets and I'll make sure nobody bullies you for the rest of the week."

And I'd take the dinner tickets and sell them for 10 pence or something in the playground to other kids. It was quite a lucrative little business; I'd have four or five of them every week.

There was one little kid, so small we called him Mouse, he used to have salt and vinegar crisps, the ones which came with a little salt sachet you'd sprinkle yourself over the crisps.

He would give me those crisps – but only so nobody would touch him during geography class, which was 55 minutes. That's how frightened Mouse was.

And I got a little gang together, two or three other hard nuts and a court jester, who was shit at fighting but made us laugh so he could be one of us and nobody would touch him.

Me, Steven Jeffrey, Matthew Curtis, Di Percival: that was my gang.

I was spending my schooldays either wasted on glue, bullying kids or being beaten by teachers. I was treated like I was thick and maybe I was, although they never identified my dyslexia. And I actually did have moments when I truly wanted to understand things.

I wasn't rubbish at everything: I enjoyed history, and I really liked, strangely, drama.

Drama for me was about going into character – and I've since learnt that's what people do when they're abused. It's a bit like the actor Robin Williams: nobody knew who he really was because he was so full of different characters.

I was similar as a kid; I would swap and change between different characters because I didn't want to be Kevin.

Kevin was going through too much turmoil, Kevin was taking drugs, sniffing glue, getting abused; Kevin was too dark, Kevin was feeling pain and dread and terror, Kevin was getting beaten; Kevin was a bully.

Sometimes, I wanted to be Willis, the main character in the American sitcom *Different Strokes*, who gets adopted by a wealthy white family and has the time of his life. I thought that was far better than being me.

I might suddenly start laughing about something and without even thinking I'd be a comic like Jerry Lewis. And that could be in the middle of a beating: without George knowing I'd pretend inside myself to be someone: perhaps Eddie Murphy, Richard Pryor – anybody who was funny or comical, never anyone that was sad or tragic themselves.

Sometimes heroes: Spiderman, Superman: people that I could never be. I would go into these characters and would instantly be in another world, out of this turmoil; fantasising the next day into a better day than it could ever be.

So maybe I liked drama because I liked playing characters. They were away from Kevin. I loved it because I was not me for a short while: we didn't get to William Shakespeare or anything heavy like that but I remember very clearly performing in *A Christmas Carol*.

I played the little kid, Tiny Tim, who's seriously ill and certain to die – until Scrooge changes his horrible ways and makes sure the child is saved. Not that anyone ever saved me.

Once, after a games lesson, I was putting my underpants on when a voice suddenly screamed: "Urr, Lueshing, you've got my pants on."

"What you talking about?" I yelled back. "These are my pants."

But it was true: the lad came up to me, Mark Smith, yanked the top of the pants round so I could see the name tag at the back – and there was his name, stitched on. My mum had bought the Y-fronts from a charity shop and they still had 'Mark Smith' stitched into the elastic.

I was totally ashamed and cursed my mother for not thinking. But I grabbed hold of Mark Smith and snarled in his face, menacingly: "If you ever tell anyone, I'll knock you out."

"I'll knock you out." Those were my four favourite words at school.

PART THREE:
APPRENTICE BOXER

Chapter Nine

LEARNING TO HIT

MY TRAINER DRAWS CIRCLES ON THE SURFACE OF AN old punch bag – one's for the head, one's for the kidneys, one for the stomach. It's perfect for me and who I am: it channels my aggression and energy and the way I feel about the world and lets me release it all, lets it all explode on to that bag. And it helps me find the points of maximum pain on an opponent's body – I'll lash into the circles on the bag, knowing I'm finding pain.

I'm not just striking a bag: that bag is my opponent, my enemy, and I'm hitting him where it really hurts.

And sometimes that bag is my dad.

Sometimes he comes to see me and hovers round for a while, watching me hitting the bag. And he probably thinks I'm imagining hitting an opponent.

But I'm not: I'm imagining hitting *him*.

Take that you bastard, and I clobber him in the kidneys, one two, blink of an eye, he doesn't see it coming.

Then, smash, right up the front of his face, so his nose explodes and there's blood flying around like a spewing volcano.

Smash, *you bastard*, smash straight into his face which boils over into an eruption of bruises and scars. Thud, *watch this uppercut George*: bang, right into the left eye, bang into his right; he can't see now as his eyelids mushroom over the slits of his evil eyeballs and he's reeling round in the dark, coughing up blood, doubled up, retching.

And he's begging now: *beg you bastard, beg*; and his corner throws in the towel and he's finished. He'll never raise a hand against me ever again.

One day, George.

****

I only got into boxing to get out of the house.

I was fleeing the hands and wrath of George – preferring instead to take my chances against an opponent who wanted to beat the living daylights out of me in a boxing ring.

But it really wasn't a calling. Despite all the brutality and pain in my life, there was never a moment when I thought: "I know, I'll take up boxing."

It just wasn't like that. A mate of my brothers Errol and Andrew, Mark Finch, went every week to the South Norwood Boxing Club, so they started going, too.

I realised my dad was giving them a bit of leniency, letting them go out in the evenings and that was unheard of. My dad's rule was: "If you're out at night on the street, you're going to be in trouble with the police. So you don't go out."

But Errol and Andrew were getting on their bikes and being allowed to cycle the five miles to South Norwood. I took the plunge and said: "Can I come'?

I was eleven, I'd just started at secondary school and I knew nothing about boxing, or boxers, other than I'd heard of Muhammad Ali, who I'd seen on TV.

I'd seen Marvin Hagler and Sugar Ray Leonard, too; I had a vague interest in them, nothing more. Boxing was not big on my radar. My brothers were going; it was a way of getting out of the house.

So I went to the South Norwood boxing club. The gym was under a working man's pub on Sunnybank Road: it was dark, dingy and perfect for hard core; perfect for victims. There were one or two black faces there but overwhelmingly it was white territory. Naked flesh hitting battered old punch bags suspended from beams; smelly, nasty, dirty, stale and sweaty.

A big, squashed-nose bloke came up to my brothers; his name was Bill. He took a look at me – in a sort of half-disgusted, half-amused way – and said: "Who's this?"

"Kevin… our brother."

"Arr, look how small he is. OK, get in front of the mirror. Which hand do you write with, son?" I told him I was left-handed and he explained that must be the hand I lead with when punching.

But my brothers thought differently. When they spotted me leading with my left, which felt natural, they immediately said: "Nah, you're doing it all wrong, do it our way." They were right-handed, so they naturally and instinctively led with their right.

I gave it a go but it instantly felt uncomfortable: "Errol, this don't feel right."

But he replied: "That don't matter, they don't like left-handers here." Which was right: boxers in those days didn't approve of 'southpaws'.

So I kept practising the way Errol insisted, even though my legs kept crossing over each other and everything seemed clumsy and unnatural. It was like playing football but only being allowed to use the leg you don't instinctively kick with.

I shadow-boxed in front of the mirror for hours on end at the club: it was painful, my arms were constantly aching; it was relentless, boring, repetitive and just when my arms were flailing a voice would yell out above all the heaving bodies: "Don't drop your hands, Lueshing, keep those hands up."

Sometimes I'd stand still in front of the mirror and stare at myself. And all I saw was a little kid. I saw nothing else: I was just a little 'Paki' called Stan. I was only doing it because my brothers were doing it, I didn't want to miss out and better still, I was getting a night away from home.

I started to do skipping to improve fitness; then groundwork – sit ups, push ups. My brothers and I would take it in turns to hold each other's legs.

The gym would be very solemn; nobody talked, everybody was concentrating on whatever they had to do. I was thrown in with my brothers, which meant I was in the wrong age group. I was in with lads who seemed big enough to be men.

It was daunting: there was a different kind of smell. I was intimidated by it all, overwhelmed by the shapes and sizes and brute force of men and the sight of men watching men, intensely. Big bulging flesh everywhere, it all felt – and looked – raw; men getting showered and great big clouds of steam coming out of the showers. I'd never seen so many huge, naked white bodies in my life.

These were my first experiences of boxing. Did I want to stick at it? No. It was cold, it was a long, long ride on my 20-inch bike to

South Norwood. But then next week would come along and I'd see my brothers getting ready, so I went back. Same the next week – and the week after.

One week I decided I was definitely not returning but George found out and said: "You not going to the boxing then? So you're a quitter are you? You just give up. Well no son of mine gives up. Lueshings do not give up."

And those words resonated with me, they still do now. *Do not give up.* That was it, I went back to the gym and carried on going back to the gym.

Eventually I was allowed to hit one of the battered punch bags. I was given some torn and tatty gloves, with horses' hair spilling out of the seams. They were primitive and when I struck the bag, my knuckles would feel the full force of each hit because they hardly had any protection from the gloves.

But the physical action of striking something, of hitting out, didn't bother me in the slightest – after all, I'd spent most of my childhood hitting other kids and hitting them hard.

This felt the same. In fact, hitting a punch bag, even with rotten old gloves, felt easier. After all, nobody was hitting back, or squirming away.

Now I could learn the science of hitting, I could aim: my eyes were like a hawk – whichever spot on the bag they focused on, my hands would hit. Eye-to-hand co-ordination. It was easy and I understood it.

I was learning how to jab, too. My reflection in the mirror became my opponent; move, jab, shadow-box, dodge. These were the basic disciplines I picked up at South Norwood.

There was no real sign of talent at this point: nobody had picked me out and thought "We've got something here." I was simply escaping home.

Sometimes I'd pretend to go to the boxing – but go elsewhere instead. One evening, I went off on my bike and headed straight for my pal's house, where I was going to play Space Invaders or something. I was just about to reach his house when I realised there was a big BMW pulling up alongside me: it was Dad.

"Where you going son," he shouted through the window. "Why you going this way? Which way is South Norwood, son? What the fuck are you going this way for, son?"

I whimpered that I was going to see my mate, Matthew George ordered me to turn straight back home and get one of his belts from his wardrobe. I cycled back; he whacked me across the palms of my hand with the belt I'd chosen and then barked: "Now get back on your bike and go to the bleedin' boxing."

Chapter Ten

YOUNG PRETENDER

FOR THE FIRST TIME IN MY LIFE, I CLAMBER INTO A proper boxing ring, elevated, in the full glare of a boozed-up audience: around 200 mainly white men, frothing with beer and steak and guffawing laughter; padded in their black suits and bow ties, with ludicrous white shirts barely able to constrain bulging stomachs; rowdy, raucous and increasingly drunk, demanding to be entertained and thirsty for some young violence as they tuck into their big, fat dinners.

The ring seems massive to me, so big it's like a gigantic playground; you could play football in here. I look to the floor, and immediately see bloodstains.

I am twelve years old, about to face my first real opponent for the first time in my life in a real boxing ring, instead of a street or school playground or a gym. The ring at the South Norwood is on ground level, it's not like this one.

I'm transfixed by clouds of cigar smoke billowing across the ring and I find myself breathing it in, gasping before a punch is even thrown. My heart's pounding – boom, boom, boom – inside my tiny chest and I suddenly want to get out of this mess. It's too scary.

And for the first time, I hear the words 'Seconds away' and the sound of a bell heralding my first steps into a boxing ring.

My fight career is about to begin. I am taking my first steps towards a world title fight against one of the world's most-famous boxers...

****

When George found out I was having my first proper fight he immediately insisted on buying me all the proper gear, and for the first time in my life I was given genuine black Lonsdale boxing shorts, boxing shoes and a boxing vest.

I was overjoyed and bursting with pride; for me to have new stuff was like: *Wow, now I'll have to make sure I do my dad proud.* The thought that he wouldn't even bother to watch me never entered my mind.

Normally I wore some tatty plimsolls, dirty old shorts and a torn vest at the gym: now I had 'Lonsdale' on my legs and that felt like the big time. I still have a photo of me standing in all that gear – looking and feeling like a champ.

I'm not even sure why George showed me that rare moment of generosity. He was good friends with a boxer called Frankie Lucas and he certainly respected and admired boxers: he loved Ali and sometimes we'd watch his fights together. Boxing was very much an accepted and honourable route out of poverty for black kids at the time. Black kids didn't do football in the early eighties; if they were fit and strong, they boxed.

My first fight was a dinner show at the Queens Hotel in Crystal Palace. For the first time I saw my name in a programme and even though it was spelt wrong, it didn't matter. What mattered was that I was official and there was my weight confirmed in black and white for all to see: I was fighting at 42 kilos.

I was ushered into a makeshift changing room and instantly started scanning it ferociously to see who my opponent might be. That's something that has never left me, and it never will: sizing up a room: who's in here, who looks dangerous, weak, who do I fear, who do I trust, who's who?

Then my trainer whispered: "Right, Kev, you're fourth on." In those days, you didn't have your own gloves – you had to use the ones from the previous fight. Mine arrived and there were spots of blood on them; they were still hot, sweaty and smelly. I battled silently with my increasing sense of anxiety and fear – and the thought that someone had just been battered by the gloves I was struggling to put on.

I was utterly on my own. No father, no mother, no brothers or sisters to see my first fight.

Sod you and your Lonsdale shorts, George.

Then I saw him. My opponent. Our eyes met, he turned away and I knew he was terrified, too. Then, as we entered the main arena, I realised I couldn't find my gumshield, so I had to borrow one from another kid, cram it into my mouth and sod the hygiene. By now the room was thick with cigar smoke and shouting and laughter and the clattering of plates.

A very adult, intimidating place for a child.

The first round passed in a whirlwind of childish punches; I sensed my opponent was backing away in the second and started to enjoy the feeling of superiority – a bully and a victim. In the third, I hit him hard enough for the ref to give him a count.

Then – 'ding, ding' – my first fight was over, met by more rowdy noise from the drunken dining tables. I'd won and people I knew were cheering, along with people I didn't know. I walked back to the changing room amid pats on the back and lots of "Didn't you do well, son; good on yer, what's yer name?; well done, boy, well done." I liked the feeling.

Then, even better, to the winner the spoils: a trophy with the word WINNER on the front – and a plateful of food. Sandwiches, crisps, a cake and Pepsi Cola.

Pepsi bloody Cola.

I'd never had Pepsi Cola at 101 Clockhouse Road and I never had praise there like I did that night.

All I had to do was hurt people to be treated like a king. That night, as I lay in my cramped bunk bed, it felt as though my future was mapped out in front of me. I knew with absolute certainty this was for me. I was addicted and it felt natural.

And I'd felt what it was like to sense adulation.

I went back to my gym the next week and there was still praise flying around: "Well done, Kev, that was great, you did us proud." Words I'd never heard before aimed in my direction.

A second show was lined up for the following week and I won again. Same kind of thing, same sort of venue, same kind of scared opponent, same kind of fear whipping me into a frenzy. Only some of the anxiety had gone now; I was one fight wiser, I had a better understanding of what to expect.

Listen: "And in the red corner, the winner is Kevin Lueshing." And there's another trophy with WINNER engraved on it. It was feeling like a roll… until –

Until Mum's car crash: the one which sent me hurtling through the windscreen and left me with a broken leg and over 60 stitches in my face. The one when George visited me in hospital and said: "Serves you right for getting in the car against your mother's wishes," and never bothered to see me again until I came home eight weeks later.

I've never forgotten my mother's words in the ambulance on the way to the hospital. "Kevin," she said, "look what you've made me do."

I woke up 24 hours after the crash with my right leg in traction, suspended – just like my boxing career would have to be for the next 12 agonising months.

I was on crutches for at least four of them and remained fragile for a long while.

But there wasn't a single second when I wasn't thinking about boxing during that enforced exile. Eventually I was allowed to do some physio: if they wanted 10 push ups, I'd give them 20. I was getting practically no sympathy at home. I just wanted to have that feeling of praise and adulation back again.

My brother Andrew kept going to the gym and had one fight himself during that period. He lost and came back home with his loser's trophy. For some reason my mum was in a bad mood and turned on him straight away, snapping: "You're useless, you've had one lousy fight and you lost." He immediately got that trophy, found a hammer and smashed it to bits. He never boxed again and that made a big impression on me: I didn't want to be a loser.

When I eventually returned, I was 13 and things had changed dramatically. The club had moved to Crystal Palace, in an old church just opposite the football ground on Selhurst Road. Now it looked like a proper gym with smart new punch bags and fitness equipment, and a new man in charge, Terry Smith. Our name had changed, too: now we were South Norwood and Victory.

Everything looked more professional, orderly, organised and disciplined. Proper hot showers, too.

Juniors and seniors weren't allowed to mix any more: there would be regimented time slots that had to be vigorously stuck to. "You late, son? Only 10 minutes? No, you can't come in. See you next week, so long as you're not late then as well."

I was an instinctive counter-puncher and that was the technique I started to adopt. I'd wait for my opponent to throw a punch, dodge – and then throw one back.

I was learning more about the art of boxing: how to parry, how to counter, how to dodge, how to take a step backwards, how to adapt to different fight situations and opponents. I was showing natural ability and I progressed, winning my first fight with Terry – then another, and another. Three fights, three wins.

The fourth fight was at The Cat's Whiskers in Streatham: a bit more heavy-duty. Tickets were £25 a head: I could tell this was a different league by what the lads were being given to eat afterwards: steak and kidney pie, gravy, proper plates and cutlery.

There were bright lights beaming directly downwards on to the ring, too. It all looked like what I'd seen on TV, a bit more big time, more showbiz.

And I revelled in it all: I put on a dazzling performance and left the ring to cheers and plenty of pats on the back. It was like people were telling me: *You're good at something.* They weren't shouting at me, they were talking to me; they weren't scolding me, or beating me, or abusing me; they were praising me.

The only person not praising me was Terry Smith. No "Well done son, you were terrific" from him. In fact I never heard him say: "You were the best boxer I ever had."

George and Terry. The two father figures in my life.

Terry looked hard, ex-army, muscular, strong – about 55 years old, brutal, a real hard bastard. In many ways he was like George: there was no softness, no sentiment or emotion. I was to have 80 fights with him; he'd travel round the country and take me to shows – some even abroad. But our relationship was military: there were no frills, precious little communication other than the essentials. He ran his life, his gym, his boxers with discipline and commands. He was the sergeant major in a boxing regime.

I remember losing a big fight in Blackpool, I'd choked on the night, and Terry never spoke one single word to me on the entire journey back home to London.

The missing link in our relationship was the same thing my real dad never gave me at home.

Chapter Eleven

EXPULSION

MAYBE IT WAS INEVITABLE, BUT I WAS EXPELLED FROM Kelsey Park when I was 14 – for fighting.

I had been goaded by another bully, Leroy Johnson, and the two of us slugged it out in front of 100 kids who had formed a human boxing ring on the lawn in Beckenham Park.

Johnson was much bigger than me but I punched him to the point where he doubled up, whimpering and groaning. As he stooped over I kicked him violently in the head, the blood splurting out of his nose instantly, like a geyser.

I won that fight because of my boxing. But there were consequences.

The next day, I was in a lesson when suddenly the loudspeaker sounded. "Kevin Lueshing to the headmaster's office. Kevin Lueshing to the headmaster's office." The whole school heard that announcement.

I walked in, and Leroy was there with his mum and dad. They thought their son had been bullied by white kids in a racist gang attack. No boy on his own could have damaged their son like that.

Leroy's dad looked at me, turned to his battered son and said: "You let this little kid do that to you?"

"Yes Dad, it was him."

I was expelled there and then and never went back to Kelsey Park. That fight was the end of my schooling and from then on, I had a private tutor. That fight was a massive moment in my life.

Years later, long after everyone had left that school, they were still talking about it. And I realised that cycling down to the park to face Leroy Johnson was preparing me for the moments I would be walking towards the ring as a professional boxer in later life.

Chapter Twelve
GETTING NOTICED

I LOST MY SIXTH JUNIOR FIGHT AND DIDN'T LIKE IT. I stared at my loser's medal and didn't like it one little bit. Back home, my brothers took the piss out of me. I didn't like that, either. I didn't sleep that night.

But I wasn't giving up, either; overwhelmingly I wanted to get back into the gym, three times a week.

I didn't lose again for another 21 consecutive fights, and I started to step up to championship level, 42 to 45 kilos. One evening I boxed twice in one night and won both of them.

I became South East champion and I sensed Terry was giving me a little more time and attention, although he never talked about it. Even my dad started to turn up, watching me train, going to a few fights.

Even though I'd been expelled from Kelsey Park, I was entered into the national schoolboy championships. That meant being the best in Surrey, then London, then England, then nationally. I quickly progressed to the final of the London stage.

My opponent that night had a record of 42 fights, with 40 wins. Not only that, he could fight southpaw and orthodox simultaneously and throw proper uppercuts like Muhammad Ali. To cap it all, his nickname was 'Sugar Ray'!

I was up against a black kid for the first time. There was a certain fear attached to that. I was used to beating white kids, but 'Sugar Ray' sounded bad news and he had a huge entourage with him. The room was full of black faces, they were chanting his name, they knew him, and they were whipping themselves up. The precious few boxing club mates I recognised there were coming up to me and saying: "Jesus, Kev, you're fighting Sugar Ray."

I looked at this kid with an Afro and a great big, shiny gold tooth glittering in his mouth and thought: "Oh my God. He's a legend already." He even had little tassles round the top of his boots.

I clambered into the ring and when my name was announced I heard a solitary voice yelling out: "Come on, son, you can lick him, boy. Come on Kevin."

My father.

I didn't even know he was planning to show. But suddenly I didn't feel so alone, and even though it was George, I was glad to hear that voice.

"Sugar Ray' pulverised me in the first round: I was getting a beating and how ironic that my father was there to watch it.

Enjoying it, George?

It was the same in the second: in fact one uppercut to my chin was so severe it jolted my head right back and I bit my tongue in the shockwave.

But in that moment, something inside snapped and I got angry. Without a second thought, I went for Sugar Ray wildly, demonically, and he started retreating. I did the same in round three: *you're not going to see me beaten, George.*

That demented thought drove me to victory, although the enormity of the result didn't sink in until afterwards. I had just beaten the best kid in London, in the London finals of a national contest. *Wow.* Even 'Sugar Ray' came over, with a bruise over his eye and a cut lip and said: "Where did you come from, man?" He carried on in boxing, too, and although we never fought each other again – he moved up a weight – we followed each other's careers.

But the biggest shock came when George walked into the dressing room and talked about me in a way I'd never heard before. "Well done, son, well done, we're proud of you Kevin."

We're proud of you.

Next came the regional final, which I won, then off to Hastings Pier for the national semi-final, where I was beaten. This time my father didn't bother to show up.

Where were you, George? Was it too far away? I thought you cared when I beat Sugar Ray. Or were you just enjoying the adulation and playing at being the proud father?

Losing at the final hurdle became a bad habit from then on. I'd battle my way to the quarters or the semis, but I couldn't seem to make it all the way to a national final.

I was 17 now and that meant moving up to senior level, where I'd be fighting men. The opponents would be nastier, older and more experienced.

The question was: did I have the will, the desire and the discipline to carry on? Or would my increasing fascination with stealing designer clothes and selling drugs to London's nightclub world push boxing into the background?

Chapter Thirteen

ARTISTRY

******

THIS IS MY FAVOURITE WEAPON OF DESTRUCTION.

I start to develop a potent combination: hard, quick-fire jabs with my right and then, crash, a sledgehammer left hook nobody sees coming. Terry helps me perfect this routine by screwing a three-foot high green cushioned pad on the gym wall, next to the right-hand edge of a full-length mirror.

And he's drawn circles on it for me: one for the body, one for the head.

Now I can fight my own reflection in the mirror: I shadow-box and just when it looks like my reflection is throwing a right-hander at me, I slip out of range and send a left hook crashing into the pad on the wall. Boom, boom. I repeat this exercise endlessly, until it becomes an instinct, second nature, something I do without thinking, like combing my hair.

It becomes a deeply-rooted part of me: jab, jab, jab; slip to the left, throw giant left hook. My eyes are drilling on to those circles, on to the head, on to the body. A perfect-yet-deadly movement so swift it looks effortless but in reality is the result of monotonous and relentless practice, practice, practice sessions in front of that mirror.

People are stopping in the gym all the time to watch and to wonder what I'm up to.

And I realise that if there is art within boxing, this is it.

Where was your artistry, George? You forced me to pick belts from your wardrobe, so you could lash them on to my frozen, open palms or across my naked back in the freezing snow.

I was your Belt Boy.

Fraud. Didn't you realise there was no beauty or science in that; no months of dedicated toil; no talent?

My act of violence is more studied than yours: it has textbook precision, it gives me grace and style and beauty. It even has morality.

Yes, we're both bullies, George; we're both evil, ruthless, tormented and sinister.

But only one of us is a craftsman.

Chapter Fourteen

YOUNG CRIMINAL

MY HEART WASN'T SOLELY IN BOXING. I'D LEFT HOME and was digging foundations and labouring on building sites for about £150 a week: I wanted to earn extra money and I absolutely didn't feel like hitting the gym after a hard day's graft. Being a teenager was probably kicking in.

Drugs became an irresistible temptation: taking and dealing. I am ashamed to say I didn't stop selling drugs until I won the British championship as a professional fighter.

There's no doubt George made me want to try marijuana: he always had it in the house and he'd usually be in a better, more mellow mood if he'd been smoking. I was naturally curious to give it a go, so I'd join up with gangs of lads in the park and we all thought we were big and tough and pretty impressive as we passed rolled-up joints between us and hung about, menacingly.

I gave Ecstasy a go, too, and there's no doubt the drugs were chilling me, just like they sometimes did for George. Maybe I was blocking out everything bad that had gone on. Maybe. I was now living rough, sleeping on a floor at my sister Lorna's council flat in Penge where she lived with boyfriend, Michael, and their baby. I never liked Michael: he was hard and ruthless and too much like George in my eyes.

Although my brothers and I took most of my father's beatings, my sisters weren't completely excluded from his hideous tempers. I remember George one night trying to cut Lorna's beautiful, long, black hair off with a knife because she was 16 and pregnant. He was apoplectic; she was desperately trying to flee the house but he leapt on her with a knife in his hand and yelled: "Nobody's going to fancy you now."

And he was slashing wildly in a demented rage, clumps of black hair tumbling on to the floor; it was barbaric.

Lorna's life always seemed to be a struggle from then on.

So, yes, I took drugs. But mainly, I dealt them. I'd buy weed for £60 an ounce and cut it up with scientific care and attention. That's how I became so good with scales and weights and measures. I'd sell it on to my mates and make at least double that £60.

I never abused drugs, I was always in control of them. I think. I could always say 'No'. Drugs meant money to me: it wasn't primarily about getting high, it was about earning notes. I was never wasted. If my mates were doing five or six 'Es', I was doing half of one but smiling and laughing as though I was as high as them. I had that discipline, maybe because of the boxing.

I eventually got away from my sister's flat but ended up in another dump above a shop close to the South Norwood gym. Damp, dirty, squalid and freezing cold: I'd lie in bed at night listening to the rats scurrying around on the floor.

Boxing was still in the background and as the ABAs approached I'd put in some more appearances at the gym. Nobody would have spotted I'd been out late at nightclubs, buying and selling drugs. Not even Terry.

But my lust for money was becoming insatiable and I started working Saturdays at R Soles, the trendy shoe shop in Chelsea's Kings Road. This was 1989 and cowboy boots were all the rage: I remember one day the shop closed so film star Eddie Murphy could come in and buy a pair without being pestered.

I started to get wrapped up in this new glam world and developed a taste for fashion and clothes. But I couldn't afford the kind of gear I saw in the shop windows – so I nicked it instead.

I'd go with my mates to places like Harrod's, Harvey Nichols and steal – either gear for myself, or stuff that I could sell on.

Kevin was good at thieving. Years of practice. I remember targeting a shop in South Molton Street called Browns. The main shop assistant there was gay: I would go in a few times, look around casually and flirt with him. Eventually he'd trust me and take his eyes off me when another customer walked in. That was my cue: when he wasn't looking, I took a pair of pliers from my coat pocket, cut the security wire off a leather jacket I wanted, and raced out. There were no security cameras in those days.

Two years later, I saw the same guy in Stringfellow's nightclub. He came over to me and said: "You were that kid who stole a leather jacket from Browns, weren't you?" Naturally, I denied it – but he was right.

Harrod's was a right result, too. We discovered a door inside one of the changing cubicles that led into a rear storage room, where there were loads of clothes, all without security tags. We'd pretend to be trying something on, sneak into the storage area and grab whatever we fancied – trousers, shirts, jumpers, jackets – and cram them into rucksacks, or put stuff on ourselves underneath the clothes we were wearing. We were nicking to order: mates would tell us what they wanted, what sizes and colours; I'd get it and sell it to them cut-price down the pub.

If it cost £160, I'd sell for around £80. This was top-quality gear as well: Comme Des Garçons; Ralph Lauren. Paul Smith in Covent Garden was easy. Gucci, too: I got an assistant there to get me a pair of really expensive shoes: once I'd put them on, I asked her to get me another pair so I could compare. Soon as she went to the store room, I scarpered with the new Guccis still on my feet.

I even started to develop my own look. Kevin would wear big colours: bold red, pink, anything that would get him seen. I'd nick a bright Versace shirt – a £350 one – and it would be the brightest and loudest and most flamboyant on the rail. I'd wear Ferrucci jeans, Gucci shoes – all of it nicked and all of it saying: *Look at me. I have style and status.*

If it wasn't clothes, it was booze. I was driving now, a VW Golf, and we'd go 'bottling' at shops like Unwins and nick bottles of champagne, whisky, Remy Martel. We'd target countryside stores and drive off to places like Cobham, where, nearly always, there'd be an old person at the counter. We'd wear big sheepskin coats, cut the inside lining and cram the bottles down them.

I became really familiar with alcohol this way and what I could sell it on for: I'd get £30 for Dom Perignon; Moet £10: Remy Martel would be £15. I had a ready market – my builder mates down on the sites.

Chapter Fifteen

AMATEUR HOUR

THE PINNACLE OF AMATEUR BOXING – THE ABA CHAMPI-
onships – was rapidly approaching: only this time I'd be in the
seniors, boxing real men. I needed some warm-up fights.

Everything about stepping up to senior level is tougher: you're
up against far older, more experienced fighters. And instead of
three two-minute rounds, it's three three-minute ones. That extra
60 seconds is a hell of a long time if you're getting beaten.

My first fight was against a 28 year-old – David Bowry from the
Eltham Boxing Club. I got stopped in the second after a standing
count. I was devastated, and although Terry tried to console me, he
knew deep down it was his fault: he'd over-matched me. I should
never have been put in so soon against such an older and bigger
opponent.

In one respect, it was a wake-up call: I was never going to beat
fully-grown men if I was hanging out late in nightclubs. I had to
man up – or give up.

That meant more gym work, more training, more intensity, more
sparring, particularly with a veteran 15-stone heavyweight called
John Pals, who was 38 years old and who became, through my
career, my chief sparring partner.

Increasingly, trainers made sure their boxers weren't pitched in
championship bouts against me. I went to Ireland once, represent-
ing London, and they would only let me fight their kid if I wore
10-ounce gloves and he wore eight-ounce ones. I agreed – and
knocked him out in one round!

I had three qualifying fights to win the ABA south east division
and won them all. I was now in the London area semi-finals at one
of boxing's meccas, the York Hall.

This had gravitas and importance; a gateway to what professional boxing must be like. This was for heavyweight, respected grown ups, who knew their boxing; not gangly adolescents with spots and unattainable dreams.

I weighed in – welterweight now, under 67kilos, which stayed my weight until my last three fights, when I moved up. Everything seemed fine, until Terry suddenly said: "OK, Kev, get your things, we're going home. We're not boxing."

"What you talking about Terry? Why not?"

"Because I don't think you're ready."

Deep down, I was overwhelmingly relieved. York Hall was too much, too soon. The drill-you-to-the-spot stares from swathes of strange faces, the overbearing male atmosphere, the crushing sense of history and the thought of boxing greats who had been here before: Terry suspected it was crushing me – and, if I lost, it would crush me for ever.

So he pulled me out and began the long process of getting me ready for the following year's championship – still unaware that I would spend most of the time pedalling drugs.

Physically, I stayed in good condition – largely because of my job. A local builder called Charlie Brecker used to come to our boxing shows and decided to sponsor me, so his firm's name was on the back of my vest. One night he asked if I needed work, so I started on the local building sites, digging footings, and hauling heavy iron and concrete beams around. It was intensely physical work but it helped build my muscle strength. After two years I became a hod carrier and many of the builders I worked with would come to see me box.

The combination of gym work and building sites was deadly: my shoulders filled out, I grew more muscular. I went from boy to man.

Again I stormed through the ABA regional preliminaries: in one night I had three fights, three knockouts: one of them, the most devastating KO I ever recorded as an amateur.

His name was Clive Dixson, from the Lynn Boxing Club, and the crash of my fist on his cheek felled him flat out, his nose and lips scrunched up against the canvas, his body utterly motionless.

The ref darted over, raised Dixson's head, and feverishly grabbed his gumshield so he wouldn't swallow his tongue. A doctor was rushed to the ring, frantic faces stooped over his prone body for at least 10 more minutes before suddenly there was a twitch of movement. He was conscious but barely in this world.

Me? I felt like Superman throughout. As doctors and trainers feared the worst, I watched the crowd watching me. Was I concerned for Dixson's health and safety? Was I hell. I was breathing in the awe, the admiration, the respect, the fear.

I even got 'Best Fighter of the Night'.

I was a ruthless fighting machine and I loved the feeling. Kill or be killed. Cold. Heartless.

I got it from George.

The kid I was meant to box in the next round immediately pulled out, which meant I was now back at the York Hall again. People were scared of me.

Now I was up against a 26-year-old, experienced boxer called Frankie Finn. I looked him up in the *Boxing News* and it said: Should go far in this year's ABAs.

But I floored him with a left in the first round. He slumped down on one knee; fight over. That meant I was now in the London ABA finals against Gary Logan, at the Royal Albert Hall.

The Royal Albert Hall! I'd never been there before: it was like being called to fight in the Colosseum. I walked down a corridor and was mesmerised by the photographs on the wall of legendary boxers who had fought there: Muhammad Ali twice in the '70s; Henry Cooper four times; Alan Minter beating Kevin Finnegan and Pat O'Dwyer; John Conteh – this was a giant hall of fame to boxing's greats. If that wasn't enough, there were the beaming smiles of showbiz giants like Frank Sinatra and Pavarotti.

The changing rooms were underground: you couldn't hear anything down there other than normal boxing banter and clattering. I even had my own room, and that's where I stayed with Terry until my fight was due.

My first sight of the audience only came when I climbed the steps that take you up, just like a gladiator, on to the main arena. The place was packed solid: the ground floor bursting with boxing officials, respected trainers, ex-boxers, promoters, famous faces like Micky Duff, hardcore fight fans. I looked up at the circle of balconies and boxes and felt the full blast of expectant gazes drilling down on me. I scanned and scanned the crowd ferociously as I walked towards the ring and was relieved and proud when I spotted around 30 bricklayers, sparkies, hod carriers – even the foreman – from my building site.

But I made a basic error: Logan was a counter puncher, too. This time I shaped to throw and he did to me what I did to Dixson and Finn – he countered with a left hook and I wobbled. Wobble.

The ref gave me a standing count but didn't stop: fight over in round one. I went mental, Terry jumped into the ring: "What the fuck, you're fucking this kid's career, he wants to carry on, there's nothing wrong with him. What the fuck you doing?"

ABA officials leapt into the ring and added to the mayhem: "Calm down Terry, stop it, you're shaming us, this is disrespectful, cut the language."

I was ushered back downstairs to my underworld, to my dungeon and broke down in tears: the first time I'd ever cried in boxing, great big soul-wrenching sobs that were deep and stretched all the way back to my beating in the snow.

Beaten, humiliated, ashamed. Then and now.

But I wanted to carry on. I was hurt but quitting wasn't in my veins. I still yearned to be a champion more than I wanted to give in.

I went back to the gym, with one obsessive purpose: to fight back. Along the way I was selected to fight for England in Czechoslovakia, and I really felt honoured and proud to be chosen and to sing the national anthem out there with my national vest on. I won eight fights that year – all by knockout – then beat Finn again to return to the Royal Albert.

Next up, though, was the loser of the previous year's national finals, 'Rocky' Bryan, who had great big dreadlocks and looked just like the giant rugby league player, Martin Offiah. I totally outboxed him and nearly knocked him flat with an uppercut that rocked his head backwards. I was over the final hurdle at last; mentally I had broken through, even though I wasn't the national champion, I had won at the Royal Albert in front of proper boxing promoters and a huge crowd.

I was the London ABA champion, I was going on to the national finals, I was the king. My finest moment as an amateur.

George wasn't there – just Terry. And he could be a right bastard when he wanted. Next up was Blackpool, where I had to qualify for the national finals but completely froze and lost tamely, probably thinking my job had been completed at the Royal Albert Hall. Terry didn't utter one single word to me during the entire 240-mile journey home.

He still didn't want me to turn professional, either, and because I had so little inner belief I let him guide me, carrying on for another two years as an amateur. The following year was devastating as well: for the first time I was knocked out cold in round one by Adrian Dobson, who had been to America, trained in Brooklyn and was simply too hard and too mean for me then.

That really deflated me; and maybe left me vulnerable to my next temptation.

Cocaine.

Chapter Sixteen

DRUG MONEY

I WAS STRUTTING DOWN THE KING'S ROAD, MEETING new people in my designer gear: I'd got new best mates, many of them older – 24, 25 years old. Suddenly I was hanging around flash nightclubs where all the cool people went – especially Browns, in Covent Garden.

I was mixing with a far more 'English' crowd, very white dominated and older, all wanting to be someone and all wanting to look good while they did it.

They could sniff the good life.

I went to Ibiza for the first time when Ibiza still felt slightly out of reach and more of a rich man's playground. But I was in for a massive shock before I got there.

I needed to get my birth certificate so I could be issued with my first passport. Of course, nobody at Clockhouse Road could find it so I had to go to Beckenham hospital, where I was born.

They checked my records and printed one out. I could barely believe my eyes: instead of saying Kevin Lueshing, born April 16, it said Kevin Lueshing – born April 17.

For seventeen years my mum had told me my birthday was on the 16th and that was the day I had always celebrated. In fact, I'd already been issued with a provisional driving licence that stated the 16th.

But my passport said the 17th.

I couldn't believe it. I went home: "Mum, how on earth could you get that wrong?"

She looked at me and replied: "It's only one day, son." Bloody hell Mum.

She couldn't understand why I was so wound up; we argued for days about it – *"For Christ's sake Mum, how could you get your own son's birthday wrong?"*

"I got it mixed up, Kevin."

I forgive her now, mainly because of her own upbringing and the chaos and turmoil of her own life raising six children in a house with George. I was just another kid she barely wanted. Now I celebrate my birthday on the 17th.

I came back from Ibiza, partying with all my new, older chums, and returned to the building sites. Almost immediately, the foreman was sacked and the surveyor – who knew me – gave me the job. It was now my role to find the sparkies, the brickies, the plumbers, and I'd get a little back-hander out of what they were being paid: the surveyor would give me £70 a day, I'd pocket £20 and hand £50 to the builders. Touch. That's how Kevin liked to do business.

Nights in London clubs, holidays in Ibiza, and scams on building sites; these were filling my days and there was precious little time for boxing. In some ways I was hanging around with the wrong people; in other ways, I was simply enjoying life.

But cocaine was waiting round the corner and with it the irresistible chance to make far more money than I could from the sparkies and plumbers. All of a sudden one of my new best friends, Al, turned out to be the only dealer in South East London: only on Friday nights, in Beckenham, conveniently two miles from where I lived.

I'd no idea where Al got it from, it was none of my business. He didn't look much like a drug dealer, either; he wasn't seedy, quite the opposite. He had a nice house, appeared clean-cut, respectable, with a shiny new car in the driveway. But he was a full-time drugs dealer; I knew him, he knew me: he even came to watch me box. We could do business.

And I knew plenty of people who wanted it, and what they'd pay: £60 a gram. I'd buy three and a half grams for £150; go home, stick a gram of glucose in it, and all of a sudden I'd have four and a half grams to sell.

Al had taught me the glucose trick: "Just put something white in it, Kev, and they won't know the difference. They'll be off their heads."

But I had another trick up my sleeve: I wouldn't give the punters a whole gram, I'd give them 0.9. That left me with another 0.4 which I could also pretend was another half gram to sell. In total, I turned the three and a half grams I paid for into five; I sold that for £300 and made 100 per cent profit.

And money was all I thought about. Money. I was hooked. Not on cocaine; on notes. This had been my upbringing; taking protection money off weak kids at school; stealing from shops to sell to mates; getting paid by the paedophile. Doing anything – stealing everything – for money. It was all I craved. Money, money, money. I didn't care if was 50 pence, or that £10 note off Derek's floor while I was fleeing his perversion. I was there for the money.

Cocaine took earning to a new level: I was mixing with different kinds of people; they were classier, sophisticated and groomed, they made drug dealing seem socially acceptable even if it was illegal. It was so easy and the rewards so much greater than anything before.

Suddenly, I wasn't worrying about bills. I didn't need to steal from Harrod's anymore because I was raking it in. I jacked the building site in, too. I made £150 a week there, tops: this lark was bringing in £500. Minimum.

So at the age of 19, I became a Full-Time Cocaine Dealer. Not the sort of job you see advertised down the employment centre:

Wanted: Full-Time Cocaine Dealer. Industry: Illegal drugs; Employment: full-time; Earnings: £500 per week with potential to earn far more; Hours: weekends mainly, late night; Location: night club; Benefits: foreign holidays, nice cars, fun crowd, meet famous people.

And I did meet and serve lots of famous people, who gravitated to Browns because they could do cocaine in the upstairs lounge, VIP style, where there were white sofas waiting and moody lighting, mirrors, and discretion in the air. This was the 'in' crowd in the 'in' place.

I'd deal up to 15 wraps on a good night at Browns: £50/£60 a wrap. Everyone was on it and I could walk out with a clear £1,000 profit stuffed into my pockets. Always cash for Kevin.

And still mixed with glucose. Nobody cared. All I would hear was: "Make sure you don't leave without seeing me, Kev."

Famous pop stars – worldwide famous ones – actors, international film stars, comedians, entertainers, TV names, sports personalities, record producers, stunning models, Page Three girls: I saw them all there and I dealt TO many of them. "Oi, isn't that so-and-so over there in the corner?"

"You bet it is and I've just sold him £500 worth of cocaine."

There was a code of conduct up there, like an Alcoholics Anonymous meeting. There were so many recognisable faces on those sofas, all protected by a code of silence. Browns' *Omerta*. What went on in Browns, stayed in Browns.

I dabbled in coke sometimes myself: I'd take a line to keep up appearances, or to keep me awake until 5am, or to keep in with the right people. I was in the toilets doing a line with a member of staff one night and said to him: "You know, I feel guilty doing this, I haven't completely packed in the boxing."

I couldn't believe his response: "Don't be so stupid, Sugar Ray Leonard was in here last week, off his head."

And he laughed.

My customers were soon telling me about their friends who wanted supplies during the week. All of a sudden I was going round the big record companies – Sony, Warner, Virgin; radio and TV stations – and dropping off packets to messengers who would meet me in the main reception areas.

Or, I was meeting the lunch crowds in bars and restaurants and serving there: city guys, investors, bankers. People in suits, all laughing and looking terribly decent and respectable.

I had a mobile phone and I was in business. I might as well have carried a business card in my pocket, with the words 'Kevin Lueshing, mobile drug dealer' in some fancy script with a telephone number, starting 0831. I was The Man.

The clapped-out, second-hand VW golf had gone, too: I had a convertible now. If you've got it, flaunt it. I was flaunting, without a care in the world and no sense of guilt about what I was actually doing. No morality. No conscience. My god was Money.

I had so much money, I took a month off one summer and went to see the 1990 World Cup in Italy. I'd never been to a football match in my life; now I was watching England in the quarter finals and semi finals of a bloody World Cup. Buying tickets, staying in top hotels: I could afford it all.

It was all so easy and glamorous: I never saw anything sinister or disturbing, although there was one customer, Robin, who was divorced and had real problems. He looked every inch the country English gentleman; Robin drove a Range Rover, was eloquently spoken, wore a neat, pin-striped suit, always immaculately groomed with little half glasses perched on his nose and stylish-ly-permed hair. He ran a very respectable tailor's shop in Covent Garden. Robin would buy an eighth off me, give me cash, and was such a reliable customer I allowed him £1,000 credit. Gradually he'd buy more and more until payment would be: "Kev, take those suits down to Oxford Street, so-and-so will take them half price and you keep the money."

Inevitably, he ran into debt and stopped answering his phone or being in the shop. So I went round his house one day and saw his car in the driveway. I knocked on the front door, no reply. I thought: "Bastard, you've had it now."

I crept round the back where there was a window with some curtains not quite fully drawn. I peeped through and there he was, dressed entirely in women's clothes, twirling in front of a mirror, admiring himself. He was off his head. He was just looking at himself, smiling and dancing.

I watched the sad bastard for about a minute and tapped on the window. The look on his face when he saw me was priceless: it was like he'd been caught red-handed by his mum. He let me in and I knew it was pointless being angry, he was in such a tragic state. "I'm so sorry Kevin, it's taken me over, I need help."

So I agreed not to serve him anymore. Shortly afterwards his elderly father phoned me and asked to meet – he'd seen me in the shop a few times. I went, he made me a nice cup of tea in a china cup, and said: "How much does Robin owe you? Can I give you a cheque?"

"Let's call it £1,000," I replied – even though it was at least £2,000. He wrote out the cheque and said, ever so meekly and politely: "Do you think you could promise not to serve him again?"

I agreed. "But listen," I added. "He will go to other people." Robin's father died about six months later, left him a lot of money and he was back buying off me a few weeks after the funeral.

I had some morals. I never served to kids: they were doing Ecstasy then and I wasn't interested in that. Not enough money. And I never got into trouble with the police. I was extremely disciplined about who I would deal with – it had to be people I knew, who I could trust, or introductions from close friends.

But even when I turned professional, I carried on with the drugs because I needed the money. Boxing wouldn't give me as much in the early days, I still needed extra income.

I never dealt in kilos, I had many chances to do so but that would have been out of my comfort zone; I feared getting caught at that level. There was a huge difference between getting caught with a kilo, and getting caught with an ounce. I had my trusted group of clients, once a week, Friday nights only – and that suited me.

But notorious gangsters and crooks have always been drawn to boxing. After one of my fights, I got talking to one of the heavyweight cocaine dealers, Bob Parsons, who did deal in kilos and who took an instant shine to me and my career. Between us we hit on what must have been one of sport's most bizarre, and I guess illegal, sponsorship deals.

I'd meet Big Bob once a week, religiously, when he was out walking his bulldog. We'd always meet in the same place on Friday evenings outside a phone box on Bushey Road in Shirley. I'd sell him about £500 worth of cocaine, even though he was a huge dealer himself – and didn't need to buy anything off me. He bought it because he knew I needed the money and this was his way of sponsoring me. We'd do the exchange, he'd ask me about my training, how I was doing, who I'd be fighting next.

"You're going to be a champ one day, Kev, and I'm going to help you get there. Then, one day, you'll look after me," said Bob. He believed in me.

PART FOUR:
NEW PROFESSIONAL

Chapter Seventeen

MY EUBANK EPIPHANY

COCAINE WAS MAKING ME RICH. I WAS LIVING THE LIFE, hanging round the coolest places with the coolest celebs. I hadn't completely thrown in the towel with boxing – I just didn't know where to go with it. The amateur scene was paling into a shadowy background: the glitzy lights of Browns nightclub seemed a lot brighter than York Hall and even the Royal Albert.

Then, out of the blue, my world turned upside down. My brother had two tickets to see a friend of ours, Gary Stretch, fight Chris Eubank. It was to be one of the pivotal moments in my life.

Even though I had risen in the amateur ranks and had become a walking encyclopaedia on boxing, I had never been to a professional fight. I really did know the sport inside out by now: I'd devour every magazine or newspaper available – *The Ring, Boxing News* – and pore through the pages, learning about all the fighters out there: who was hot, who was not; ones to watch; young pretenders, former greats; their triumphs and tragedies, everything.

I began to realise so many great fighters had drug problems, or came from broken homes. Many had psychological problems that stretched back to deprived childhoods and I definitely saw a lot of myself in their stories. I'd read books about the black fighters in particular and marvel at how they'd beaten the odds to reach the top. I was intrigued to understand why black fighters were usually better than white ones – not always, but it seemed to be the case. I decided we had more to fight for.

Fighting as an amateur had whetted my appetite but I still didn't fully comprehend just how different the professional world was. Until that night on April 18, 1991. Stretch v Eubank for the WBO middleweight title.

As soon as I walked into the Olympia arena, I was enthralled. I instantly spotted lots of famous celebrities in the crowd – boxers, as well as showbiz and football faces; I was thinking 'wow', when a few people started recognising me and asking what I was up to. The words "When you turning pro then, Kev?" started to repeat themselves around me.

"What you doing as an amateur, Kev? You're wasting your time, man."

I took my seat amid lots of handshakes, hallos and how-are-yous – and then Olympia was dramatically plunged into darkness, the ultimate boxing anthem started booming across the arena…

"De, de, der… de, de, der… !"

The *Rocky* song. I swear it changed my life there and then: I turned professional in that razzmatazz moment. My entire body shivered, I can feel the hairs on my arms tingling right now; I was utterly entranced by the showbusiness and the roars and the excitement and the drama. I wanted to be walking out, I wanted that noise, I wanted this. Gary was soaking up the roars and the adulation as he headed towards the ring and I wanted to swap places with him there and then.

When Chris Eubank appeared and 'Simply the Best' blasted out, I felt a different kind of awe. He was the man the crowd loved to hate, everyone was booing and yelling at him: but he played to it masterfully and although he was the pantomime villain, he had Olympia in his hands. The more the crowd booed, the bigger he appeared to be: by the time he reached the ring he looked 10 feet tall, and the place was in uproar. Unbelievable.

And Eubank wasn't finished, either. As he got to the ropes, he stood still, gave a 360degreee stare of defiance to the crowd and then acrobatically leapt over the ropes straight into the ring. Pandemonium. 'The ego had landed', and I was hooked.

The fight was over after six rounds, Eubank stopped our pal and my brother said: "Come on, let's go see him in the dressing room."

When we got there, Gary was sat on a bench, shoulders slumped, head down, completely deflated. I remember going to him and saying: "Don't worry, mate, you weren't meant to win. But you learnt from that. Don't feel sorry for yourself, Gary, look for the lessons."

And he turned and hugged me – me, amateur fighter and professional cocaine dealer, Kevin Lueshing – and suddenly I was getting mutual respect from a professional who had just given his all at the top of the sport against one of the country's best fighters. I had an overwhelming sense that this was my world now.

Then Gary said it. "When you turning pro, Kev?"

"I'm not ready yet, Gary, I want to win the ABAs."

"Forget them, man. You're wasting your time."

My destiny was sealed. I still have to this day one of the old black passports everyone had to travel abroad with in those days. Inside is a visa to Thailand, where I was meant to be going for a jolly with a bunch of mates six weeks later.

But the combination of Olympia, Gary Stretch and Chris Eubank put an end to that trip. I never went.

Instead, I told Terry the next day: "I'm turning professional." Deep down, I knew turning pro was also an attempt to pull away from selling drugs. Olympia was brighter than Browns after all.

Terry didn't want to turn professional with me, even though I offered him the chance. "I don't like those people. They'll rip you off, Kevin."

"Well can you help me?"

He reluctantly recommended a pal of his, also called Terry, who, co-incidentally, was related to a girl I had just met at the time, Jackie Hillier. A girl I would go on to marry and have two children with.

Terry was still an amateur boxing trainer who also worked with a few professionals. He knew the big managers and promoters and soon announced: "I've got an in with Frank Maloney – do you want me to fix up a meeting, Kev?"

So I went to see Maloney. He'd just taken on Lennox Lewis and signed him to Sky TV, who were emerging as a big boxing broadcaster. Maloney, perhaps understandably, was a bit full of himself.

Jackie and I went to his pub in Dartford. I was nervous. I knew this was a big moment in my life but I had no father figure by my side, nobody to say, "Kev, be careful, don't get ripped off here." The only thing that stuck in my mind was 'don't commit to three years' even though that was a standard boxing contract.

Maloney at least knew of my amateur reputation and knew I had a following and could sell tickets. "OK, I'll take you on, but I want a three-year contract." Exactly what I didn't want – I didn't like someone having that amount of control over me. But Maloney was proper big time.

He said: "We'll put you on Lennox's undercard, Kev, we'll turn you into a champ, you're a great prospect, your style is best suited for pro boxing, I wanted you a couple of years ago but your amateur trainer blocked me; you're a good looker, too, maybe a bit of modelling on the side."

But he didn't tell me specifically how much I'd be getting paid to fight and I was too scared to ask – even though that's what turning professional was supposed to be all about. I was on my own and so overwhelmed by the thought of signing for Mr Maloney that I didn't even dare ask such an impudent question. "Take it or leave it, Kev. You can trust me."

Somehow I found the courage. Mumbling and ashamed to even look him in the face, I said: "I only want to sign for two years, Mr Maloney."

"Alright, this is what we'll do. Sign for two years but I'll have the first option to sign you again at the start of year three."

"Fair enough, let's do that, Mr Maloney." The deal was agreed there and then, I didn't shop around, I didn't go to any other managers, I just went with him. Probably because he had Lennox – and I couldn't face that ordeal all over again.

Next, I had to go to the Boxing Board of Control and sign with them to get my professional licence. That meant having a full medical, brain scan in London's Harley Street, eye tests, heart tests, AIDS test, all sorts of stuff I'd never experienced before and that I had to sort out on my own. Maloney agreed to pay for it all – about £400 – but then took it out of what he paid me for my first fight.

My trainer was still Terry, although I was starting to have doubts about him and whether he was right for me. We trained three times a week at the famous Thomas A Becket gym in the Old Kent Road but I wasn't convinced his manner and style suited me. There was no art or science or fluency there, very little technique, it was wham-bam boxing, hit the pads, everything aggressive and route one. There was no space for my style and how I boxed. My instincts told me he wasn't paying attention to the way I naturally jabbed and moved.

"Hit 'em hard, Kevin." I wasn't happy with that, it wasn't enough.

Two months later, I was on the Lennox undercard at the Royal Albert, just as Maloney had promised. "Right Kev, your fight's booked, how many tickets you going to sell for me?"

So now my job was to sell tickets, collect the money and give it to Frank Maloney. And although that sounds like I was being ripped off, it was completely normal for boxers to sell their own tickets for their own fights to their own mates and hand over their money to their own manager.

It wasn't a shock: I knew I had lots of friends who would want to see me and I sold £6,000 worth of tickets very quickly and easily. That was a hell of a lot considering it was my professional debut. "How much?!" roared Maloney. Even he was impressed.

I was on 10 per cent. In fact I earned more money from the ticket sales than I did from the fight itself, which only paid me £400. But that all quickly diminished because Maloney took out the costs of my medical and getting my pro licence. It didn't matter. I wasn't in it solely for the money then: I was in it to start a career and get away from selling drugs.

As the big day approached, people were ringing me up, local papers wanted interviews, my name was next to Lennox on the fight posters. I was news and I was nervous.

Although I'd been to the Albert Hall before, this was different. I'd have to box without a vest now; there'd be six rounds if it went the distance. I'd never gone that far. And I was up against a Welsh fighter called John McGlynn, a rugged, tough-looking boxer. But when I first saw him at the weigh in, I thought he looked out of shape, like someone who'd just been dragged out of a pub. He was a journeyman and I was the prospect.

Even Andrew and Errol decided to see this one but George couldn't have shown – even if he'd wanted. He was still inside a Jamaican prison.

I'd persevered with amateur boxing in the confused hope of impressing George but turning professional was for Kevin and nobody else. And here I was, back in the underground changing rooms at the Royal Albert, about to make my first step into the big time.

I went up, just like I had for the ABAs, but the arena wasn't as packed as it had been then. I was the Lennox Lewis support act and it was only 8.30pm. It felt like a different kind of audience, too; lots of official-looking grown-ups – probably from the boxing board – lots of chiselled faces belonging to men who had been in the fight game all their lives and either couldn't let go, were trainers themselves, or had the desk jobs.

It instantly felt professional and serious. But among all those ex-pro stares I could hear the raucous cheering I was more used to: I looked up to the pigeon seats, the balconies way on high that stare down on the arena and there were all the mates I'd sold tickets to, leaning over dangerously, waving down at me, shouting and hollering and really making themselves heard above all the sobriety. "Kev-in, Kev-in, Kev-in." The builders, friends I'd grown up with, my new best mates from the cocaine crowd.

You can't lose now, Kev. Not in front of them.

I climbed into the ring and even the announcements sounded different. "Kevin Lueshing, making his professional debut and weighing in at 10 stones, 12 lbs; John McGlynn, with a professional record of eight fights, six wins and two losses... seconds away... "

I dominated the first round and quickly got him against the ropes in the second. He was a standing target, soaking it up, nowhere behind him to run to. The punches poured out of me and suddenly the referee stepped in and stopped the barrage.

I'd won. I was exhilarated; really tired but more from nervous energy than anything else. Above all, above all the cheering and the jubilant slaps on the back and the "You clobbered him Kev, you're on your way" – was an overwhelming sense of relief that it was over and done with. My first professional fight was out of the way.

Maloney was happy, too. "Well done, Kev, you looked great, I told you it'd be easy; we'll have you back here in a month's time."

I hung around for the Lennox fight. That was a different entity altogether. The Royal Albert was heaving, he came out to massive booming music – just like I'd heard before Gary Stretch and Chris Eubank.

Chapter Eighteen

RAY OF LIGHT

I WAS 14 WHEN I SAW SUGAR RAY LEONARD FIGHT FOR the first time. It was on TV, against Roberto Duran, and he dropped his hands, he impudently opened his face to Duran as if to say: "I don't need to defend myself against you." I'd never seen anything like that: it was art and poetry all wrapped up into a boxer. He looked like he enjoyed fighting and I enjoyed watching the joy on his face: I could imagine watching him box to music; he was bedazzling, electric, he made boxing seem less brutal and more beautiful.

His balance had me spellbound. And his control: the way he could slow it down, then instantly turn up the heat before you even registered what he was doing.

And what I really, really liked was that he never showed pain. You would never know from his face whether he was hurt or not. Even if he was mimicking being happy, it looked real. I was so impressed by that and I tried throughout my career to be the same. There were occasions when I was hit hard and I wanted to wince and curl up in the agony of the moment: but Sugar Ray taught me to keep that pain hidden, even when it was crawling all over my body.

Boxers have to be chilling, cold, ruthless, executioners. But my God, Sugar Ray did it with style and grace and elegance and entertainment and I wanted to do it that way, too.

The speed of his hands, his timing, his poise, how he would lead an opponent into a false sense of security, in control, always knowing what was going on. Oh, I liked that.

Then, the killer instinct. The cold, ruthless destroyer. Sugar Ray never took punches to throw punches, that's what I particularly liked. So, I never deliberately said to myself: "I'm willing to be hit twice here, because it might force an opening so I can throw a punch back."

Sugar Ray was the blueprint for hit-and-not-get-hit, and that's what I tried to emulate. I went back into the ring after seeing the Duran fight and tried to dance a bit more, smile a bit more, have more charisma. Just like Sugar Ray. Make opponents miss, then make them pay. Kevin would maybe only throw 50 shots in a fight, but he'd throw them with 80 per cent accuracy.

I didn't really have the self-belief to be as flashy as Sugar Ray but I could work on the style of his boxing: move, dance, hit, move, use the ring. That was me. Everything that I thought was missing in boxing he supplied; he was flawless, he was a dream to watch, he looked good, he talked well and I wanted to be him, to emulate him. He was my definition then of the perfect boxer.

In later life, I discovered he, too, had suffered sexual abuse as a child.

There were other fighters who inspired me, but in different ways and for different reasons. I admired Barry McGuigan because of his passion and his following and his patriotism. I can never forget his fight at Queens Park Rangers football club when he beat Eusebio Pedroza to win the world featherweight title.

I was sat watching it on the TV with my mate, Frankie Cocozza – whose son went on to star in Simon Cowell's *X-Factor* – and we were marvelling at the crowd, and the noise and the excitement and he turned to me and said: "Just think, Kev, one day this could be you." And we laughed!

McGuigan was nothing like Sugar Ray, of course; he was a 'come-forward' fighter. But the relentless volume of his punches that night impressed me: he wore the world champion down by giving him nowhere to hide, no refuge from a relentless barrage. I learned from that.

I was also amazed how a slightly-built fighter like McGuigan could command such heavyweight respect and loyalty among such a huge following. He understood his fans and he knew how to connect with them. Getting his father to sing 'Danny Boy' before his fights was a masterstroke: it whipped everyone into a frenzy, the weight of noise and excitement were like hefty body blows into an opponent before a punch had even been thrown.

Errol 'Bomber' Graham was another: one of the greatest fighters to never win a world title; should have won a world title and was winning a world title until he dropped his hands.

But there was only one stand-out fighter for me: only one Superman. Only one Sugar Ray.

Chapter Nineteen

A FATHER'S VOW

WHEN I FIRST SAW THE WOMAN I WOULD MARRY, SHE was arguing loudly with some bloke in the Drummond pub in Beckenham. She had very dark hair, blue eyes, cute freckles – she sounded passionate and feisty – and was wearing a bright red top that made her stand out from the crowd. Her name was Jackie. I'd just finished with a girlfriend; I was turning professional and I needed a soul mate.

We got chatting and Jackie came home with me that first night – nothing physical, we were just getting on with each other. It wasn't long, though, before we were living together.

We quickly got into a routine, largely based around my boxing and training. Jackie worked as a hairdresser in Dulwich, she'd get home, drive me somewhere about five miles away, drop me off and I'd run back from there. I'd get home, Jackie had dinner ready – and that became our way of life.

But we argued too much. I'd always be on a short fuse before a fight and I'd take it out on Jackie, looking for the tiniest reasons to shout and yell at her. But she could give it back and some part of me liked the fact she'd stand up to me. I'd never seen my mum properly do that to George: she cowered when he got angry.

About three months into our relationship, after my first professional fight, Jackie told me she was pregnant. With a baby on the way, I got it into my head that we needed to stop paying out rent and take on a mortgage instead. So we bought our first house: two up, two down, a classic Victorian wreck – 23 Bromley Crescent in Bromley. But we made it perfect: Jackie had a fantastic eye for interiors and colour. She masterminded all the décor; I got my builder mates to help with the construction.

We knew Jackie was expecting a girl – in fact, it was going to be twins but she lost one of them very early on. We decided on a name – Ruby – and Jackie got her room made up beautifully: yellow and sky blue, lovely lampshades, matching curtains and a little cot all ready and waiting.

Then came the time for Jackie's last scan and I went with her to the hospital. I was sitting in the waiting room when she came out, pale and anxious, and said: "Kev, there's a problem. The doctor needs to talk to us."

He told us Ruby had a heart defect, the chances of her surviving were extremely slim and even if she did, she'd almost certainly have Down's Syndrome. I went into a cold, heartless, emotionless place. My defence mechanisms kicked in and there was no room for sentiment. 'We can't have it, Jackie." Suddenly Ruby had become 'it'.

We were taken to a room, alone, Jackie was given a tablet and went through labour in the normal way. Our stillborn baby was instantly taken away from us and then brought back in a little white box with a red rose. And there was a little girl, a girl called Ruby, with perfectly-formed little features: lips, nose, ears, hands, eyes tightly closed – everything there in a tiny form. Ruby, not 'it'. Jackie took her from the box and held her: I did the same. Our perfect little girl, our miniature little doll with her eyes closed. I took a polaroid which I still carry with me today.

Suddenly I felt unbearable sadness holding our little Ruby, who never existed in this life but was now in my hands. At that moment I felt infinite loss, and thought I saw the life she should have had flash before me.

We had Ruby buried; every year a book of remembrance with her name inside and a psalm next to it is opened at the chapel. Jackie and I would go and put some fresh flowers out.

I didn't react well to Ruby's death. Jackie was completely down and depressed and I wasn't there for her. I switched off: I wasn't mature enough to deal with it. I should have helped Jackie, be the shoulder she needed. I didn't.

Five months later, Jackie was pregnant again but from that moment we both had the same fear: would the baby have a problem? That worry, often unspoken, overshadowed any sense of joy. Jackie had endless tests, I'd come back from training – "You OK, luv?" – but the anxiety never went away.

We'd kept Ruby's bedroom pretty much the same, the scans had revealed it would be another girl and we decided to call her April Ruby. The moment she was born I instinctively babbled: "Is she all right, is she OK, is everything normal?"

"Yes, Mr Lueshing, all's good, don't worry, you have a beautiful girl. Do you want to hold her?"

Suddenly all the emotion that had left the room when Ruby was born came rushing back in. I instantly felt taller, prouder – more responsible.

I looked at April and started talking, nothing rehearsed, and it was though we were the only two people in the world right then. 'I'll never let you down, my sweet, I'll never hurt you, I'll never leave you, I'll be by your side for ever, I'll protect you, no-one will get to you, you're safe my little April."

I didn't know where these words were coming from but they poured out of me. It was like my manifesto to my daughter and I heard myself vowing I would never let happen to her what George did to me.

"I promise you, April. No, daddy's not crying, honestly, he's not."

Nothing in my life had ever come remotely close to how I felt in those moments for my daughter. This was something I had been starved of for 23 years; my life had a new purpose that would keep me going when I was running back home in the pouring rain or freezing cold.

"I'm going to be a champion now, April."

And the great irony of it all was that April was white-skinned and looked more like George than anyone else.

******

Chapter Twenty

THE LOOK

ALTHOUGH I'D WON MY FIRST PROFESSIONAL FIGHT with Terry, I knew deep down he wasn't for me. Too 'Jack the Lad'; he didn't give me enough attention, he didn't push or encourage me. We didn't gel.

Then one day I was in the gym and a bloke came up to me called Gary Nichols, a chirpy little East End guy with a jolly face, an ex-featherweight professional with a really broad Cockney accent. We started chatting; he knew his boxing. Before long, he asked me outright whether I wanted a manager. I replied: "No, but I might want a trainer."

I'd liked the interest Gary had shown, I felt it was sincere so I phoned him back the next day and said: "Will you train me?"

"Yes, but you'll have to sort it out with Frank Maloney first."

Frank didn't like it. "You can't sack Terry, you can hand back your bloody contract if you do that."

"Alright, I will. I'll pop it in next week. I'm not going back to him, I want Gary and no-one else."

I told Gary what had happened and he reassured me: "Who's Maloney working for – you or him? Tell him I'm training you and if he doesn't like it, we'll go somewhere else."

So I went back and told Frank he could have his contract back. 'Don't be so stupid, Kev. I only said that for the sake of it. Who do you want training you?"

"Gary."

Maloney was way too busy with Lennox Lewis then to be bothered about this. "Yeah, he's not bad, alright then, that's fine, off you go."

And for the first time, I had a trainer who talked to me morning, noon and night, who made me feel good, who built my confidence and who helped me banish all the self-doubts, who diffused my anxiety. I needed this badly.

"You're unbelievable, Kev; you can knock these kids out all day long, they're all petrified of you, boy."

Gary started writing stuff down for me, he'd do groundwork with me, show me how things were done, stuff I hadn't done properly before. I learnt how to duck, to move and to jab with speed; Gary gave me a rhythm to my movement, showed me how to be more co-ordinated, just like Sugar Ray. He'd tell me to do something and I'd do it immediately; we were on the same wavelength, we understood each other's language.

Overwhelmingly, he gave me confidence whereas all my life I'd only been left deflated and broken. He believed in me like no-one else ever had, no-one at home, school, even at South Norwood Victory. Not belief like this. If he'd said, "Do some press ups on your head," I would have done. I believed in him because he believed in me.

Training became far more personalised than ever before: Gary would spend half an hour just bandaging me up, then watch me stretching before I even started on the serious stuff.

All the while he'd be talking to me, hugging me – "We're going places you and me, Kev" – bigging me up or making little adjustments, getting me to try different things. Four rounds shadow-boxing, 10 rounds pads, four three-minute rounds on the bag, then skipping, then groundwork. I was training like a machine under Gary; my body was turning into solid rock, I was looking ripped. I was violent, hungry for violence, pumped up – mentally as well as physically – and I was ready to go.

I hadn't let go of the drug deals, though. On the way back from training I'd still stop off, buy some coke, knowing I'd be making enough on Friday night to pay the mortgage and look after April.

My routine would be go to training; take a detour on the way home to get the merchandise; go home, play with April, see her to sleep; slip out later, do some selling; head back home. I didn't hang around the nightclubs like before and I wasn't taking the drugs myself. It was simply a slick business operation that suited me and my small group of clients. "There you go, Kev, same time next week. Good luck with the boxing."

I won my second fight comfortably with a round-two KO. I'd sold £5,000 worth of tickets for that: I got paid £600 for the fight – and 10 per cent of my ticket sales. Gary only got 10 per cent of that, even though he'd been training four days a week with me intensely for six or seven weeks before the fight. I quickly realised Maloney was making at least £3,000 profit out of us, even though I was selling most of the tickets for him.

"Your job is to fight, Kevin; I'll worry about the figures."

I cruised through my third fight, too: in fact, I noticed Nigel Benn in the audience, giving me a bit of attention. I asked for his auto-graph afterwards. "Sure man, hey, you're not bad. You can bang." I would become his manager ten years later.

Although Lennox was taking up most of Maloney's time, he started to realise I was worth a bit more attention.

He also noticed I looked good, so he pushed me into a bit of modelling work. I did some catalogue shoots for £300 – sportswear, trainers, that sort of stuff – and even landed some extra work for TV dramas, like *Minder* and *EastEnders,* just background roles. Then I was asked to do some stunt work for a low-budget film: I was a pirate and had to get shot on a beach in Wales! There'd be a bang of smoke and I earned an extra £100 for falling back dramatically on to a giant mattress hidden under a load of seaweed. It was all very exciting and different and felt very glamorous to what I'd been used to. The papers even picked up on it.

Then, one day I was chatting with Maloney in his pub when he said: "Listen, Kev, we've got to find a name for you now – every top fighter has a ring name, the fans love it, it's part of the show."

At the time, Maloney used a cut man everyone called Mick the Rub. He was listening and immediately chipped in: "Well look at him, he looks the part, he's done a bit of modelling, the ladies like him – it's obvious. He's got to be: "Kevin 'The Look' Lueshing."

Maloney instantly liked it. "Done." But now I had a name, I had to have a theme tune to go with it that could be blasting out when I walked towards the ring. My signature tune, the one that said: The Look is in the building.

There was one stand-out-obvious choice at that time: "You've Got the Look' by Prince became my anthem. My 'Danny Boy', my 'Rocky'.

My next fight was back at the Royal Albert on the Lennox Lewis-Derek Williams undercard. Gary and I went there around midday on the day of the fight – only to be told my opponent had pulled out. 'But I've sold thousands of tickets, I can't give them the money back."

Gary started making frantic calls and after several dead ends finally beamed: "Don't worry, I've sorted an opponent."

"Who'?

"Chris Eubank's brother, Simon." I was terrified. Chris Eubank's brother. *He must be good.*

"Don't worry, Kev. Listen to me: I will never put you in with someone I don't think you can beat. Never. Believe in me and believe in yourself. You will knock this kid out, he is slow."

Another voice piped up: "Anyway, if you can't beat the likes of Simon Eubank, you're going nowhere Kev."

"OK, OK." But deep down I was in a right state: deep down I felt like I'd be fighting Chris Eubank, not his brother. I could feel the same old Lueshing fear and anxiety and dread sweeping through me. I went home trying to conjure up any tiny excuse to pull out. "I've got a cold, my hand hurts, I've had a fall." None of it sounded plausible.

I even picked up a hammer and held it over my knuckles, poised, willing myself to crack it down and smash my hand sufficiently to call off the fight. *Tap… tap… then a bit heavier across my knuckles… come on Kev, just one more proper blow.* And I was actually lifting the hammer back in the air, holding it still, looking down on my reddening knuckles, summoning up the insanity to do it.

You can't do this Kev, come on, put the hammer down. Enough.

And I was talking out loud to myself: *"Fuck it. You shitter, Stan, you fuckin' coward shit. What the fuck is wrong with you? How you planning to explain this shit to Gary?"*

I dropped the hammer.

Before the fight, Gary started bigging me up in his normal way: "Kevin, you are supremely fit, this bloke is an old man. Just because his name is Eubank doesn't make him Chris Eubank. You will destroy him."

And just before I went out, I posed for pictures with the legendary trainer Angelo Dundee, there to watch the Lennox fight. I chatted him with – the man behind Muhammad Ali and Sugar Ray – and he was so polite and decent. I kept thinking: "He'll be out there watching me, watching how I do."

I had my new 'Look' to show off as well: I was groomed, my hair was styled, jet black, greased back. I even had my own designer outfit, thanks to the woman who had been my private tutor after I was expelled from school. Her son was a talented costume designer and he made me a waistcoat with 'The Look' written across the back – only the two 'O's were made to look like two eyes.

It was perfect, black and red to match my shorts, which now had the words 'April Ruby' sewn on them. I also decided to have the initials NSPCC sewn on the other side of my shorts. I'd seen a very disturbing Christmas advert on TV for the children's charity that featured a little boy alone and crying in a room, with angry parents shouting in the background. It resonated; it looked and sounded very familiar.

And for the first time I heard the MC, Mike Goodall, deliver the words: "Ladyees and gentlemen… introducing: Kevin – The Look – Lueshinggggggggggggggg."

I knocked Eubank down in the third, he quit halfway through the count, but as I walked back to the changing room I heard a few seasoned trainers, all part of the Maloney camp, saying: "Well done there, Kev, you've surprised a few people tonight: we didn't think you were going to win that one. That was a 50-50."

I looked at Gary and he just smiled his Cockney smile. "Don't you ever fuckin' doubt me again. Now start believing the hype."

Fights four, five, six, seven – four wins, although I was taken the distance on the sixth for the first time and I was finding the opponents were getting a little bit harder and craftier. They knew a few tricks of the trade, like holding me, giving me no room, closing me down and not coming forward themselves so much. The Look was looking good but was having to wise up. "Don't throw wild shots, Kev."

I was caught by a right hand during my ninth fight, I actually felt it pummel into my chin and for ten seconds or so I was sore. Then I knocked him out, but it registered with me that I had been caught.

It wasn't so much the pain, I had learnt to absorb that during George's beatings. It was the shock and the breaching that hurt.

My fan base was growing substantially with every win and local supporters were starting to show up in Kevin 'The Look' Lueshing T-shirts. My name was spreading far and wide in boxing itself. I was being talked about where it mattered: articles were appearing in all the right papers and magazines.

Gary and I were getting on really well; we were becoming quite a little team and everyone could see that. I got his undivided attention and I loved it. Everything was 'Kevin and Gary'. Seven fights, seven wins, five by knockout. And I was on £1500 a fight now.

Kevin's parents on their wedding day
.

Kevin with his sister Sharon and brother Andrew.

Looking for trouble with his primary school gang

12 years old and the trophies are piling up

Slugging it out at a schoolboy semi-finals on Hastings Pier

Kevin with the 'Cockney Rebel', trainer Gary Nichols

Kevin delivers another amateur knockout punch

With legendary American trainer Lou Duva

In Australia, on the set of I'm a Celebrity Get Me Out of Here *with Nigel Benn and Darren Day*

Frank Bruno drops into Kevin's training camp before his British welterweight title fight

In Vegas for a Lennox Lewis fight

Lifting the Lonsdale Belt after winning the British title

All smiles with Mike Tyson in London

Kevin joins Prince Naseem Hamed and Chris Eubank to celebrate Muhammad Ali's birthday in London

With Nigel Benn at his emotional reunion with Gerald McClellan

Beating Chris Saunders in the Fight of the Year

With April and Louie at an awards night

All grown up – Louie aged 17

Sharing a kiss with my soul-mate

Chapter Twenty-One
CRUSHING KIRKLAND

I WON MY TENTH AND ALL OF A SUDDEN GARY SAID: "I think you're ready."

'Ready for what?"

"Kirkland Laing."

And he added: "They've offered you Kirkland Laing for the light middleweight southern area title."

Kirkland 'The Gifted One' Laing beat Roberto Duran in 1982; he was a former British and European champion. He was 33 now, maybe past his best, but everyone knew and respected him. He'd had 34 fights, won most of them; I'd had ten but Gary said I was ready.

I'd be getting £6,000, too, and the fight would be live on Sky TV. Plus, there was a belt at stake.

"You'll catch him, son, we're ready for this one."

'You sure, Gary?"

"I'm sure Kev."

It was all serious stuff but I actually fancied it because I'd spotted Laing fought with his hands down all the time. Ha! I didn't realise how good he was until I was in the ring with him.

There was no doubt this was the acid test: the put-up-or-shut-up moment for Kevin – The Look – Lueshinggggg. A lot of people would be coming just to see if I was the real deal. And I wasn't nervous: *he drops his hands, I'll catch him.*

First round, and I didn't get anywhere near him, all my punches missed hopelessly, farcically. Laing was so far out of my range he was almost out of sight. Yes, he dropped his hands, but he was moving and dodging so fast I couldn't get close.

It was then I realised there were ten three-minute rounds of this. All my other fights had been six-rounders but this was a title fight, with a belt at stake. Laing had all the experience, he'd been here before. While he was moving backwards and dropping his hands, I was swinging into clear air, sapping my energy, and letting frustration build up.

Gary in the corner: "You're doing fine, son, don't worry but listen, here's what you've got to do. Aim for his neck. His neck, Kev. Look son, look at me: Fuckin' aim for his fuckin' neck."

And that's exactly what I did, and I started catching him – not always on the neck but I was suddenly hitting what seemed like a bigger target, maybe catching his chin, or his chest, but making contact where before I was hitting nothing.

Now we were going through exchanges, it felt more like a regular fight: I was hitting him, he was hitting back, the crowd were getting excited, standing up, swinging their arms as if they were in the ring, too. At one point I caught Laing in the right eye but the ref waved to carry on.

The frenetic pace was tiring me, though, and I went back to the corner, puffing. Gary: "Stop chasing him, Kev, conserve your energy; you don't have to go looking for him now. Let him come."

But I'd lost my rhythm, he was connecting more than me; I'd take swings but they were wild, without precision or class. I was directionless. I could even hear the commentators just below me: "Lueshing is starting to lose control now. Laing's got him against the ropes and he's connecting with big body punches."

Desperation. Nothing hurt, there was no sense of pain, but everything felt feeble and inadequate. My energy was deserting me, seeping away with the effort of every wasted blow.

Back in the corner, end of round four, slumped on the stool. "Composure Kev, composure. You're working too hard, you're using up too much energy. Relax." But it was in one ear and out the other. All I could sense was despair. Then Gary started slapping me and shaking me: "Don't quit on me. Kev. Not now. Not here. Go on, son, fuckin' kill him. Go for the eye."

And those words landed. I hadn't heard "Go for the eye" before. But it gave me a target and I threw everything in that direction: punches, elbows, my chin, anything. I was deranged by "Go for the eye". I connected, connected again, again, a left hook – something squashy – and then Laing was going back, wiping his eye, there was blood, I could smell something. I was stalking and pursuing and striking and connecting and all of a sudden...

The referee stopped it after one minute and 25 seconds. He pointed to Laing's eye, took a towel, rubbed over the bloodied area. I watched, frozen, inwardly praying – I knew I was spent – and then the ref waved his arms in the air. Fight over.

Jesus, I'd won.

I was the southern area champion, I'd actually won a title and got a champion's belt.

I put it on in the middle of the ring. People were cheering for me: And the Southern Area champion is... Kevin – The Look – Lueshingggggggggggg.

PART FIVE:
TEMPTATIONS

Chapter Twenty-Two

BETRAYAL

I WAS STILL ECSTATIC AFTER BEATING KIRKLAND LAING when Gary took me aside and said: "Kevin, I'm going to have to let you go. I can only take you so far."

Talk about body blow. Gary was a black cab driver when he wasn't training me and the combination of juggling boxing and driving was too much. "My missus is sick of never seeing me. Besides, you need someone to look after you all the time."

But who? I didn't trust anyone. Gary had been my mentor for nearly two years.

Just as I was reeling from this news, Frank Maloney announced: "Kev, we're sending you to America to train with Pernell Whitaker." At that time he was one of the best pound-for-pound fighters in the world, a household name, an Olympic champion. It would be the equivalent of spending a month with Sugar Ray Leonard.

Pernell, or "Sweet Pea" as he was known, was about to fight Julio Cesar Chavez, which meant I'd be mixing, sparring and training with some of the biggest names in welterweight boxing. But my contract with Frank was coming to an end and he wanted it renewed before I flew out. I wasn't so sure, Frank was too preoccupied with Lennox Lewis for my liking, I wasn't earning much out of him and I'd just lost my trusted trainer. But I really fancied the trip to America, even though I'd heard stories about how tough it would be, and how sparring sessions were treated like real fights.

"Don't worry, Frank, I'll sign for you when I come back. I'm not going anywhere else."

Maloney reluctantly agreed and I decided to have a savage skinhead haircut before I left. I wanted to look horrible and mean because I knew this trip would be hard. I knew I would have to get beaten up, that was part of the deal.

I was picked up at Virginia airport by the legendary trainer and manager Lou Duva, which was an honour, taken to a Hilton hotel and told to rest easy for a couple of days before they came back to get me. I was totally on my own, so I went out, turned a corner and there was the beach right in front of me, heaving with bodies, heaving with women. What a playground.

Two days later I got a call telling me to be in the hotel lobby for 6am. There, I was met by six other fighters and we went for a six-mile run along the beach. Then we headed to the gym and for the next couple of days I did some relatively gentle pad work. But all the time I had the feeling I was being watched, being weighed up – and prepared for something brutal.

I was nervous, tense, and badly missed Gary's encouragements; I was shadow-boxing on memory. At one point Lou came up to me and said: "Heh, Kev, you sure you're black, man? You don't look too black to me, you ain't got any rhythm."

But I was willing and hungry to learn: when Pernell got in the ring, oh my God, it was like watching ballet. Everything he did looked natural, like flowing extensions of his body and soul. And that underlined the gulf in class between what I'd experienced back home and how it was in America. It was like going from the top of Division One to the final of the Champions League. These people were like Lionel Messi and Cristiano Ronaldo. Everything was inspirational and I was being spoilt – until they suddenly said: "Kevin, we've lined up some sparring for you – nothing heavy, a southpaw."

I pretended to be delighted but my smiles were fake. *I'm going to get ripped apart here.*

My opponent arrived the next day: tall, skinny like a rake, nothing on him. *Nothing to fear.* We went into the ring – I was overly desperate to throw some commanding blows but missed every time; he was relaxed, cool, moving effortlessly, like he was having a stroll on the beach.

Then all of a sudden… blackness. To this day I have no memory of what happened up until the point where I found myself sat on the edge of the ring, taking my gloves off, glumly. I remember Pernell came over and said: "Heh, kid, stop feeling sorry for yourself, get up and go skip it off."

Some time later, Pernell's trainer, George Benton – a legend who trained many champs, including Evander Holyfield – spoke to me in a very calm and philosophical way. There was no attempt at blame, just cold, stark analysis. "This is boxing son. Learning to hit and not be hit, learning to use all that energy wisely and not wasting it in a rush. We all knew what was going to happen back then – but you didn't."

We were inside the gym but Benton was still wearing his trademark white flat cap as he spoke and although his words were judgemental, they were eloquent and softly spoken.

"We need to strip you back, we need to get you right back to basics and rebuild from there. You've got power, you've got style, you've got speed, but you're not using them intelligently."

I took it all in. This was the top level, Benton's words were poetic and I wanted to learn from him. And he taught me from scratch all over again: how to jab, how to breathe, how to train properly. Day in, day out. At 7pm each night everyone in the camp would get together for an evening meal, and we'd just talk and talk and talk about boxing, training, great fights, great fighters. It was magical to be in such company. I was shoulder to shoulder with the elite, feeling like I belonged.

By the end of two weeks I was outsprinting Pernell. Then: "Right, Kev, we're all off to Texas now." That's where the big fight was being held and I was invited to join them.

A couple of nights before, though, I betrayed Jackie. My days were full, my midnights empty. I'd noticed girls in the gym giving me the eye, my body was looking good and they adored my accent. "Hey, Kev-in… have you met the Queen?!"

One night I went to a local bar with a couple of the other sparring partners and started chatting to a girl, an air hostess who was staying in my hotel: she had a drink, then another, then another. It was easy. We went back to her room, she could barely stand – "Don't worry, Kevin, I'm on the pill."

We completed the act functionally, as though it was fulfilling some basic chore that couldn't be put off any longer. We didn't even kiss: Kevin was cold and heartless again. She turned over and I went back to my own room. I never once thought about Jackie.

Two days later I was in Texas where I sparred so confidently that Mr Benton came over to congratulate me. I was improving, Mr Benton said. He could see potential, he said. He could see me fighting for a world title one day.

"Thank you Mr Benton."

But after six weeks away, I was missing April. And even though the big fight was only a week off, and excitement levels were rising by the day, I decided I had to get back. I can't now believe I made that decision: I could have been in Pernell's changing room, it would have been one of the biggest experiences of my life.

Frank Maloney couldn't believe I was heading back, either. "Don't forget, Kev, we've got to sign that new contract."

But as I stood at the check-in desk for my flight home, something happened that would utterly change my boxing career: I bumped into a former fight referee, Mike Jacobs, who was just beginning to establish himself as a promoter. "Hello Kevin, good to see you, what on earth are you doing here?"

The plane wasn't full, so Mike came over for a chat once we'd taken off. During the following nine hours he convinced me to ditch Maloney and sign with him and his new partner – a boxing promoter and financier called Roger Levitt. "Drop Maloney and we'll give you a salary, £800 a month, Kev. We'll pay your phone bills, your medical bills, we'll do everything for you, set you up for life."

Jacobs explained his job was to find eight fighters from around the world to form a stable of champions whom Levitt would fund. I vaguely knew Levitt – he'd brought Lennox Lewis over from Canada and had selected Maloney to be his day-to-day manager.

I'd met Levitt briefly a few times at the Lennox press conferences: he did everything with panache and theatre, very OTT, always smoking expensive Cuban cigars melodramatically. His expansive droopy moustache seemed to run parallel with the droopy bow ties he always wore; his debonair eyes and sharp nose made him look like an upper-class Freddie Mercury.

Levitt didn't come without baggage, however. He'd been arrested after an investigation by the Serious Fraud Office into the collapse of one of his companies. Famous celebrities had apparently lost millions of pounds. All the major allegations against him were eventually dropped, however, and there was something about him I really liked. He was always smiling, always larger than life; a give-you-the-time-of-day character and razor-sharp at remembering people's names

Jacobs explained that they already had two fighters from Nigeria; one from New York; Spencer Oliver – who nearly died in a title fight years later – and they were going to be called the KoPro camp.

They'd even fix a trainer for me – Graham Moughton – but our gym would be in Weston Super Mare, near Bristol, where we'd all have to live Monday to Friday. Jacobs even assured me everything with Frank Maloney would be sorted. "We'll just send him a little letter."

I could smell the money, the salary, the security. I got home, told Jackie – "£800 a month, that's what he promised." She was worried about Frank and the drama but agreed it was a great deal. The following week I met Mr Levitt in an office in Bond Street and it was like meeting royalty. Everything was ostentatious: framed pictures on the wall of Lennox, framed pictures of Roger with celebrities, Roger's stunning PA floating around with smiles and coffees. Levitt himself was magnetic and mesmerising; everything was bullshit but I accepted every word of it. I was entranced.

I even summoned up the courage to ask him about his fraud case. "Kevin, do you really think I'd take people's money?" I didn't really care, so long as I got my £800 a month.

He wanted to know all about me, whether I was married, had kids, family and the like. He took an interest in me and I was always gullible to that sort of attention. "You're going to be a star Kevin. I've always wanted to sign you, I've always believed in you, I've been watching you progress but we're going to make you a proper champion. Keep on winning son, and we'll make you a millionaire. I promise."

I signed with him there and then – for three years. *Screw you, Frank Maloney.*

But first Frank tried his damnedest to screw me. "I'm going to get your licence taken away, I'm going to the Boxing Board of Control, you ain't walking out on me for Roger bleedin' Levitt. Who the fuck do you think you are? I'm getting all the money back that I've spent on you. You know what? There's hundreds of Kevin Lueshings out there. You're fucked. You'll regret this son: I'll see you in court."

I phoned up Mr Levitt to tell him how Maloney had reacted and he calmly said: "Listen, Kevin. I do not want you to mention that guy's name ever again. I will deal with him tomorrow: you just concentrate on boxing – and winning."

So I started my new life, which meant getting up at 6am Monday mornings and driving three hours to Weston, where I'd stay until Friday with the other fighters, a right mix of nationalities, weights and sizes but all real prospects. We all lived together in a cramped bed and breakfast just off the seafront; we took over the whole building and although we got on, it very quickly became a lonely and torturous existence.

Every day became the same. We'd get up at 6.30am, a van would be waiting outside to drive us six miles away. Then we'd run back to the bed and breakfast, eat and either go back to bed for an hour or so, or just kill time. It was boring, hard, isolated and repetitive and nothing like as glamorous as America. We'd spend our afternoons in the gym but the trainer, Graham, couldn't cope with so many different styles and demands and couldn't give us each the personal attention that I, in particular, craved.

In the end I told Mr Levitt. 'The training's shit, Graham can't cope, he's not giving us enough time. He's telling me to lead with an uppercut. I never do that, Mr Levitt, it's wrong for me."

"Who would you like, then, Kev?"

I mentioned Duke McKenzie's trainer to him, Colin Smith, only because he'd once complimented me after a fight and I hadn't forgotten that. "OK, Kev, this is what we'll do. We've got a fight lined up for you in Wales – get that out of the way and we'll get Colin."

Chapter Twenty-Three

SUICIDAL

THE NEW LIFESTYLE INEVITABLY TRIGGERED ARGU-
ments between me and Jackie, who understandably grew sick of
being left on her own all week with April. Our relationship disin-
tegrated into a once-a-week tense call from a phone box; I was
feeling increasingly agitated, short-tempered and unhappy about
the set-up. I was sexually frustrated, so much so, I went to a
massage parlour in Bristol knowing full well what would happen.

It was seedy and dirty, just like Derek's house. I knocked on a
sinister black door down a dark alley – there was a security camera
slung on a brick wall opposite and I remember turning away, half
embarrassed, half excited to be walking into a depraved underworld. A dyed-hair woman failing to conceal her age and hips
answered and led me up some dingy stairs that seemed to climb
sharply into eternal blackness. "Follow me luv, we've got a nice girl
waiting for you."

I was led to a bedroom: a single red light struggled to glow from
a short, stumpy lamp and a young girl, about 24 years old, sat on
a scruffy single bed. *Had I been here before?* I stared at her face;
she was desperately trying to look sexy and inviting under layers
of make-up but struggling, just like the lamp, to glow. Next to her,
splayed across the bed, were pornographic magazines.

Everything Kevin associated with sex was here: it was dirty, it
was not nice. The girl felt like home: her depravity, her complete
physical surrender, the dirty bed, the red light, was comforting and
familiar. We were both victims and this was all we deserved. I gravitated to it. Animal sex without commitment. An act: filthy, seedy
and raw and disgusting. Her hands, Derek's hands; flesh exposed,
the shameless invasion, the vague guilt.

Then payment: £40.

131

Afterwards she gave me her phone number and said: "I want to see you again. I think you and I connected." But that's not why I called her back: I called her because it meant next time I'd get it for free.

She invited me to her house this time and said: "I can get us some crack." That sounded dangerous: in Virginia a couple of the fighters had said to me: "See that guy over there… he's a crack head. He'll fuck you up completely."

"I know all about cocaine," I replied.

"No, no, Kevin. Coke is for rich people; crack is for dead people."

She lived on a council estate in Bristol, the cold, graffiti kind full of hopelessness and misery. Rough. I parked up, my breathing getting anxious, danger. *I've been here before as well. Grey stucco walls.* I knocked on her door, number six; she ushered me in with furtive 'shush, shush' gestures.

"My little boy's upstairs in bed."

Should I be doing this?

I'd brought a cheap bottle of champagne with me and she brought out an old battered coke can, crumpled almost flat in the middle, where a hole had been pierced through the tin surface.

Then she got some tin foil, spread it over the hole, and tipped what looked like pellets out of an old envelope on to it. Next, she took out a Bic lighter, flicked on the flame and held it against the pellets until they started to smoulder. She looked like she'd done this many times before. She looked like an addict.

Then she put her mouth over the end of the can where the ring pull had been opened, and deeply sucked in the vapours coming from the burning crack, holding her breath for what seemed like ages. I looked to her eyes – just like I always did in moments of danger – and they freaked me out; they looked empty and dead. Zeroes. Next, she exhaled – calmly and slowly. She looked like she'd been tranquilised.

My turn. "Go on, darling, suck it up, suck it up." She wanted to hold the Bic for me but I wouldn't let go of it: I needed to keep a sense of control. I held the vapour in, exhaled, nothing happened; she urged me to do it again, I did, and same thing – nothing, other than I didn't want to be part of this any longer. Something inside was screaming: "No, Kevin, get out of here, Kevin." She could see I wanted to go, and just as she tried to cosy up to me, a child's crying started from upstairs. "He'll go back to sleep, Kev, don't worry about him."

I insisted she went up to see her son; soon as she left the room, I fled. I never returned.

Damned right we had a connection. We were both victims. But she'd made it to the graveyard, I hadn't.

I rowed ferociously and unreasonably with Jackie the following weekend, my temper spewing out of me, raw, volatile, poisonous, looking for tiny reasons to be angry. Everything in me was boiling.

I drove back to Weston early on Monday and spent the entire journey sinking into blackness: Jackie wasn't for me; the prostitute crack addict wasn't for me; the trainer wasn't for me; driving backwards and forwards wasn't for me; living in a bed and breakfast wasn't for me; lonely nights without a woman wasn't for me. The more I drove, the more possessed I became until depression seemed to ooze through me like an ugly, spreading slime.

I was on the long Avonmouth road bridge that carries the M5 from Bristol towards Weston and I was staring manically at the low-slung metal barrier on the left that stops you swerving off and dropping 30 metres into the river below.

The more fixated with the barrier I became, the more my foot pressed down on the accelerator; life and death separated by a thin, steel strip that seemed to be shrinking and shrinking the more I stared at it. There had to be a speed where I could smash into that barrier and the car would flip over and fall uncontrollably into death. When I was nine, I'd tried half-heartedly to kill myself: for the next 30 seconds I contemplated suicide.

I was seedy, dirty, unfaithful, untrusting, incapable of love; I was worthless, my life was therefore worthless. I wasn't crying for help. I was craving death.

My foot presses down more: 70, 80, 90… rising so enticingly… I hit 100mph. I'm in the middle lane – *Come on Kev, get past those lorries – there's a gap ahead – just keep the speed going, then pull over but don't level off, keep going to the left, keep the foot down, go on son, slam the barrier, hit it, the car won't stop, there's nothing it can do, it'll somersault and fall; Kevin, now, do it.*

I pass the lorries, check in the mirror to see them fading away, then start to pull over – I'm doing it, this is it, my foot's flat down, my eyes are nailed to the barrier, I can see the speed, 110 maybe, the metal's becoming a blur of horizontal lines, it's so low, so inadequate.

Then I hear a child's cry, like the child in the prostitute's house, only it isn't a boy.

I hear April. "Daddy." The image of her being told "Daddy's dead," the thought that no father can protect her ever again, that she'll be for ever abandoned and vulnerable like I was, hurtles through me in a flash. My foot shoots off the accelerator, the spell is broken; I straighten the car frantically in a frenzied twirl of hands and arms and stay on the inside lane, parallel to the barrier all the way to the Weston turning.

*****

Chapter Twenty-Four

VALE OF TEARS

NOT GIVING UP ON APRIL SAVED MY LIFE.

I got to Weston, back in control of myself, and was told my fight would be in five weeks and it'd be on late-night BBC. Suddenly I had something to fight for again, and I was instantly happier – even though I was still stuck with the same inadequate trainer.

I was to face another southpaw called Chris Saunders, from the Brendan Ingle camp, in the Ebbw Vale sports leisure centre – every bit as unglamorous as it sounds. I didn't bother trying to sell tickets: it was a horrible place to get to from London. Errol and Andrew showed – and about nine other mates. That was it. This was Conference League stuff compared to the Champions League Mr Levitt had promised. I went into that fight weighing 10 stones 12lbs, which, as a welterweight, was too much. It was undisciplined and betrayed the life I'd been leading. Nobody had been pushing me, there was no father figure around, just mates and macho talk. "Just knock him out, Kev."

I hadn't fought for over a year, just training erratically for about nine months. I got into the ring – "All the way from London, Kevin – The Look – Lueshingggg" – and what sounded like a solitary hand-clap feebly crawled towards me. It was like being on Hastings pier. Nobody knew who I was and nobody cared.

I was absolutely ripped to shreds. Everything I learned in America deserted me. I was a distant memory of a fighter I had started to be. I was too heavy – Gary would never have allowed that. I knew nothing about my opponent – Gary would never have allowed that, either. After three rounds I had nothing left, no strength, no energy. Knackered and desperate. I went out, tried to throw some shots when suddenly, *bang*: I was down on my knees. I bounced right back up, too quickly of course, like that amusement arcade game,

Whack-a-Mole, when you bang the top of the animals' heads with a hammer but they keep springing back up.

Suddenly a swarm of punches were all over me and I was down again, crouched on one knee, disorientated, not in control of my body – everything looking and sounding other-worldly, distant. I was vaguely aware of faint voices from somewhere and every-where. I looked over to my corner: "Get up Kev, get up, move." I dragged myself up and the ref asked: "Are you all right?"

"Yeah, I'm alright." Only there seemed to be two refs stood in front of me right then; everything was smudged and shadowy and blurry. "I'm alright." Within seconds, I was knocked down again and the ref waved his hands high; it was over. There was no need for a count.

It was amazing how quickly my senses came rushing back as soon as the ref ended it, as if to punish me even more. Suddenly I was totally aware of how devastated I felt; I could now hear acutely and clearly the cheering, and I could see vividly my oppo-nent jumping up and down with joy. I went back to the white-tiled shower rooms that had been converted into a makeshift dressing room for the night – and sat alone with Jackie, who held my hand and tried to soothe me. "Don't worry, Roger will sort you out Kevin, he'll get a trainer for you."

Bless her.

But this wasn't in the bloody script, Mr Levitt. I learned then that when you lose, you lose alone. I was the only one from our stable to lose that night. Nobody knew what to say to me.

At least I was thinking clearly: I knew I had to learn from this, to accept responsibility for my own training and lifestyle, what I ate, what I inhaled. I went to see Mr Levitt the following Monday in his office and told him everything. "The training's shit, I don't like trainer, I'm not right mentally, I'm not looking after myself physi-cally. I would sacrifice everything if you sorted my training out."

"Kevin. I am not going to let you down. This is nothing, we will both learn from this. Whatever you want, whoever you want, you'll have it. Go get the trainer you want. You don't have to go to Bristol any more, either, you can go down the Henry Cooper gym and train there. Just don't let me down."

Redemption. Did Mr Levitt want me to give up? No, he wanted me to win.

I went down the Henry Cooper in The Old Kent Road the next day and asked Colin Smith if I could speak to him. We went outside and sat in a nearby McDonalds: "Colin, please train me," I begged. "I'll give you 10 per cent of everything I earn – Roger will pay you on top – and I promise I won't let you down."

"OK, son, we'll give it a go. Start next week over at Crystal Palace."

After four weeks, I was transformed, on a different level. Colin had taught me to jab in a way I'd never learnt before; he spoke calmly, methodically, but with microscopic detail – everything clear and precise, nothing left to chance or misunderstanding. Textbook, to the point of no mistakes.

I liked his personality. There was nothing loud, brash or flash there: he was short, an ex-fighter, mid-50s with a big shock of hair which I always took the piss out of. But he gave me respect and talked to me like an adult. I wanted to do well for him; he put the spring back in my step, I was running in the mornings and winning the sprints against the other fighters, like in America. "You're going to be a textbook counter puncher, Kev: move to the left, to the right, step back, another step back – then on the third… hook."

And he started to tell me what to expect from my opponents, what their moves would be. I started knocking out sparring partners regularly – step back, step back… third time – wham. KO. It was working. One day my ex-trainer, Graham Moughton, was watching and I knocked down a kid who'd come over from the Bronx and who was meant to be tough. Back, back, back… strike. I looked over to Moughton as if to say: "See, that's what you could have had. But you weren't in my league."

Colin then took me back to his headquarters at the Henry Cooper and let me train alongside Duke McKenzie, who became a world champion at three weights, a British champ at two and a European at one. "This will be your second home now."

Chapter Twenty-Five

FIGHTING BACK

THE BOXING NEWS WROTE ME OFF: "SAUNDERS EXPOSES The Look" was the headline after the fight in Ebbw Vale, and it hurt just as much as the defeat. My brothers took the piss – "You got beat by a bum, Kev" – and I felt totally ashamed and embarrassed by their acid comments. I even thought I could hear Maloney mocking me from far away.

I knew how I reacted would define my future – I had to learn quickly and fortunately I now had the perfect trainer to help me do that. Working with Colin was what I imagine it must have been like for Manchester United's footballers to learn from Sir Alex Ferguson. He spoke to me calmly and reassuringly, he rebuilt my confidence and made me believe again in my strengths rather than my weaknesses. I believed in him and wanted to prove a worthy student.

He patiently explained to me what I'd been doing wrong and I absorbed every word of it. And he drilled into me the 'three Cs' – courage, composure, conviction. I became a different person, a different fighter, in those days immediately after the Saunders defeat. And I didn't have to worry about money – Roger was paying me the monthly salary he promised.

But he and Colin didn't know that my drug dealing remained an important source of revenue. One afternoon I had to meet my supplier in the McDonalds outside the Henry Cooper gym. I bought quarter of an ounce of cocaine in a plastic bag and stuffed it inside one of my boxing gloves. I then ran over to the gym and was ordered straight into the ring to do some sparring against a boxer who'd been waiting ages for me to turn up. I went three rounds with the charlie still stuffed in a packet deep inside my glove – nobody knew. That's how it was.

My next fight was at the York Hall, my favourite venue: I never lost there. It was intimate, the crowd was pressed in tightly and their excitement, their drinking and their cigarettes created a frenzied atmosphere that rose above the clouds of smoke and always left me with goosebumps. It felt like boxing to me, familiar, like some of the venues I first boxed in as a child.

I was fighting Dennis Berry although quite frankly I would have taken on Mike Tyson that night if Colin had wanted me to. That was how much belief he'd given me post-Saunders.

I sensed this would be a night when everyone would think "Is Lueshing finished, is this the end?" I hated that pressure; it fuelled the anxiety attacks I could be prone to. Annoyingly, we both turned up with the same coloured shorts – black and red stripes – and my camp had to pay £200 to persuade Berry to change into plain black ones. That really pissed me off.

Colin spoke to me for a full 30 minutes non-stop before the fight – something he would do for all my future bouts afterwards – methodically and meticulously bandaging my hands as he chatted. The whole routine was calming, almost hypnotic. Then, just as I was being lulled, he applied some pressure: "This is the big one, Kev, everyone in boxing is waiting to see whether you've still got it. You can't fail tonight, Kev, this kid will come out and try to throw big punches – but he's not in your league. Just do everything I've taught you Kev."

The hall was heaving that night and insufferably hot. "Calm, Kev, breathe easy, relax son, use your jab and show him what you have to offer." I remember seeing Roger in the crowd, and seeing him wink at me, and I desperately didn't want to let him down. The fear of losing was driving me.

Berry came out and started swinging big, wild punches recklessly with little impact. His hands were down, he left open gaps and I started filling them with jabs that connected. Colin's voice: "That's it Kev, that's it: this is easy, isn't it, there you go. Remember the three Cs, Kev." I was repeating everything he had drilled into me in the gym and it was working.

I caught Berry even more in the second round – all the while moving backwards as he came forward, waiting to throw a big one at the first glimpse of an opening. Colin's voice again: "It's coming

Kev, not long now, son." And almost on cue, Berry dropped his left hand, I saw the gap, and – crash – my left hand smashed right on to his chin and knocked him out, pole-axed, flat on his back. "Perfect, Kevin, well done, now stay calm." For a few anxious moments Berry was too still and the crowd fell quiet: he eventually struggled up and returned to his corner. Only then did the applause return – mainly relief for him that there was nothing seriously wrong.

I was back.

Two months later I was back in the ring, this time in Middlesbrough. This was live on Sky, which meant more publicity and hype, against Peter Waudby – a fighter I should have faced in the ABA national final if I hadn't been beaten at Blackpool in the qualifier. I wasn't even nervous, he looked like a bloke from the pub – the sort who has a permanently broken nose. Dopey.

I was so confident I was starting to play up to the cameras: as soon as the little red light sprang on, I knew we were live and The Look would give a little look to the viewers back home. This was fun – Waudby couldn't even look me in the eyes, he had no muscle tone and had even struggled to make the weight.

So I used him to try a new shot I'd been practising with Colin – the double left hook. Hook to the body and then, wham, one to the head. Vicious, a classic Mike Tyson combination but difficult to execute. My moment came when he fell onto the ropes under a barrage and put his hands up for protection.

I struck in a flash: a thunderous blow exploded onto his stomach, his hands instantly dropped and I followed with a spontaneous and venomous blow to his head that sent him crashing to the canvas. It was one of those moments when the crowd gasped and stood up in one giant movement of shock and awe. Colin: "Perfect Kevin. Stay calm now, son." Waudby got up but I finished him in round two – first with a vicious body shot that crumpled his remaining strength and then a series of hammer blows straight into his face that left him covered in blood and nursing a broken nose.

"There is a different look to The Look now", said the Sky TV pundits afterwards.

Colin and Roger were now convinced I was ready for an eliminator that would give me a shot at the British welterweight title. There were four of us in the frame but only one of us could fight for the title, so we had to fight each other for that right. Who fought who would be decided by which promoter offered the biggest purses. I thought Roger would win the bidding hands down but Frank Warren came in with a colossal offer – £26,000, massive than – because his fighter, Michael Smyth, was considered the clear favourite.

I started serious training but two weeks before the fight, Smyth pulled out, injured. It happens but it's incredibly deflating when you've been preparing so intensely. The fight was rescheduled – but not for another three months – and I needed all Colin's wisdom and experience to keep me focused. "This is boxing, Kev, it happens, don't worry."

But disaster struck twice and the re-match was cancelled again about a month later. 'I can't take this shit Colin."

"Stay strong son. What you going to do, throw everything away? You must carry on training and not worry about whether it will be cancelled. Get it into your head Kev: this fight will happen."

Fans would even turn up to watch me train during this period: when Colin and I were on the pads it was breathtaking: right jab, double jab, move, uppercut, move back, step: it was fast and furious, pummelling my strength, science and artistry into those giant pads on the end of Colin's hands – mesmerising to watch, exhilarating to perform. Move, move, rhythm, rhythm – dancing to background music in the gym: I'd changed my signature tune to U2's 'Even Better Than The Real Thing'. Lou Duva's words would creep sometimes into my mind: "Heh, Kev, you sure you're black?" *Well, look at me now Lou.*

Colin and I would do pad work for eight rounds, 40 minutes, and he'd nurse me between each one, giving me a drop of water, massaging my shoulders, wiping the sweat from my brow. I liked that: by the end, my adrenalin would be pumping and I'd be ready to take on the world. Like I was a gladiator.

Chapter Twenty-Six

MY AFFAIR

MY GLADIATORIAL INSTINCTS WEREN'T CONFINED TO the gym: while I was waiting for the eliminator, I began an affair. Each time the fight was on the horizon I persuaded Roger to let me stay in a hotel, so I wouldn't be distracted by Jackie. I ended up staying close to the Docklands Arena in London – even though my home wasn't far away at all.

I had a little top-floor penthouse and one afternoon bumped into a model I vaguely knew called Suzie. She lived just round the corner from the Henry Cooper gym. "What you doing here, Kevin?" We chatted in the street outside the gym and she gave me her number.

I phoned her that night and we met in a bar. We laughed at the same things, we shared similar views, we didn't need to argue because we didn't disagree with each other. I told her about Jackie: "We're not really getting on." Suzie was fun and sexy but I didn't even try to kiss her that first night.

We met again a week later and this time played tennis together. It was summer, I was on a high despite the cancellation setbacks, and this girl playing tennis never seemed to disagree with a word I said.

We sat in my car afterwards, talking and laughing, and I never gave Jackie a second thought. There was no sense of guilt at all, even though she was at home nearby looking after my daughter all on her own. Suzie mentioned Jackie and said: "She must be mad to let you stay in a hotel, Kev."

My eyes fixed on to Suzie's lips – I saw the slightest flicker there and kissed her. I stopped and pulled back to look at her glowing face. "What about our friendship now, Kev?" she enquired. I instinctively opened the car window and replied: "It's just gone out there, that's what." We laughed. Our affair had begun.

We met constantly from there on. Jackie would phone and ask, "What you doing tonight?"

"Nothing much, I'm really tired. I'll be going to bed early." Then I'd go straight out of my room and head to Suzie's flat and continue a double life.

On the rare occasions I went home I wasn't interested in what Jackie had to say, or how she was coping on her own with April. It was me, myself, I. And I'd even sleep in the spare bedroom. 'Can't have sex before a big fight, Jackie."

PART SIX:
BECOMING CHAMPION

Chapter Twenty-Seven

WELSH WIZARD

THE ELIMINATOR WAS EVENTUALLY RE-ARRANGED FOR June 17 at the Cardiff ice rink and this time there were no cancellations. Suzie came over to my hotel the night before and I said I wanted her to see me fight. "No Kevin, it's not my place, you go there and win for me but you don't need me to be there." I knew Jackie would be, she never missed any of my fights – bless her – but inside I was aching for Suzie to be in the crowd.

I arrived in Wales tense and agitated and Colin worked overtime to soothe me and find a way of calming my nerves. "What does Smyth do Kevin?"

"He comes forward."

"So what do you do, son?"

"Drop backwards."

The arena was packed solid that night and they were all Welsh. I had about 25 fans rooting for me; Smyth had around 12,000 boozed-up Welshmen. When I walked out, and 'Even Better than the Real Thing' was blasting out, I was met by an avalanche of hostility and booing that even drowned out U2: objects were hurled towards me – plastic beer cups with the dregs spraying out in mid-air, coins – drunks spitting as ferociously as they could muster, their grey phlegm landing uncomfortably close and choruses of "Fuck off back to London you black bastard."

It didn't bother me.

I glimpsed my brothers near the front and as I passed them Andrew's hand reached out and slapped me heavily on the back: "We're here for you, Kev."

I couldn't believe my ears when Smyth came out: not because the boos suddenly turned to waves of Welsh euphoria but because he had also picked a U2 song – 'Where The Streets Have No Name'.

I remember thinking to myself *"What a shit tune!"* When he eventually got in the ring I knew I was going to be OK: I could see and smell he was more intimidated than me. He was frightened, even though he had his own fans and Frank Warren in the front row, urging him on. Nerves: worse than mine.

The Boxing News had predicted I'd put up some early resistance and then fall in the fourth. *Sod 'em.*

The first round was cat and mouse – he was coming forward, swinging, I was moving back, weighing up his movements, getting used to his style – which became increasingly predictable. Back in the corner Colin said: "You're doing fine, Kev, keep patient, this could be a ten-rounder, don't use up all your energy. He's making mistakes, isn't he, so work that double jab, right hand, Kev."

Round two and I started to connect: I saw the gaps and I picked him off: one left hook to his body hurt him badly. Colin: "Calm, stay calm Kevin." The crowd knew their man was wobbling – they started chanting Smyth's name and I could distantly hear: "Fuck off Lueshing, you bastard, fuck off ."

I went into the third with Colin's words again swirling through my head: "Step it up now Kevin, don't show him any respect, let him come." Smyth went to throw a right hand, missed, his hands were momentarily down, I saw the gap, and smashed my fist down on the top of his head: it wasn't a clean connection but it was a sign of things to come.

Five seconds later we were in the corner, he threw a lame punch, missed, left an opening and I was straight in – *smash!* I clobbered him with a brutal left hook that disconnected his brain from his legs and sent him falling into the gap between the ropes, so his body was actually dangling horizontally on the rope, unsure whether to fall on to the ringside seats below or back into the ring itself. Right in front of Frank Warren.

Hands from the crowd frantically pushed him back into the ring, the ref checked he was tuned in enough to continue and Smyth came towards me again. Suddenly Colin was screaming: "Don't wait for him Kev, go for him, finish this."

I crowded Smyth back to the ropes and smashed him with four consecutive left hooks – bang, bang, bang, bang. There was no response, the torrent was too rapid and too relentless. The ref had no option but to step in, push us apart and stop the fight. But my adrenalin was still erupting and I ran, demonically around that ring, yelling and screaming at the pissed-up Welshman. "Yes, you bastards, yes, fuckin' yes." I was beating my chest like King bloody Kong and then I spotted Warren and he got it as well: "Yes, fuckin' take that, yes." Warren didn't like that at all: he looked severely pissed off, like he'd really got the hump. His man had been annihilated and I was rubbing it in.

Jackie was waiting for me in the changing rooms and she was really happy for me. But it wasn't her I wanted to be with: my mind was on Suzie as soon as that fight ended. I was desperate to tell her I'd won and to be with her. Instead, I stayed in happy family mode, went home with Jackie and spent the night watching the fight over and over on the video recorder.

Chapter Twenty-Eight
JOINING FRANK WARREN

MY VICTORY OVER SMYTH EARNED ME THE RIGHT TO fight for the British welterweight title. Every boxer wants to win a Lonsdale belt and I was acutely aware of its glorious heritage: I'd stared for hours at the famous names for ever inked into boxing history – Bombardier Billy Wells, Jock McAvoy, Tommy Farr, Randolph Turpin, Ronnie Clayton, Henry Cooper, Billy Hardy, Lennox Lewis, Carl Froch – all of them among the true British greats. Now it was my chance to join their ranks and that felt like a dream. I never quite made it as an amateur; this was my chance to do so as a professional.

Roger was elated but his KoPro team was beginning to crack. The other boxers in the stable were unhappy that I had a great trainer and they were still stuck with Moughton. Spencer Oliver defected and joined Barry Hearn; slowly but surely the others got picked off. Even Mike Jacobs left.

It was unsettling but I didn't want to betray Roger, who I felt incredibly close to. We talked every night, or he'd invite me to his big house in swanky St John's Wood. He made me feel special – not just as a boxer but as a human being, as though he genuinely valued our friendship. He became increasingly the father I never had, he always found the words I most needed to hear when I was down, or doubted my own abilities. Our nightly chats became something I anticipated and looked forward to: I was always vulnerable to anyone who took an interest in me but this time there didn't seem to be a sinister, ulterior motive. Yes, he was a businessman and yes, he was hoping my success would earn him money – but he made no secret of that.

The difference was he stood by me, even after my heaviest defeat, even if that meant digging deeper into his own pockets to keep me on track. I genuinely believed he cared about me – he certainly showed he cared many times – and I responded to that. I wanted to prove he was right to show me such faith.

I even told him about my affair although, ironically, he was even able to cast his spell on Jackie, too; she would often phone him and pour her heart out like I did. There were times when she believed as much in him as I did.

While Roger's role was to make money for me commercially, and carry on being my mentor and sponsor, I still needed a boxing manager and promoter.

So, with his approval, I went to see Frank Warren – I'd just destroyed his prize kid, Smyth, and maybe he could claw back some of his money if he took on me. But going to his office was an intimidating experience: he really was boxing's top promoter then, he had Sky TV; I was in awe. I sat nervously in his office, we shared some small talk, and then he came straight out with it: "How much do you want from me to be your manager for one year?"

I thought I was being smart and bold when I straight away answered 'Ten grand." But even quicker he snapped: "Done. Do you want it now?"

He'd done nothing wrong – he was just smarter and wiser than me. But as I walked away from his office, I suspected I'd lost the negotiation. It was a lesson I never forgot, especially in later life when I started negotiating deals for other fighters and celebrities. The expression 'whoever starts the bidding, loses' couldn't be truer.

Chapter Twenty-Nine
FOUND OUT

FRANK ASKED ME WHETHER I WANTED TO FIGHT THE reigning British champion, Del Bryan, who had dominated the welterweight division for some years, winning, losing and regaining the title. I said: "No, let him fight Chris Saunders first, and I'll fight the winner." In the meantime, I asked for two more warm-up fights, which Frank would give me £10,000 each for.

And that was when Jackie found out about my affair.

I was in the Britannia hotel in Docklands again, pretending I had to be away from home to get ready for the first warm-up fight. But on this particular night I had to attend a boxing awards dinner and Jackie was expected to come along as my guest. I told her to turn up to my room – with my suit – for 2pm, so we could get changed and go off from there.

I lost track of the time and was on the phone in my room, chatting away with a mate about Suzie, and what she was like and what we did together. I even said stuff like: "Do you reckon I should ditch Jackie?"

Suddenly, there was a knock on the door.

I looked at my watch and stared in horror: it was 2.15pm. Jackie was meant to show at 2pm. Had she been stood outside the door the entire time, listening to every word I'd said?

I ended the call, walked nervously to the door, opened it and the moment daylight appeared, Jackie burst forward. She'd heard every single word.

I don't blame Jackie for being so furious. As we argued, I realised how much shit she'd had to put up with because of me. I'd rarely shown her the love and devotion a woman should expect in a relationship; she'd remained loyal and raised our child and been by my side throughout. In return, I'd been unfaithful.

It was my worst nightmare – and then I started thinking: "Christ, I've got to attend the awards' night and Jackie *has* to come with me. Colin will be there with three-times world champ Duke McKenzie, everyone expects Jackie and me to be together, we're a team, Jackie and me." And in the middle of all the chaos I realised I had to not only calm her down, I had to get her into a party mood.

"Jackie, we'll sort this, I'm so sorry – I didn't mean it, I was just showing off to my mate, talking shit – Jackie, we've got to go to this boxing thing, come on now, let's calm down, let's talk about it all tomorrow."

I carried on begging, shamelessly: "We must be there, it's important for my career Jackie, please." Unbelievably, she relented.

So we went and Jackie put on a smile and shook people's hands and played Kevin's doting partner for the night. It was horrible for her. And when the night was over, we parted: she went back home and I went back to my hotel room, where I phoned Suzie and told her what had gone on. I told her Jackie and I were finished. "You'll have to tell her that to her face, Kevin, it's your decision, your responsibility – nobody else's," she replied.

But I was more worried about what was best for my career and poured my heart out to Roger the next day. "Listen Kev, you've got to decide, not me. If you want Suzie, I'll back you; if you stay with Jackie, I'll back you also. But Kevin, you must understand this. If you leave, you won't be able to see your daughter so much, you'll become a stranger to her and it will never be the same for you again."

He'd got to me: I knew straight away that I had to stay – for the sake of still seeing April. I grovelled and begged Jackie for forgiveness; once again she relented and I returned home.

In a bizarre way, all the chaos wound me up perfectly for the first warm-up fight. By the time I reached the ring – and Jackie was there again, as she was for all my fights – I was ready to cause damage. Danny Quacoe hung on for the full eight rounds but I put him down twice.

I went home afterwards, my relationship with Jackie still thorny. All the while, I carried on seeing Suzie whenever Jackie wasn't looking. Then, one afternoon, another calamity. My mobile rang,

Jackie spotted Suzie's number, grabbed the phone, ran into another room, locked the door – and started talking to her.

All I could hear was: "Is that so; really; did he; oh, is that what he said; did you; no; you're joking; what a shame; well, that's certainly not what he told me; yes, I'm sorry about that, really."

It was horrible, I couldn't force open the door and end it. Their conversation ended, Jackie opened the door and we argued again, only now April could see and hear it all. I really don't know how Jackie held it together; I was a bastard, I was selfish, egotistical, cold, cut off and emotionless, utterly unapproachable.

Still, I carried on seeing and talking to Suzie: she was happy to go along for the ride – so long as it suited her. She was in control. She was the female version of me.

I had to go to Barnsley next to see the Del Bryan/Chris Saunders fight, knowing I'd be fighting the winner for the British welterweight title. Sky TV had invited me down to commentate; Saunders won an absolute war, beat Bryan on points, and said to the camera: "Now I'm going to do the same to Kevin Lueshing."

It was all part of the hype, it was box office and I was raring to go. What could be higher than fighting for the British welterweight title – against the only kid who had ever beaten me as a professional?

Chapter Thirty

UNFAITHFUL IN MANHATTAN

BY NOW ROGER HAD LEFT THE UK AND WANTED ME TO fly out to see him in America for two weeks. "One day this will be your home, Kev."

I told Jackie. She wasn't overjoyed but accepted I had to do what Roger wanted. And as soon as that conversation was over, I was on the phone to Suzie, saying: "Listen, you're coming to New York with me."

I flew out with a heavyweight fighter Roger had just taken on, Richard Bango, and we were met at the airport by Roger's driver, Al – who we dubbed 'Driving Miss Daisy' because he was absolutely like that character from the film. He took us to an apartment in Brooklyn but on the first night we heard gunfire outside and sirens in every direction. Bango was huge – 6ft 6ins tall, 240 pounds and an African champion – but he was so terrified I had to phone Roger and beg him to put us somewhere else. 'Driving Miss Daisy' returned in the limo and took us to the New York Palace. 'Five star' barely described the luxury: I'd never seen anything like it. And we weren't even champions – yet.

Roger met us for breakfast the next morning and mapped out the regime. "You're going to do some training at Mike Tyson's camp in the Catskills – he won't be there – but you can use all his facilities."

That night I explored New York and was instantly intoxicated: from the bright lights to the red lights, from the penthouse suites to the seedy alleys. Over in Brooklyn I saw familiar things: the hookers and the dealers; I spotted the furtive eye contact as people crossed the road, hands moving, drugs exchanging and I desperately wanted to be involved and see how good the cocaine was. So I stood on a street corner I'd noticed and in no time a kid came over. "What do you want, dime bag or nickel bag?"

"Dime," I replied, and he told me to go to the sweet store opposite and tell the "Puerto Rican behind the counter" what I wanted. It was like walking into a village store, but with homeboys standing menacingly outside looking like they had guns stuffed inside their hoodies and pockets. I knew why they were there: to protect the shop. I went to the counter as directed, asked for a dime bag, handed over 20 bucks and walked out, like I'd just bought some Black Jacks and Fruit Salads from the newsagent where Derek worked.

Inside, the cocaine was top quality, flaked – not mixed with anything. I gave it a go later that night but threw it away – it was way too strong for me. But I knew now how easy it was to get and how cheap it was. I knew I'd be back to deal.

I went to the airport the next day to pick up Suzie and she spent the next week with me, watching me train during the day. At night, we'd hit Manhattan, laughing, strolling through Central Park, dining out, nightclubbing until 3am. Suzie and I shared almost everything. 'Almost' because there remained one secret I still couldn't confide – even though I truly wanted to.

Derek had to remain a closed door, so I simply carried on living the dream in New York. Even training was fun: every day we'd be picked up in the limo, there was a massive swimming pool at the training camp, an outdoor barbecue area, Suzie was there, there were iced beers in the fridge and we could help ourselves to it all. I felt like I was in a movie set and I couldn't sleep because I was so excited. I remember Roger seeing the smile on my face one day and saying: "This is where you belong, Kev." He was right, he'd whetted my appetite – which was exactly what he'd hoped to do. But I'd also seen the seediness, I knew there was a dark side here and I was certain I could make lots of money out of dime bags.

Once or twice I'd phone Jackie, but always pretended I was in a rush and couldn't spend long talking. "It's boring here Jackie, hard work, how's April, put her on. Heh babe, daddy misses you, I'm going to bring you back a big present, got to go now, tell Mummy I'll call her back." Then I'd go straight back into Suzie's arms.

It had to end. I had the biggest fight of my life coming up and I wasn't ready to split with Jackie. So Suzie and I came back, and carried on in secret for a while, just as we'd done before New York.

But not long after she went backpacking with a friend to Australia; that was a turning point and I think we both knew that it would spell the end, and that I would stick with Jackie.

So I switched off, coldly and clinically Suzie wasn't that important to me. Boxing was all that mattered now.

My final warm-up was at the York Hall against one of Saunders' stable-mates, Steve Goodwin. I knocked him out, breaking his nose in the second round, before turning to the TV cameras and proclaiming:

"This is what you're getting Saunders. I'm coming for you."

Chapter Thirty-One

LIFTING THE BELT

I HAD SIX WEEKS TO GO BEFORE THE SAUNDERS FIGHT and decided to head for Tenerife, where Nigel Benn had invited me to use his training camp. He was getting ready for a huge fight against Thulani Malinga – and Frank Bruno was there, too, preparing to face Mike Tyson.

I took Del Bryan with me to be my sparring partner – although he'd just lost to Saunders, he was also a southpaw, which could be useful. My new best friend and gofer, Paul Stockton – who had been my sparring partner in the past but had increasingly become a trusted pal – also came along. Everything was paid for by Roger.

It was four weeks of gruelling, relentless, hard-as-it-gets training – every day I'd be running six miles up Mount Teide, then back for sparring, pads, gym work, circuit training. And all around were the temptations of a Spanish holiday island: I could hear the pounding music as I lay awake at night in my bed, and during the day I could see the women, barely wearing a stitch in the blazing sunshine, bodies glistening with sun oil; some strolling dangerously close to the training camp in their bikinis and flimsy tops.

One Friday evening, I spotted Del Bryan and another sparring partner getting all suited for a night out. 'Where you going," I asked desperately, knowing full well what the answer would be. "To the strip, Kev – you coming?" Colin my trainer was downstairs – I was under a strict 10pm curfew, how could I possibly sneak out? But I wasn't a boozer, I knew I wouldn't be tempted to take drugs so close to such a huge fight, and I desperately wanted to see what was going on out there. "Sod it, I'm coming." And I crept out with the others to hit Playa De Las Americas – where I spent the night flirting with pissed-up girls.

I crept back at around 3am, desperate not to wake Colin up, and sneaked in through an open window. *Got away with it.* I was up on time the next morning, walked out of my bedroom and there was Colin stood outside, waiting.

"What did you get up to last night, Kev? D'you watch the fight on TV?"

"You bet, it was terrific."

"Tell me then, Kevin, what round did he win in?"

And before I could stammer back some sort of response, Colin hit me with the following tirade: "I'm going to say this only once. If you go out again, I will pack my bags and get on the next fight home and you and I will be finished. Do you understand? Are you listening to me? Del bleedin' Bryan can go out any night he wants; he's already a loser, he ain't fighting for the British welterweight title, he's just a sparring partner getting 70 quid a day. Are you with me, Kevin? Del Bryan don't care, it's not his responsibility this. It's yours, boy. So tell me, Kevin: what do you want to do? You've disappointed me, son. What d'you go and do that for? You're not taking this serious."

I felt ashamed – for myself, for my own standards, and for letting Colin down after all he'd done to get me to this point. "I'm sorry, Colin, I got tempted, distracted, it won't happen again."

"You're damned right it won't, because I'm gone, I'm out of here if it does. I trained Duke McKenzie and he doesn't do this sort of shit to me."

And that was it: I was switched back on; Colin's speech had put me on track and both sparring partners got beat up heavily the next day for getting me into such a mess. I saw Del Bryan as a different person now, he was just a punch bag and I wanted to hurt him. My training intensified as well: halfway up Mount Teide, Colin, who was driving a little car alongside me, told me to stop – but I kept going. In the end he had to say: "Listen Kev, you're doing too much now. You're going to leave it all here if you overdo it. Hold some back."

And Colin relaxed about the women, who started hanging around the camp during the day to watch Nigel, Frank and me training. In the end I pulled one of them, a young 20-year-old party girl on holiday. I can't even remember her name. All I did was wink at her while I was hitting the punch bag and that was it. Easy. 'How long you here for, babe?"

"Two weeks, Kevin." *Bang. Don't need to pay 40 quid for this one.* I was boxing, sweating, training, steamed up and I needed a release. It was pure sex, she'd come in for a couple of hours, then go. *Sod Jackie and Suzie.*

I came back to England and Roger found me a stunning penthouse by the Thames in Wapping, which belonged to Mary Bonham, who had made £millions from the DIY market with products like WD-40 and J-B Weld – and who went on to sponsor me.

Jackie and April were allowed over for brief visits but most of the time I was training ferociously. Colin even brought in a powerful African sparring partner who had apparently knocked me down during training in the dim and distant past, although I had no memory of that. I staggered into a third round with him, wondering why I was being put through such a tough ordeal and Colin whispered: "You need this, Kevin, trust me. The fight you're about to have will be harder than this."

Colin was doing textbook work with me so I'd be equipped to face a southpaw; he was teaching me different movements and responses and it was all beginning to make sense and click into place, even though it was brutal.

And every night after training Colin and I would talk, for hours, dissecting everything that might happen – how Saunders would come at me, which angles he'd use, where his gaps and weaknesses would be; how I must respond; how I must handle the pressure; how Duke McKenzie coped in these situations. Roger would phone me every day, too, making me feel special, bigging me up: "Win this one, Kev, and you and I will be earning some serious money. Serious." And every day he'd get a driver in a stretch limo to pick me up at the penthouse, drive me to Battersea and drop me off so I could run back. Luxury penthouse, luxury car, pre-fight medicals and scans in Harley Street – Roger took care of me. I was being treated like a world champion, even though I wasn't one.

Then one night Suzie turned up – she wouldn't be going to Australia until after my fight. We talked and laughed and got on all over again, exactly like before. She visited regularly after that, eating with me, having fun and helping me forget the pressure.

I was eating the same food every single day a week before the fight: breakfast would be half a cup of mint tea – no sugar – muesli, with semi-skimmed milk and a banana. Then I'd go for my three-mile run, come back and have lunch: always a jacket potato with tuna and no butter. I'd then train for about three hours in the afternoon – everything would be light, I'd done the heavy stuff in Tenerife and Belfast – and absolutely no sparring, to avoid injury. Just light work, like skipping, to keep me ticking over.

Then, I'd head back to the penthouse for evening dinner around 8pm – jacket potato and tuna again. No butter. I followed that diet and regime religiously for seven consecutive days. I was tight on the weight, there wasn't a sliver of fat on me. I was five foot 11ins tall, my weight should have naturally been nearer 12 stones but instead it was 10 stones 7lbs. I was starving myself to be a champion and I had to be severely disciplined to make sure I did it. Every single night I'd weigh in to make sure I was on track. I'd always go to bed at 10pm so I didn't have to spend any more time thinking about what I ate, although I would often dream about food – mainly steaks and Mars Bars and ice cream.

And, oh my God, the cravings. I'd crave every food, not just any food, but boring stuff like lettuce and rice – although mainly biscuits. And Pepsi Cola: I had to drink flavoured ice water instead. Sunday roast dinners were constantly on my mind. Suzie was eating with me one night and tucking into the works: beef, Yorkshire pudding, roast potatoes, the lot. All I could do was watch and carry on eating my jacket potato with tuna and no butter.

Two days before the fight, I attended a press conference and saw Saunders for the first time since he'd beaten me. *He looks smaller, definitely smaller.* I went over to shake his hand: "How you doing?"

"I'm alright Kev. I'm looking forward to this one."

"Yeah, let's hope it's better than the last one," I replied, cheerily.

I'll never forget his response: "Don't worry about that Kev. You're going to fuckin' get it."

We went for the head to head, so the photographers could take their pictures, stood toe to toe with each other, naked from the waist up, our noses so close they were almost touching, our frostiest glares drilling deep into each other's eyes, searching, hoping to laser the soul, looking for the weaknesses and the fear. "You're going to fuckin' get it, Kev." Boy, he looked confident; I didn't win that psychological battle at all. He was the British champion, and although he was smaller than I remembered, he seemed big and imposing. He was beating me.

I went back to the penthouse and I was scared. *Have I done everything properly? Have I done enough training? Have I run far enough? I've hurt all my sparring partners, every one, but is it enough? Am I ready for all his moves, his shots, can he hurt me? He's beaten me before, he's the champion now, what if he's better than before?*

Roger wanted to see me in his big house the next day and sent his driver to pick me up in the limo. It was the Jewish Sabbath: Roger was wearing his kippah, and ceremoniously placed one on my head as soon as I arrived. Next I was sat at the kitchen table alongside his wife and their three kids and we were all praying. It suddenly felt like a sombre, deeply religious moment and in the middle of it all Roger started talking, as though he were a priest giving a sermon: "This is it Kevin. I can't be there but I will be alongside you in mind, spirit and soul and I will be watching you and we will win this together, Kevin, you and me." But unlike your average priest he continued: "We're going to do this and we're going to fuck all those people who said it wouldn't happen: you and me, champions of fuckin' Britain. Out of all the fighters I signed on, I knew you were the kid who would make it and we're going to make serious money after this. Just don't let me down."

Some sermon.

I went back. Colin was staying in the penthouse with me now. It was early evening, I was sat on the sofa and, despite Roger's sermon, my mind was succumbing to fear and self-doubt. *You're going to get beat, you're going to let everyone down, you're going to let Roger down.*

My eyes grew heavier and heavier, like I was falling into a troubled sleep and I almost nodded off: vaguely aware of distant sounds and sirens, and then suddenly a massive thunderous bang, like an explosion, so loud it shook me out of my reverie and I yelled to Colin: "Did you just hear that? What the fuck was that?"

"I dunno, power station or something," and the pair of us thought no more about it.

The next morning, we turned on the TV news and straight away the screen was full of ambulances and sirens and police cars: there'd been an explosion at the Docklands Arena. The IRA had detonated a truck bomb in London's swanky financial centre, Canary Wharf, destroying buildings, killing two and injuring 39. It was horrendous and devastating.

And it also meant my fight was off. My thoughts should have been with the dead and injured but they weren't, although I understood the horror of the moment. Instead, I was thinking: Shit, what now, will it be re-arranged, when for, where will it be? *Oh Christ, I'll have to go through all this over again, the eating, the training, the abstinence.*

I was so frustrated I went out that night and headed for Browns, where I'd done all my drug deals. I was deflated: it felt like everything was over. I didn't even want to go home and be with Jackie; she wouldn't know how to handle all the pent-up adrenalin and energy boiling away inside me. I'd dreamt about winning, the elation, the crowd, the belt – and now it was all shattered.

I woke up in the penthouse the next day and the phone rang. It was Frank Warren. "Listen, the fight's back on – York Hall, Tuesday. You'll be topping the bill and you'll have to weigh in again on Monday."

My reaction wasn't great: I didn't want to fight any more, I was deflated and couldn't face the thought of raising myself again, even though it was only a couple of days away. In the space of 24 hours I'd put on weight – 10 stones 11 now after binge-eating on pasta and chicken – and I couldn't face the sheer enormity of getting back to jacket potatoes and tuna. I phoned Roger, he sent his driver over to get me again, and he spent an hour calming me down and getting me back in the right frame of mind. It worked: I went out running that night with a sweatbag on. I weighed in on the Monday: "Kevin Lueshing... 10 stones 7 pounds." Bang on the limit.

I was back in the penthouse again but this time a couple of girls had moved into a flat opposite and I started flirting with them in the corridor the night before my fight. 'You're going to see me on the TV tomorrow girls, and when I come back I'm going to be the British welterweight champion." They thought that was hilarious and we were laughing and giggling with each other.

It was only a bit of fun and I slept well afterwards. Then, the day of the fight, Roger's driver arrived again in the limo and took me off to my moment of destiny at the York Hall. My favourite venue, where I'd never lost.

I went to the changing room – 10 foot square, plain and basic with a mirror and chair and nothing else – with Colin and our cuts man, Paddy Burns. On the door a sign read: "Kevin Lueshing – Challenger." I liked that. I was nervous, but the *Boxing News* had tipped me to win in the fourth round. I badly wanted to prove myself.

Straight away, my mind went back to those days as an eleven year-old when I went, reluctantly, with my brothers to the South Norwood club – just so I could flee George for the evening. A small boy thrown into a steamy, raw, savage underworld, looking for sanctuary but finding instead an escape route.

I thought back to my first fights, the dinner shows in front of fat, boozed-up audiences, baying for kids to beat the living daylights out of each other; my amateur career, OK but never quite good enough; turning professional after seeing Gary Stretch fight at Earls Court. I thought about my life: my dad – in prison in Jamaica; my mum and my brothers – none of them present to see me; the paedophile; 101 Clockhouse Road; the violence at school; nicking stuff from swanky London stores; labouring on building sites; dealing drugs; Jackie and Ruby and April; being unfaithful with Suzie; the fights I'd won and the fights I'd lost; drifting in and out of trainers and managers but finally ending up with the best I'd ever known, Colin and Roger.

And I had an overwhelming understanding that these were the component parts of why I was about to fight for a British title; I knew that losing would blow the logic of it all to shreds and make everything utterly meaningless and futile.

Roger couldn't be there but he'd demanded I entered to a different song for this fight: a re-mix of one of my earlier signature tunes, 'You've Got the Look'. It was more of a rap-style version and cost him £2,000 to put together. Another reason why losing wasn't an option.

I was really happy with my gloves, Rayes: eight ounces, really tight, proper 'punchers' gloves' that fitted me, excuse the phrase, like a glove. They made my hands feel like weapons of destruction, like specialist tools I would have picked up and used for heavy-duty work on the building sites. I looked at myself in the mirror, looked at the boy who had come all this way and thought to myself: *I'm ready.*

I switched on some music – 'War' by Bob Marley – and the loud, booming base rapidly got me into an ugly, tribal, state of mind as I shadow-boxed, practising the moves and punches that would destroy Saunders.

Then suddenly: "Five minutes, Kevin. Five minutes son."

The fight before me had finished far earlier than expected: I thought I had at least another half an hour to look at myself in the mirror. But there wasn't enough time to start panicking or self doubting. Colin looked at me and said: "Come on, Kev, let's go to work."

I walked out of the changing room immediately into a corridor and everything seemed eerily quiet. One or two stray faces looked at me, I didn't know who they belonged to and nobody talked. Then I saw a Sky TV man and I watched his hand as he counted down: "Four" – suddenly, I'm aware of my breathing – "three" – heavier now – "two" – my chest heaving – "one"… and… " Walk."

The doors behind him immediately burst open onto a heaving arena. In a flash, I could sense the sweat and the smoke and the excitement and the bloodlust. It was indisputably masculine: hard and tense, rowdy, raw and primitive. It was where I belonged. As I walked forward a channel opened in front of me as fans shovelled to the left and right, forming a corridor out of bodies. Some reached over to pat me on the back, others shouted out my name "Kev-in, Kev-in" but my eyes fixed on the ring that was quietly waiting above all this mayhem in the middle of the arena. A camera man walked backwards in front of me, his camera zoomed on to my face, hoping to find something there that might add to the intensity. Roger's re-mix of 'You've Got The Look' swirled alongside the crowd's roar.

Suddenly, fleetingly, I saw familiar faces – one of the builders, one of the drug clients, a former girlfriend, an old trainer, a sparring partner, a mate – their smiles flashing before me, then disappearing just as quickly, but enough to say: *We're here for you. Your friends are in this 1500 throng.*

I clambered between the ropes on to the ring and raised my arm. Immediately I spotted Roger's wife and kids in the front row; I glanced to the left and spotted Jackie but my eyes rushed past her. I didn't want to see negativity. Instead they picked out Liam Gallagher and Patsy Kensit.

Then my music died down and Saunders started his grand approach towards the ring. He did a dramatic back-flip over the ropes when he won the British title: but this time I spotted something significant. Just as he moved into position, he hesitated and changed his mind, ducking between the ropes instead. *Noted.* My confidence soared.

Everything felt familiar until the master of ceremonies announced: "Fighting for the British welterweight title." The stakes rocketed with those six words; I then tuned into the roar that erupted when he said my name – I had never seen or heard so many people in one arena backing me.

This is it, Kevin; win, win. Lose this and you can never, ever, climb back into a boxing ring.

I went to the middle of the ring and touched gloves with Saunders but didn't bother giving him the evil eye. I just wanted this war to start; I just wanted to kick the shit out of him. Back to my corner… "Seconds away, round one."

****

Saunders throws a lead left hand – one punch – I see it coming, I dodge, move back and make it miss. Everything Colin's taught me is instantly tuned in; Saunders has left a gap, I see it, I hit him with a left – crash – he's down, on the canvas in seconds. The crowd go ballistic; Saunders scrambles up but then goes down on one knee in his corner to take a count – and get more rest.

What do I do now? The fight's only just started.

I can hear Colin's voice from my corner: "Don't panic, Kevin; calm, stay calm – don't rush." So I return to my back foot, Saunders is coming at me, doing exactly the same thing, missing me, leaving a gap and I'm picking him off, just as I've practised. His punch is coming, slow and predictable, I dodge, let it miss, there's the gap, I counter – and strike. I am like lightning, everything is flowing: I am eleven years old winning my first fight; I'm the seventeen year-old who won the London ABAs; I'm beating Frank Warren's boy to win the eliminator; I'm in America getting the rhythm from Lou Duca – it's all coming together, all making sense.

It's all art and precision and science and beauty; Saunders is now being lured towards the ropes, he doesn't even know it, he swings wildly and – *bang* – I clobber him viciously; his body gives way and crumples to the floor. He's down again.

He gets up, takes a standing count, it's still the first round and he's been down twice already, and Colin is screaming towards me: "Kevin, look at me, look at me. Kevin, for fuck's sake, look at me."

But I won't; my eyes are glued on Saunders. I want to finish him off. I am a fingertip away from being the British champion, my gloves are stretching out to take the belt, I'm so close now.

Saunders comes back at me, swings, misses, I hit him with a left hook, and – crash – he's down again. *Fuckin' hell, man, stay down, what's wrong with you?*

The ref starts counting but for a third time, Saunders gets up. *Christ.* I've had enough of this and I rush at him, I want to slay him and to hell with the science, to hell with Colin's wisdom, to hell with the weeks and weeks of training and talking and planning. I want this over right now.

I throw a wild, uncontrolled punch towards him, I miss and in a flash he clips me on the top of my head. I'm wobbling, stop it, my legs buckle, they disappear, I feel my body fall, but as soon as it hits the ground, it bounces straight back up, involuntarily, as though someone else is pulling the strings. I've definitely touched the floor. *What the hell was that?*

And now my back's up against the ropes, the audacity, and Saunders is loading up on me. How? What? This isn't possible. *Stay calm Kev.* But Saunders is hunting me, I'm not seeing so many gaps suddenly and I'm not throwing so many punches as before. I'm not in control. The bell comes as a relief and I can try to fathom out what just happened.

Colin is calm. "Son you're doing perfect, you've knocked him down three times, you're winning this." Every reassuring word restores my senses, I'm back in the room. Next Colin is taking deep, animated breaths, getting me to do the same, buckets of oxygen pouring into my lungs and empowering me afresh. All the while he's saying: "Keep that jab going, Kev; he's lazy, he's making mistakes son, you're doing everything perfectly."

Ding, ding... Round Two – and it's the same again, I'm moving backwards, he's coming towards me and he's not learning. He thinks my backwards steps are weakness. *Stupid sod.* And he walks straight into it: he throws a lazy left hand, misses, his hand goes down – there's an opening – and I smash a straight left into his numbskull face. He's down – again. For the fourth time inside two rounds.

This is it, this is it, I'm going to get you now, I'm not letting you off the hook this time. Once again, I ignore Colin and I rush back in, I'm a street fighter now and Bob Marley is pounding inside me – "Everywhere is war, me say war" – but I'm wild and ignorant and uneducated and I hurl a grenade, it misses and then... the aftershock.

I'm on the floor. Saunders has knocked me down. He's got me bang on the middle of my jaw and I've gone crashing like a dead weight, not subtly, not gracefully or gently, but brutally and violently, like I've stepped off a cliff and plunged straight down, dropping, unable to stick out a hand or anything to break the fall. As my body smashes to the canvas, I dimly notice the bodies in the front row seats leaping up as though we're connected and they've been jolted upwards by the heaviness of my fall.

I haven't got a clue where I am, my senses – all of them – are blown; I exist, I breathe, but everything is jellified. And here's a strange thing: as soon as my pole-axed body hits the floor, somebody tugs my strings again and I bounce straight back up, my body vertical but my mind still flat out on the floor.

This happens with such rapidity that Saunders still has his eyes on the floor where I landed – he thinks I'm still there, he hasn't seen me bouncing straight back up. Nor have I.

The ref, Mickey Vann, grabs me by both hands and barks: "What's your name?"

"Kevin Lueshing."

"Box on."

And now Saunders is hurtling towards me, like a great steam train, trying to find the killer blow just as I'd tried earlier. But all my switches are down, nothing is coming on, there's darkness everywhere; I know I must move, get out of this danger but the power supply has cut and all is still.

Then suddenly I'm aware of a colossal surge of lightning that flashes across my eyes from absolutely nowhere and sends my senses surging back – like a gigantic electric current. I have movement and response in my body although my mind is still cut off.

Saunders is trying to hit me, but my body instinctively reacts on its own, doing all the right things, as though on auto-pilot. It dodges on cue, it steps back, it sees the gap and it sends my own left hand smashing into him. My brain has no part in this; my brain remains disconnected. I am watching myself fight.

Saunders starts wobbling, he's hurt, and a part of me registers a smear of blood under his chin – and the effect is like smelling salts under my nose. I smell blood.

The round ends, I stagger back to my corner, but whatever Colin says during the next 60 seconds is wasted: I couldn't even register sounds from the crowd, never mind a single voice. I feel hypnotised, in the room but not in the room.

I get up for the third, and my eyes see Saunders making the same mistakes again: he's coming forward, he thinks I'm retreating, he throws, he misses, he leaves the gap. My body keeps moving, my body is saving and protecting me and giving my mind time to rejoin the fight.

And then it happens. Saunders lurches forward, leaves the gap, my left arm rises and smashes straight into the corridor that leads to his face. Thump. He crumples to the floor, again. I walk away and just stare at him, and watch him – yet again – pull himself back up. But I'm more alert, more aware now and I can hear Colin saying: "Kevin, take your time. Precise now, be precise."

I go back in and my punches are accurate now, like arrows peppering a big, round archery target. Smash, I hit the bull's eye

– his chin – and his blood smears across my glove, the spoils of this savagery. Bang, smash – the hunter closing in on his prey – kill or be killed. Nothing misses; his resistance disintegrates, his legs are immobilised.

Smash, smash, smash, smash: my assault is relentless, vicious, accurate, remorseless and just as I'm about to launch another bombardment the ref leaps in and ends this attrition.

Twenty-six years of abuse; 26 years of anger; 26 years of cruelty; 26 years of being branded worthless; 26 years to prove bastard teachers and bastard parents wrong; 26 years waiting to be proud; 26 years to become … a champion.

Screw you George, screw you Derek, screw you Kelsey Park, screw you Mr Davis – I knew I could do this but you didn't.

****

I paraded triumphantly round the ring, beaming, my adrenalin flooding through me as I soaked in the applause and the hysteria. As I walked round I spotted Jackie and saw she was crying and that instantly brought tears to my eyes. Of all the people in that arena right then, she was the only one who truly *understood.* Her eyes seemed to be saying: "I'm happy for you, Kev. You can have this, it's yours," and in that moment we shared something that was bigger than physical contact, that over-rode all the rows and my infidelities. Fleeting – but real and tangible. My glove touched my heart and I mouthed in her direction *"This is for you."*

And then someone appeared with the Lonsdale belt and put it round my waist; my tears became uncontrollable, unashamed, and flowed freely – drowning all the abusers, the back-stabbers and the doubters.

I leapt on to the ropes at my corner and yelled, "Thank you, thank you, thank you" at my supporters and then I was ushered over to the TV cameras where the interviewer, Gary Norman, was desperate to talk to me.

"Congratulations – champ – but that was a war. Tell us about your second knockdown. How on earth did you get up from that punch?"

I looked at him blankly and in total honesty replied: "What punch?" I genuinely didn't know what he was talking about and listened in disbelief as he described how heavily I'd been put down. It was though I was being told about something that had happened to somebody else.

And then I switched the conversation. "I just want to say something. I want to say thank you to my girlfriend, who has always been by my side, who has never failed to come to all my fights, who has had to suffer my terrible mood swings and who's had to raise our child on her own for most of the time. I just want to say: 'Thank you, Jackie'."

Twenty minutes later I found a public phone box and called Suzie. I even sang 'I'm so Excited, I just can't hide it' down the line to her. Then I headed off to Browns – where else? – to have a victory party with my closest pals, fans and Jackie, who – sadly – was very quickly sidelined. Although we'd had that connection immediately after the fight, she was back on the outside again – struggling to be seen or to be heard. I barely knew she was there – everyone wanted to talk to me.

It had been like that for most of our relationship and it was no different in Browns. One week before the fight she'd had her hair cut and dyed and I didn't even notice until she told me. I had no hugs or kisses for her.

The limo eventually turned up to take us home, although I didn't want to be with Jackie even then. All I wanted was to get back to my penthouse with my Lonsdale belt and fall asleep with it; but Jackie insisted on coming up with me. We got to my front door and I stared in disbelief – the girls who I'd flirted with in the corridor had dressed it up like a Christmas tree, there was a bottle of champagne on the floor and scrawled in big red lipstick the message: "Well done champ, come and see the girls in number five." Kiss, kiss. *Oh Christ.*

I stood frozen, barely able to look Jackie in the face. We started rowing; it was yet another fight between us, probably of my own making but symptomatic of our relationship and what always seemed to happen whenever we were together.

And that was how the greatest moment of my fight career ended. It had started with a war – and it had ended with a war. Two fights in one night – one that would be voted Fight of the Year, with seven knockdowns, a fight that I won; and one that was tragic and desperate and sad – that nobody could win.

PART SEVEN: EMBRACING DEFEAT

Chapter Thirty-Two

CHAMPION AMONG CONVICTS

I AM BEING CHEERED, LOUDLY AND RIOTOUSLY, BY people who won't be allowed home tonight, who are making the explosive noise of a boxing crowd but who can't go to any of my fights. They're packed together in a bleak, depressing room with no decoration and no natural light; they are all wearing identical clothes and they all have hardened, granite faces, many with ugly, disfiguring scars – the remnants of too many knife attacks. They come from streets where there is no weakness, just brutality and drugs and crime and, in the end, heartbreak.

And I feel overwhelmingly at home among these dregs; they do not intimidate me, and they do not look at me with resentment, either, even though I am wearing clothes that have come straight off a catwalk. We are, in this room together, at this very moment, equals. In fact, I could so easily be one of them and not just an outsider momentarily lifting their gloom: I'm so comfortable here because here is where I could belong.

I am in the visitors' room at Her Majesty's Prison Bristol, to thank the man who helped me win a precious boxing title. I've even brought along my beloved Lonsdale belt to prove to him, to me and to the inmates in this room and their prison officers that I really am the British Welterweight Champion.

******

I'd thanked my fans after beating Saunders but there was somebody important missing – Bob Parsons, the heavyweight drugs dealer whose unusual way of sponsoring me was to buy cocaine off me – even though he already had his own hardcore suppliers, way beyond my league. He didn't need my coke; it was just an excuse to give me money to help my fight career. I couldn't forget that. He'd shown me loyalty and belief.

Inevitably, he'd been caught and sentenced to fifteen years in HMP Bristol – for category A offenders in those days. He'd been found guilty of importing over £500,000 worth of drugs, that's how big-time he really was, but I had an overwhelming urge to visit him and show him my belt. So I tracked down his wife in Elmers End, not far from where I was living, gave her some money to get by and said: "I want to go see Bob and show him my belt. Can you give me the governor's number so I can arrange a visitor's permit?"

I phoned the prison the next day, explained I wanted to visit and they were fine about it. In fact I sensed they were even excited. Two weeks later I drove down and pulled up outside the prison's massive wooden gates, domed at the top, looking like something out of the 1970s television series *Porridge*. It was every bit as grim as I imagined. The tall brick walls either side of the doors were cold and a lifeless dull red: there was even a watchtower looming above the doors, with a great big clock halfway up as if to remind the inmates how slowly time passes.

I got out of the car and picked up the black executive-style case that had my prized belt inside. Just holding on to that gave me the courage to go in. I'd already experienced the impact it could have not long after my victory. I was walking along the street after a gym session at the Henry Cooper, when I noticed a lad, hoodied and booted up, walking with a bit too much attitude towards me, flaunting his meanest 'I'm-looking-for-trouble-Paki, what've-you-got-there' look.

He headed straight towards me, glaring, intimidating; I put the case down, stared straight into his snarling face and said: "What the fuck you looking at – mate?" He made to square up and I said: "Stop. I want to show you something." I opened the case and said: "That's my Lonsdale belt. I won that last month, you might have seen it on Sky. But listen, I'm happy to close the case now and you and I can fight. What do you want to do? '

"That's wicked, no problem mate, I didn't mean anything: I wasn't looking for trouble, honest." *Diffused.*

Back outside the prison doors, I rang the visitors' bell and was immediately met by wardens who were expecting me and let me by-pass the long line of families, wives and partners also waiting to get inside. "Kevin Lueshing? Over here champ, we've been looking forward to seeing you – come on, this way, follow us. Now son, when you get in the main room, people are going to want to touch you, get your autograph, have a photograph, talk about the fight. There's a few lifers waiting to meet you but no murderers today."

Suddenly I was nervous, like I was walking out to a fight arena, only nobody would be leaving.

They led me into a big room, not unlike a hospital ward but with long tables and chairs and rough, hardcore faces. Absolutely everyone inside instantly stood up in unison and started applauding and cheering: even the prison wardens. The inmates were calling my name, so were their wives and girlfriends – and many of them looked even rougher than the prisoners. I stood still, beaming in my Gucci shoes, sharp Ralph Lauren jeans, my fancy black leather jacket and a Cartier round my wrist; looking rich. I had made it big and I was walking down their avenue. I felt every inch at home, like I belonged, like I could so easily have been one of them but for a pair of boxing gloves. I was far more comfortable there than I ever was in some suited business meeting, or even with Roger in his big North London house.

My eyes scanned the room and halfway down I spotted Bob. He looked at me, opened wide his great big polar-bear arms and mouthed: *"Come here, son, come'n give Bob a hug."*

He had tears in his eyes as we embraced and that moment between us was so special it felt like one of the best things I had ever done in my whole life. I desperately wanted to sob, too, but managed to hold the tears back for fear of shattering my champ status. But absolutely everyone was smiling and cheering as Bob and I hugged, like they needed to see it as much as I needed to do it and we clung on to each other for what seemed like an eternity.

"I can't believe you're here, Kev. But I told you that you'd do it, didn't I? I knew." And he reminded me of a poem he'd sent me while he was in prison and we laughed at the final line: "By hook – or by crook – you'll be a champion."

There was so much emotion in that room among hardened faces who'd grown up without weakness and fragility in their lives and yet there it was, breaking out in bucketfuls.

"Sit down champ, let's see your belt, tell me all about it." And Bob grabbed the belt, slung it over his shoulder, and did what everybody does in a situation like that: he became Rocky for 30 wonderful seconds, holding his arms wide, elbows bent, fists pumped up to the skies like a champ. The room went berserk, like he'd won the title himself; even the wardens joined in the fun and laughter.

And I thought to myself: *"You've earned this moment, Bob."* Over two years of loyal 'sponsorship' he must have given me nearly £15 grand, which made a huge difference to my lifestyle just when I needed it most. I must have stayed at the prison for about three hours: everyone wanted to get a photograph with the belt – guys with more tattoos than visible flesh, violent but suddenly crumbling into humanity. I didn't care who touched the belt, even though some weren't allowed. "Oi, 512, sit down right now."

It overwhelmingly felt right: we were all from the dark side of the street yet we were all enjoying a rare moment, together, in the sunshine. God knows, they needed a bit of that.

Chapter Thirty-Three
WINNER TAKES IT ALL

I POCKETED ABOUT £25,000 FROM THE SAUNDERS FIGHT and I was centre of attention; it seemed everyone had seen the fight. I'd be stopped in the street, fans wanting an autograph, fans wanting to talk about it, fans wanting a quick photo. I was being treated like a celebrity but the line was crossed when strangers started knocking on our front door wanting to see my belt – that was a bit too creepy. I told Roger and he said: "Kevin, go and find somewhere bigger and more secluded to live. Go and buy somewhere around £250,000."

So Jackie and I headed off to the countryside – Westerham in Kent, which I'd always thought picturesque. An estate agent showed us round a stunning Grade II listed building, built in 1776 with a little cobblestone courtyard outside, and sold it to me the moment he declared: "Winston Churchill used to meet a friend here and have a glass of sherry in the front room." It was such a gorgeous property we had it featured in various society magazines and the television series, *Through the Keyhole*. I even bought a black Range Rover to complete the country-gent look.

Frank Warren wanted me to defend my British title and set up a fight in Newcastle against Geoff McCreesh. I headed out to Tenerife again for a training camp, this time four weeks. The first thing on my mind was women: who would look after Kevin for a month? I found a chubby little holiday rep, *that'll do*, and was sorted – phoning Jackie once a week to listen to her, then back for some extras off the rep.

After three weeks, though, I got an unexpected phone call. The boxing board of control wouldn't sanction McCreesh to be my opponent and Frank was having trouble finding a replacement at such short notice. I really wanted the fight – the champagne lifestyle and country comforts hadn't made me soft. More than anything I wanted to keep my Lonsdale belt for ever, and I knew that meant successfully defending it twice.

There's a famous scene in the film *Pulp Fiction* when a suitcase is opened and the contents inside are so bewitching they leave everyone mesmerized and awestruck. That was how I felt each time I opened the case that contained my Lonsdale belt. It was like possessing the crown jewels. Every little detail bedazzled me: the picture of Lord Lonsdale encased in an ornate gold frame, the gold chaining against the red, white and blue silks, the names of famous fighters inscribed into the gold plates. I never tired of looking at it, of feeling I had a part in its history now. It took pain and work and disasters, as well as triumphs, to win one; it represented the sheer will to win and the sheer refusal to be beaten. I didn't want to let go of that.

The only fighter prepared to face me was a journeyman called Paul King, and we met in Newcastle – four months after I'd won the title. Before the fight his own manager phoned me up and said: "Look, you've got our Paul up next. Now listen, he knows he's going to get knocked out but when you do it, would you hit him on his body – and not his head. As a favour, like. He's had a hard life, he didn't know he'd be fighting you. He was on the piss only last week."

I told Colin but he shrugged it off and said: "Don't believe that Northern bullshit, son. It's trap to make you go soft. You kill him."

I went through the motions in the first round – ping, ping – bit of footwork, but my mind wasn't in it at all. Back in the corner Colin started laying into me: "For fuck sake's, Kevin, wake up will you?" But while he tried to shake me into life, I noticed a sexy ring-card girl climbing between the ropes and parading around the canvas. Our eyes connected, she looked fully into my face and I winked at her.

The second round started and suddenly King clipped me. That was my wake-up call – *Who the fuck d'you think you are?* – I switched on in an instant and raging bull was back in the ring. King tried to throw a big one, missed, and – wallop – he was pole-axed with a left hook. Straight in his fuckin' face.

He staggered back up and tried holding me. So I gave him what his manager had asked for: a thunderous left into his kidneys. He crumpled on impact, gulping frantically for breath, like a bomb had just taken half his stomach away. After the fight, his manager came over and said: "Thanks chuck, I appreciated that. You're all right, you are."

I got changed after the fight but wanted to go back to the arena in my sleek suit to see my mates, sign some autographs – and check if the ring-card girl was still hanging around. Jackie wanted to get back to our hotel for some peace and quiet. We argued and she left.

I went back down, saw the card girl immediately, took her into a quiet room and we kissed and groped: "Oooh, you are naughty, Kevin." Fortunately, a mate had spotted me and came running in when he saw Jackie re-appear in the arena. "Kev, quick, your Jackie's outside and she's asking where you are." I tucked my shirt in, brushed myself down, went out and told Jackie I'd been doing another interview for Sky television. We headed back to the hotel.

Chapter Thirty-Four

FROM THE BROTHEL TO THE ALTAR

I GOT BACK TO LONDON AND ROGER IMMEDIATELY SAID: "Pack your bags, you and I are going to New York. Business – I've already told Jackie. I've got you a world title shot."

'What you talking about, Roger – a *world title shot*?"

And he explained that he'd arranged a fight with a new boxing body, the International Boxing Organisation, and I was to contest one of their first world title bouts. The words 'world title shot' were swirling in my brain but deep down I knew this wasn't really one of the prestigious crowns I wanted. However, it was a start and the IBO did eventually become a mainstream body with famous champions like Floyd Mayweather.

"You'll earn another £100,000, Kev," he added.

"What you talking about Roger, how?" I asked.

He explained that I was now sponsored by Mary Bonham's J-D Weld company and the contract clearly stated that if I fought for a world title I would automatically be entitled to the extra cash. It occurred to me Mrs Bonham may have been a bit naïve about boxing.

But I knew I had to sort out my relationship with Jackie before leaving. I didn't want the endless arguments, any more than she did, and I knew she had devoted her life to me and my boxing – with precious little to show for it, other than our daughter.

I had two choices and I was too much of a coward to choose the right one. We were too combustible together but I couldn't face the upheaval of separation and I absolutely couldn't face the prospect of not seeing April. So, I proposed, instead. 'OK, Jacks, we'll get married. Let's do it after the fight."

"Do you mean it, Kev?"

"Yes, babes, I do and I'm going to get a ring before I leave."

If I stayed with Jackie, I stayed with April and marriage was a means to that end. No big deal. I told Roger and he promised to sort a registry office. "Just win the fight, Kev."

I arrived a month before the fight and was booked into the Millennium Hotel on Broadway. I went through the motions of training but Colin wasn't with me yet and I was bored. So bored, I flew my mate Paul Stockton over to break the tedium.

His arrival triggered a sex and drugs orgy – literally. It was so bad, I was still taking charlie six days before the fight. It started when I hooked up with a woman called Stephanie, a PR from Birmingham who Roger instructed to look after me. She introduced me to the New York social scene: I met celebrities and went to a Calvin Klein fashion show; I went to parties and then one night Stephanie took me to a freaky little nightclub, with topless women gyrating on raised platforms and dingy lighting that made dark shapes out of couples as they openly groped and entwined with each other.

It smelt of sex and drugs; it was eerie, psychedelic and in-your-face vulgar. There were no rules or limits and everything was on display: men kissing women; men kissing men; women kissing women. Everything and anything. I was gripping on to Steph's hand and she started introducing me to some of the girls: "This is Kevin, the champ, from London, isn't he cute?" Suddenly she pulled me up and led me down a corridor without saying a word. My heart was exploding with excitement – all the ingredients Kevin associated with sex were here: dark lights, dark girls, dark alley-ways, seediness, danger. Steph led me straight into a cubicle in the ladies' toilets while all the other women were outside powdering, fiddling with hair, trowelling on lipstick and gossiping about sex.

Later that night I went to the gents and there was a smart-ly-suited bloke, still wearing a tie, sat in one of the cubicles, door wide open, smoking crack out of a little gold chillum, sucking in the vapour. *Wow.* "Heh, buddy, do you want a hit?"

"What is it?"

"This is cream, man, the best quality flake, from Colombia." And he handed me a gold straw, but the alarm bells rang immediately. If he'd stuck that up his nose, he could have had a nose bleed and I could be infected with something. "That's OK," I said, "I'll use my own 20 bucks." And I rolled up the dollar bill and snorted straight out of a little gold box he kept the coke in. It even had a mirror underneath the lid so you could watch yourself. I was six days from a world title fight; I had never ever taken anything before any of my previous fights but this felt good. It felt sexy. Maybe I wasn't taking the IBO seriously; maybe I desperately needed Colin's discipline to get me back on track – whatever the reasons, I succumbed to the moment and the temptation.

I came out and sensed everyone was looking at me with dirty eyes or with ulterior motives. *Who is he? What's he got? Can I suck him? Can I fuck him? Can I rape him? Can I nick something off him? What's he doing here?*

But it was Steph's job to keep an eye on me; Roger had told her what I would like and what would keep me happy. The next day she phoned me at the hotel and said: "Have you ever been to a swingers' club, Kev. Howsabout we go there tonight? But Kevin," she continued. "We have to go as a couple. We pay 75 bucks but you can only have a girl if her partner is willing to look after me."

"OK, let's do it."

Steph picked me up later that evening and we went to what looked like a very classy members-only sauna club; from the outside it could have been a restaurant, on the inside you had to sign a visitors' book at the reception desk, which Steph did for me. Not at all like the previous night's venue. As soon as we walked in, there were naked bodies everywhere – either walking around or writhing around; lots of stunning model types sipping from champagne glasses, but also older women caked in make-up, and flabby women who just didn't give a damn what they looked like. Scattered on table tops were hats and bowls with condoms piled inside; lubricants everywhere. There were even nibbles and canapés, little open buns with exotic toppings and fishy substances on them: it was decadent and seedy but, unlike Bristol, incredibly upmarket, even posh and sophisticated. Dark, expensive, mahogony furniture.

Steph told me to "Go upstairs and grab a shower" which I did, returning with just a bathrobe on. Now all I could see was sexual depravity: in one room alone there were at least sixteen people in various contorted positions, naked and groaning and oblivious to anything but their own physical pleasures. I noticed a stunning

Puerto Rican girl, naturally beautiful, no make up – and no clothes. Next to her was an old man in his mid-60s, at least, with long, dyed, permed hair and a gold chain dangled across his hairy, grey chest. Naked. I looked hopefully at Steph, a bikini struggling to contain her fleshy folds, she looked back at me and mouthed: *"Don't even think about it."*

But eye contact had been made and the Puerto Rican came over to me. "Hallo, honey, you can't touch me unless my guy can touch your lady." Steph wasn't having it, though, and pointed towards another couple, who were looking our way. That girl was nowhere near as stunning but I knew it was going to be my only chance. 'Alright, Steph, go for it."

We all went into a room on a giant bed and performed. But it was sterile and awkward. I didn't really want to be there. Afterwards, I sat on my own in a lounge area and watched people eyeing each other up, whispering, touching and then disappearing into rooms where the doors always seemed to stay slightly open and you could see glimpses of sex and flesh.

A woman sat next to me who looked the spitting image of Mrs Robinson from the film *The Graduate*: classy, short-ish dark hair, elegant, mid-30s, with a gorgeous, alluring voice, immaculate nails. "Tell me, how does it work here?" she whispered. As soon as she heard my English accent, that was it: she started touching me. We never even moved to the privacy of a room: it was like being in my own porn movie. Hands and bodies and mouths and legs all around us. I looked around at the writhing mass and thought: *time to go now*. I'd seen enough and left around 3.30 in the morning – five days before my next fight – and six days before I was due to get married.

Chapter Thirty-Five

FAKE FIGHT, FAKE MARRIAGE

THERE WAS SOMETHING ABOUT THE FIGHT THAT I couldn't take for real and when I saw the venue, I knew why. It was like a stage set straight out of the Hollywood movie *The Sting* – the scene where they make up a room to look like a betting office. In a similar way, Roger had found a dingy little New York basement gym and done it up so it looked grand enough to be a world title venue – which it definitely wasn't. It barely held 100 people; the ceiling was so low I could touch it by just raising my arms.

It felt like a giant illusion: a fledgling boxing organisation's title in a fake arena for the benefit of a woman who was giving me £100,000 to fight for a title nobody – including me – had ever heard of. I was even fighting a Mexican opponent, Nino Cirilo, who I'd never heard of, either. Mrs Bonham would be there and she would be treated to a world title fight, no matter how false the surroundings.

To be fair to Roger, it was what he did best and, as I mentioned before, the IBO did go on to become an important and serious boxing federation. But none of us knew that then. Or maybe he did.

At least Colin – who'd been absent throughout because Duke McKenzie had a fight – was back by my side. He saw me sparring just four days before the fight and there was no fooling him. "You fuckin' idiot. I can tell you ain't been training properly, your mind isn't in this, you're not fit, you're not switched on. What the fuck you doing Kevin? You big time Charlie now in New York, that it? You been partying? Think you can pull the wool over my eyes? I've not come all this way just to get beat because you can't be arsed. You understand?"

It jolted me back into life and the same sparring partner took a beating the next day. Then Jackie arrived – she was nervous about the fight; nervous about the wedding; nervous she hadn't yet sorted a wedding dress. Two nights before the fight we both had to attend dinner with Roger and Mrs Bonham, who'd flown in all the way from Texas anticipating a grand occasion.

Mrs Bonham was clearly elderly and clearly very wealthy with pendulous diamonds and pearls covering her exposed areas of skin. She was a billionaire having fun and Roger came up with a slogan to justify the unlikely association between a British welter-weight champion and one of the world's biggest DIY products. "J-D Weld – all the punches stick."

She and I bonded over dinner, I was flirty, she was touchy-feely. Ridiculous really, but it was all harmless given the substantial age gap between us. But once again, Jackie was left on the sidelines, with nobody really including her in the conversation. I sensed she was feeling marginalised but instead of involving her, I turned on her.

"If you don't like it, fuck off." I didn't care.

Roger got her a car back to her hotel and then took 2,000 dollars from an inside jacket pocket, handed them to me and said: "After the press conference tomorrow take Jackie down Fifth Avenue and go buy her a wedding dress." There was no hero in me, though; I didn't even give her a farewell cuddle. That night I slept in one of the Big Apple's swankiest hotels, the New York Palace. *You're in the Edison, Jackie.*

But I did as Roger said, met with Jackie during the day and headed for Gucci. The second dress she tried was stunning, we paid 1,000 bucks for it, which was a lot in those days; next she had her hair done. I had to leave so I hugged her – weakly, like I was hugging a mate. She desperately needed some love and strength in that hug but I couldn't give it.

I was still agitated going into the fight: I glanced over at my opponent and he looked irrelevant, a nobody. Like he was just turning up, as requested. I went into the 'arena' and could easily have remembered everyone's name in the crowd, it was so small. There were TV cameras dotted about – undoubtedly for Mrs Bonham's benefit – but they were clearly channels nobody had ever heard of and nobody ever watched.

The ring announcer tried to sound loud and important but he was no Mike Goodall. The fight started, I went through a few slow-motion moves, but all my shots were lazy and tame. Midway through the second round I threw a half-hearted punch that almost connected but Cirilo still managed to collapse theatrically to the floor on impact, like he'd been sledgehammered. I heard Roger's booming voice "Way to go, champ" and Mrs Bonham applauding heartily. *What a charade.*

The Mexican staggered up, I knocked him down easily again, but this time he stayed down until he was counted out, indicating his head was hurting to the ref. "And the new IBO world welterweight champion... Kevin 'The Look' Lueshinggggggg." I lifted up the belt and beamed at Mrs Bonham: plastic smiles for a plastic title.

I got paid £5,000 for winning that belt. Mrs Bonham paid me £100,000 because it was a 'world title'. And that was back in 1996.

I was in a better frame of mind after the fight. Jackie had me back, some of her family had come out for the wedding and Andrew was over as well. We went out for a meal together that night and talked about getting married the next day.

Roger had sorted out a downtown registry office and when we arrived it felt like the whole of New York was getting married that day, too. The queues ran outside the building.

Mrs Bonham turned up, Colin and his wife, too; Roger was my best man and our allotted time was 2.15pm. The words 'I do' were starting to pound through my brain, though, like a series of punches I couldn't ever escape from: *I do, I do, I do, I do, I do.*

As far as I was concerned, we were just mates, getting married. It was just another charade, like my fight the night before.

The next day, Roger phoned early and said he had a surprise for us. His car picked us up and drove us to a heliport, where, to our astonishment, he had a helicopter waiting to fly us to New Jersey and drop us off at the Giants Stadium to see the Three Tenors perform a live concert. It was a beautiful summer's day and even I felt more romantic as soon as we heard Luciano Pavarotti, Placido Domingo and Jose Carreras. It was like being at an outdoor Oscars ceremony: there were red carpets, men dressed in bow ties and tuxedos, ladies in beautiful gowns, dripping in jewellery that sparkled and glittered in the New York sunshine. In that magical moment I was happy: I was only 25, I didn't know what love was, I hadn't learnt to link the idea of it with sex. But hearing those three sing together was the closest Jackie and I came to peace and calm during those few days.

Before we went back to the UK, Roger took me aside for a chat about finances – and how they would work. "Kev, I sorted you a contract with Mrs Bonham for £100,000. I take 20 per cent of that, leaving you with £80,000," he explained. "The middle man I used gets 10 per cent, so that leaves £70,000, then there was £4,000 for hotels, but I tell you what, Kev, we'll forget about those."

"Thanks, Roger, thanks a lot.

"So, Roge, tell me, when will my £70,000 be wired to my account?"

"Don't worry, Kev, it won't!" And he continued: "I'll keep it and send it over to you only when you need to spend some of it. That way you won't blow it all in one go. How's that sound, buddy?" I was surprised, but it sounded logical, I trusted him implicitly, and I agreed. To be fair, Roger upheld his side of the arrangement: he'd put money on my American Express card if I was about to use it; if I needed £5,000 to buy something, he'd pay for it direct.

Then he told me Mrs Bonham was close to investing another £2 million to sponsor a showdown between George Foreman and Larry Holmes. "Kev, you'll be in for 20 per cent if that fight happens."

Chapter Thirty-Six

GEORGE IN JAIL

I'D WON THE LONSDALE BELT AND NOW I'D WON A dubious world title. It was time to make another trip to prison – this time to see my father.

Jackie and I flew back home from New York, picked up April and went straight off on honeymoon to Jamaica, where George was still serving time for fraud. My mum had been nagging me to see him – and deep down I saw an opportunity to show him who I'd become, what I had achieved – and maybe, just maybe, hear him utter the words: "I'm proud of you, son."

Remember me, George? I'm the one you beat to a pulp and said was no fuckin' good.

We stayed in the Half Moon resort and lived like kings and queens in what looked like our very own manor house, complete with maids, butlers, driver, a nanny for April – all paid via Roger's accountancy system.

In no time at all I was puffing the best weed out there; I was chilled, swaggering, enjoying myself, but also counting down each day until I would see my father. My uncle, Neville, came to collect me when the moment came and I noticed a small, badly-wrapped package on the back seat of his car as I climbed in.

"What's that?" I enquired.

"Weed, Kevin. For your dad."

The Mandeville prison was like a scene from the film *Papillon*; decaying whitewashed buildings looking crumbled and beaten and derelict against a brilliant bright blue horizon. The only concession to the modern world were incessantly-whirring fans, high up on the ceilings that looked dangerously close to crashing down on someone's head at any moment.

Rusting iron grilles dominated tiny window holes that exposed the thickness of the prison walls: nobody would be digging through those with the ends of a concealed fork. But this was Jamaica, there was nowhere to escape to even if you did escape. Inmates wore allowed to walk freely around the rough dirt grounds. There were a few laid-back guards in shabby shorts and T-shirts with ferocious looking rifles casually slung across their backs. That was enough deterrent.

Neville and I were ushered into a long, battered, stone room with rickety wooden chairs, small tables and more bloody fans whirring too loudly from on high. There were other prisoners already sat around talking above the din of the air conditioning to their wives and families and somewhere in the distance a radio was belting out reggae.

Then I saw him, over by the far wall, sitting by a table, on his own. He was wearing the same dark prison pyjamas as everyone else and, as I walked towards him – our eyes yet to meet – it struck me he looked smaller than I remembered.

He stood up as I reached the table; we shook hands limply, feigned some weak smiles and hugged awkwardly, in a way neither of us was happy with. He looked weary but not especially sad; we sat down and I took off some Ray-Bans I was wearing and put them in front of him on the table.

Before I'd said a word, Neville started fidgeting with his bundle of weed and tried whispering: "George, George, got something for you man."

I noticed the top of one of my father's fingers was missing, from where he'd been shot. I tried immediately to look him straight in the eyes: I tried to search there for a glimmer of humanity, a scrap of remorse, a fragment of emotion. More than anything I wanted to see pride.

But George wasn't having that; his eyes kept darting around – in fact, he was more interested in the Ray-Bans and the bundle of weed Neville was still nervously trying to conceal. "For Christ's sake man, just hand the fuckin' stuff over and stop sweating." He took one quick look and snarled: "What you bring me this shit for in any case? I can get better stuff than this from the other prisoners." *He hasn't changed.*

It was the first time we had seen each other for seven years and we would only be together for 45 minutes; 45 minutes to absolve a life of cruelty and torture; 45 minutes to find a connection; 45 minutes to be a father and son. Had I really thought that would ever happen in 45 minutes when it hadn't happened in 25 years?

Instead we had 45 minutes to realise we couldn't find much to talk about.

Our conversation was tortured. There was no "Thanks for coming, I really appreciate it, such a long way, you're looking well." Just a few half-hearted questions: "How's the family?"

"Fine."

"Good. How's your bothers?"

"Fine."

"Good. How's your sisters?"

"Fine."

"Good."

There was no momentum or flow or depth to our questions and answers; we were trying to catch up on two separate lives without knowing how to find the words to do so.

There was nothing confrontational; I didn't bring up the past, I didn't seek an argument. I wasn't there to be a judge. I was there searching for something and I quickly realised George wasn't going to let me have it.

I rambled on about winning the title, praying he'd interrupt and say: "Well done, son, I'm really proud of you." I was dying to hear that, but it never came. He just sat, listening, and looking at the Ray-Bans. The only moment he spoke was when I mentioned Kirkland Laing, who he'd heard of. His ears twitched when I mentioned that victory and he muttered: "Yes, that's a very good one." I heard nothing I was due from him; there was no concession to the past and there was no acknowledgment of the future.

Our complete failure to find words that connected left me irretrievably convinced I never really knew the man. If we had the slightest spark, there would have been so much history to flow between us. Just a word would have been enough to start the avalanche, a year, a name, a place – any one person, incident or thing would have been sufficient. But we couldn't even find that; we couldn't find a common denominator to start a simple conversation.

I was sitting with my dad in a prison and realising I had nothing in common with him, just blood. It felt crushingly sad.

It wasn't long before I started to look for a way out. 'Neville, I need to be getting back to Jackie and April now." Then, I picked up my Ray-Bans, kicked off my Gucci sandals, looked him in his evil eyes and said: "You can have these."

"Thanks, son, they'll come in useful here." With that, we stood up, shook hands, embraced weakly and I left.

On the drive back I tried unloading my feelings to uncle Neville, tried analysing a bit what had occurred. "Christ, he's just the same, isn't he?" I said, not really looking for – or expecting – an answer, just talking aloud to myself, really. "He's still the same cold, ruthless bastard, completely sterile, unwilling – or is it unable, Nev? – to display emotion. Will that man ever show remorse? Will he ever say: 'You've made me proud, well done son'? It's too much for him, isn't it? He can't bring himself to stoop so low, to become human, to be something softer than the vicious fucker he's always been. He's incapable of giving love, Nev, I'm telling, he can't fuckin' do it. What'd you say, Nev?"

Poor old Nev tried to defend him a little, tried to explain life was hard on Jamaica, even harder in a Jamaican prison, and that I was the champ now, therefore I had a duty to be the bigger person. And he added:

"But *I'm* proud of you, boy. We're all proud of what you've done."

I phoned Roger that night, explained what had happened and asked him to put $5,000 into my dad's bank account so if anyone else from the family went to visit him they could withdraw some and give him it to spend in prison. Five thousand bucks was no big deal to me anymore.

We all returned home not long after. While I'd been away Roger had been stirring up the boxing scene among other promoters, bragging about how hot I was, and how important my new IBO title would prove to be. He was making waves and I unexpectedly received a call from Frank Warren: "All right, Kev, how you doing?"

"Fine."

"That's great. Now Listen. I've got you a world title shot."

"You're kidding – who against Frank?"

"Felix Trinidad. And it's serious money. I'll give you £150,000 but you've got to be on a flight in two days' time to Nashville to promote it. You up for it?"

"When's the flight?" I replied.

I told Roger and two days later I was on my way to Tennessee for what, in my heart, I knew was a proper world title showdown.

Chapter Thirty-Seven
WARREN HITS BACK

I FLEW OUT TO TENNESSEE THE NEXT DAY: IT WAS TO BE a huge Don King promotion with the main fight a WBO heavy-weight championship showdown between Henry Akinwande and Scott Welch. Five world title fights all on the same bill and I would be one of them.

Roger turned up at the press conference, loud and brash as usual. He even told Don King that he was my manager now, and not Frank Warren. Frank got word of this and phoned me from London to ask what was going on. 'Don't worry, Frank," I said. 'It's just Roger, he can't help himself." Little did I know what was to come.

I saw Felix Trinidad for the first time there and instantly felt intimidated, although I never went eye to eye with him. I was too scared for that. I knew he was the best fighter at this weight in the world and I was just an imposter. I was over-awed by what he was; like everyone else, I also believed he was the best. I am certain he would have smelt my fear there and then because that's what animals do.

I had to make a little speech in front of all the assembled report-ers and explain why I believed I would win. I was terrified and mumbled: "I believe I can be a hero." When I'd flown over I'd been listening to the song 'Search for the Hero' by M People and the words had stuck in my brain.

The fight was scheduled for January 11, which meant there'd be no Christmas in the Lueshing household in 1996. It was only July but I spent every second of every day for the next six months in fight mode. My training regime was immaculate, I did everything right, I ate all the right food, I kept away from drugs. I was lean, there wasn't an ounce of fat on me and I was as ready as I could be.

But I knew I lacked the one quality that separates challengers from champions: confidence. Colin, though, had identified a possible weakness in Trinidad – he'd been knocked down before, he was susceptible, even though he'd always got back up and never lost a fight.

"He goes down, Kevin."

So, we worked relentlessly on one routine in training. I would hit Colin on the pads, he would go down and at that point I had to race back to a neutral corner as quickly as possible because only then would a referee start the count. Once that count was over, I had to storm back in and throw absolutely everything I had to fell him again while he was still foggy. At this point I had to do the opposite of everything that was instinctive to me. I was a counter puncher; I always waited for an opponent to make a mistake before knocking them down. Now I had to learn to go forward. I had to practise hitting Felix Trinidad everywhere and anywhere and to get in first. It wasn't about knocking him down, it was about keeping him down.

I was so in the zone that I went back to being remote, cold and heartless at home. I put Jackie through hell again before eventually flying out to America three weeks before the fight, convinced I was in great condition, convinced I could knock him down – but also convinced I would lose. I had trained to win, but *believing* I was going to win was a different matter. I only ever won in my dreams, when I would clearly hear: "And the new champion of the world… Kevin – The Look – Lueshinggggg." Then, I'd collapse on to my knees, screaming: "I've done it, I've done it." I would have this dream every night but unlike my childhood dreams, when I was a superhero saving the world, I was partly living this fantasy. I was actually about to fight the man I was dreaming about, I really was going to have a shot at doing something heroic.

Then I'd wake up.

I was constantly searching for little moments of inspiration. One came as Colin and I were being chauffeured to the gym in Tennessee; our driver said "Hey, Kevin, listen to this" and put on the song 'I believe I can fly' by R. Kelly. The three of us fell stony silent, none of us said a word, as we absorbed the inspiring lyrics.

I was very tempted to have that song for my entrance but in the end opted for 'Search for the Hero'. But I will never forget the three of us in that car, lost in thought, daring to believe.

I went for the weigh-in the night before the fight and felt totally lost. It was my second sight of Trinidad; physically we looked the same, ripped, not an ounce of fat between us, similar height, honed and ready. I was quarter of a pound inside the weight; he was bang on it, 10 stones seven pounds with not a sliver to spare. Add a feather – an ant – and he wouldn't be able to fight: that's how utterly in control of his weight he was.

I noticed Roger in the room and heard a whisper that he wanted to demand a bigger say over the way I should be paid for the fight. I went over to ask him if that was true, when suddenly Warren appeared, charged straight up to Roger and said: "I want a word with you. In private."

Five minutes later Roger returned, blood seeping from a cut on his lip. "Frank Warren's just slapped me in the mouth," he bleated.

"You what?" I screeched, genuinely shocked. I didn't know what to believe – in fact I never knew for sure until I later saw Frank quoted in the papers, saying: "He challenged me to hit him on the chin – so I did!"

Pandemonium broke out and reporters started chasing after me. "That's it, the fight's off, I can't have this," I said to anyone who wanted to hear. *I wish.*

Word reached Frank that I was threatening to pull out and he summonsed me to his room. Understandably, he insisted I signed a new contract there and then, one that would commit me to fighting on future Don King promotions if I beat Trinidad. That was fair enough – after what had just happened he needed some extra security.

"You'll still get the same money, Kevin – half a million for the first defence; £1million for the second and if the third's a unification fight, you'll pocket double that," he said.

It was four pages long, so I just picked up a pen and signed. I walked out and told nobody, not even Roger.

I didn't sleep well that night: I was scared. Make no mistake, I wanted to win. But that night I was too petrified to win. It was exactly the same anxiety I felt when my dad made me go upstairs to fetch a belt. I knew I couldn't win, I couldn't fight back or resist, I was too small. I knew that night I still couldn't conquer that fear; it had stolen into my soul when I was a child and was still deep in my psyche, too embedded to shake loose.

Chapter Thirty-Eight

SURRENDER

IT'S THE MORNING OF THE MOST IMPORTANT FIGHT OF my life. I am consumed by dread: I clamber out of bed, draw back the hotel curtains and see thick, heavy snow outside. Blanket upon blanket stacking densely over the ground, giant flakes cascading down, adding to the deepening pile and creating a dazzling white drift across Tennessee.

I haven't seen snow like this since... since... I lean, motionless, against the window frame, my memory instantly falling like the snow into a deep, hypnotic trance. I am eleven years old again; George is lashing me viciously.

The jump leads in his hands are red, just like boxing gloves; red against the white, my body curled on the floor, my entire being crushed and broken, naked and humiliated. The image is too powerful, it invades my head as I stare out, utterly dominating my mind and soul. Kevin was outside then and I need to be out there now; I grab my bright red parka from the wardrobe, and walk into the icy blast on my own – not really questioning why, just feeling compelled to face it, to feel its freezing bite, to let the snow bury me so that I vanish – just like the ground is doing as the downfall continues.

Christ, it's cold out here: colder than when I was a child. The flakes are huge and stick to my coat, until all that's left of the material are dots of red poking through a white skin. Dots of blood.

I am lost in this bleak reverie, re-living the worst moment of my childhood, seeing the evil eyes of my deranged father and then seeing them turn into the cold eyes of Felix Trinidad. I realise the animal stares are identical: two vicious beasts eyeing their prey, waiting to strike; weighing up and calculating the moment to pulverise and destroy. I have never felt so utterly lost in the build-up to a fight, so utterly frozen by fear. No other opponent has ever reduced me to this.

I am sinking deeper into my depression when I become vaguely aware of a voice I recognise. My friend, the British fighter Glenn McCrory, has seen me and is standing in the hotel entrance, yelling: "Oi, Kevin, get out the fuckin' cold, you'll freeze out there." I smile weakly and head back.

But I've seen a vision of hell in that snow.

*****

Back in my room I tried some shadow-boxing in front of the mirror but the reflection was still a little boy. I didn't see a 26 year-old, I didn't see a man: I saw a beaten and battered child, trying to stand but not being able to cope with the blows. A little Paki, called Stan. I saw myself talking to myself, in a horror-film whisper, ghostly and rapid and insane. *It's going to be all right; don't worry, you can get through this; stay standing, come on man, come on Kev.* Then horror-film breathing, a terrified victim about to be brutally attacked.

My reflection looked like a vision of insanity – and sounded like a breakdown.

I was rambling; I was patting myself – on the head, *Come on Kev;* on the heart, *You can do this man;* on my fists, *You can punch;* on my forehead, *Outsmart him, Kev.*

A knock on the door broke the spell: it was Colin. He was in fight mode, thank God, and raring to go. "Come on, we've got a job to do, we can do this."

We eventually left for the fight arena and sat together in my dressing room. 'I need a lift, Colin," I said, looking at him pleadingly. So he found a stack of Post-It notes from somewhere and scribbled messages on them which he stuck around the walls – *Win for April; You can do this Kevin; Believe in yourself; This is your destiny; You are the champion of Britain; You will rock the world; This is where you belong; Kevin Lueshing, the new welterweight champion of the world.* He stuck these notes absolutely everywhere and each one chiselled away at my self-doubt until a rare smile crept across my face.

God bless you, Colin. You were the closest to Kevin.

Frank Warren popped in and wished me luck and that helped, too. I actually believed he thought I might do it. Then a camera crew appeared and I knew the moment had come. I was as ready then as I ever could be, given the torture I'd put myself through in the snow that morning. I was led down a maze of corridors that seemed to snake here, there and everywhere but never reach a destination. Suddenly a pair of doors burst open and I heard: "Search for the hero inside yourself..."

The arena was massive, very American, decked in stars and stripes and some Puerto Rican flags. I felt alone and started mumbling 'I'm going to win, I'm going to win' as I clambered between the ropes into the ring. Then I watched Trinidad arrive but when he climbed into his corner it felt like his entire family were climbing in with him, too. He was completely surrounded and someone was even holding a cake because it was his birthday. He was bouncing around like this was his party and I wasn't on the guest list. He was smiling; he was coming to play, not to work.

Jesus.

I was spellbound and watched, overawed, as Trinidad punched his fist into the air when the MC read out his chilling record – 34 fights, 34 wins, 31 KOs, and I was his 11th world title defence. Then I heard my record – 19 fights, 18 wins, 15KOs – and I tried punching the air, too. But it just wasn't the same.

We touched gloves and he gave me the stare. George's stare. The stare of the bully. My eyes instantly dropped, as they always did when I knew I was beaten and I looked at the floor as he carried on annihilating my soul. *Don't get trapped in his eyes, Kev, you've been there before: that's where dread and fear and pain and brutality and defeat are lurking.*

The first round was dull; both of us danced round each other, barely making connection, throwing insipid punches that hit air and little else. The first round was a phoney war: I was waiting for him, he was assessing me.

Still, I felt good going back into the corner, I hadn't been humiliated and Colin said: "Well done, you're looking good, Kev. But he's going to step it up, so be ready. He'll leave an opening and that's when you must drop him. Soon as that happens, Kev, look for me and get over to the corner as fast as you can."

Round two started the same way but I connected a couple of times. I went back to the ropes, Trinidad threw a lazy left hook and my instincts snapped in: *bang*, my left bit back and he wobbled.

I switched into attack and hurled three rapid left hooks – *bang, bang, bang*. And it happened: he fell, slumping back against the ropes, legs splayed out. I had knocked down one of the world's greatest fighters. *Jesus Christ.* Colin's routine kicked straight in: I ran so fast to the corner the ref must have wondered where the hell I was going. The count started and Trinidad scrambled back up at six. I watched him look towards his corner, then he turned towards me and locked on to my eyes with a laser stare that drilled me to the core. *Fuck, it's George.* The referee said something Spanish – "*Estas bien?*" – as much to me, as to Trinidad.

Colin screamed: "Make contact, son, get in there, finish him, make contact!" and I tried desperately to do everything we had practised. I practically ran at Trinidad and threw every single grenade I carried; but I was too frenzied, I was like a drunken soldier, everything was whirling and whizzing but nothing was hitting the target in the way it needed to. There was no precision, composure or discipline, just a wild bombardment. I was hitting, hitting, hitting, but it wasn't measured or controlled. One left hook shuddered into his body, a clean connection that would have felled any other boxer. Not him. My hand just bounced back to me. And in the middle of my deranged assault, the chill hit me: I realised his eyes were still boring into me and the more he stared, the weaker my punches felt.

Years of being a counter puncher had deprived me of the ability to force Trinidad's hand. I needed him to make the first false move and he wasn't doing that. Our plan wasn't working any more.

Back in the corner, Colin urged me to believe, to finish it off. "He'll come at you now, he'll open up and you must pour in the moment he does." But deep down I knew I had missed my chance.

Trinidad stepped it up right from the start of the third, like he knew I was a bit of a threat after all and now it was time to get rid of me. His trademark attack was a double left hook – one to the body, one to the head. I'd watched it, I knew it was coming, but when it did I froze and he caught me. My ears instantly filled with a buzzing that sounded like an electric drill boring into my skull: he'd burst my left eardrum. I went down but it wasn't pain that disabled me, it was the incessant drilling, so loud – getting louder – that I couldn't shake it away. It kept gnawing away deep inside, driving me insane.

I saw Colin urging me to stay down, to take a breather and take the count. But I wasn't having that: I got back up, even though my head was still reeling from the relentless battle zone exploding inside my ear. Then he was on me, hurling bombs, just like I'd tried to do to him. My body went into counter mode and as I moved back I caught him with a vicious shot that landed squarely on his chin. *For fuck's sake, why didn't you just go down?*

It was though he'd suddenly sprung a force field around himself; an impregnable armour I could never smash open. I caught him again with two left hooks but they were repelled by his defence shield. He responded with an uppercut – *Christ, I hate those punches* – and a left hook that put me down again. I was dazed: I looked round hoping to register something recognisable that would snap me back into the room but nothing seemed familiar; everything was distant and indeterminate. I pulled myself up but the shuddering thought swept through my scrambled brain: *I'm only getting up to get knocked down again.*

That was the moment I gave up.

I was falling at the final hurdle; a weak and inglorious surrender, not a brave hero fighting to the last. That second knockdown reduced me to the ten year-old, naked in the snow, begging for the torture to end, unable to take the pain and humiliation any longer. Every good fighter will recognise this defining moment; it is the choice you make when the abyss is there: do I fall in, or am I going to slug it out to the last? I chose the easy option. I still regret it to this day.

Trinidad clipped me straight away: I fell back, like I'd rehearsed it, waiting for the slightest contact to knock me over and make out it really hurt. I didn't want to get back up. *I didn't want to.* There was a three knock-down rule and I knew going down signalled my submission. I lay on the floor and watched the ref stopping the fight – thinking: *Thank God, it's over.*

I wasn't in any physical pain but my cowering soul had thrown in the towel. Now I knew. I wasn't the superhero of my dreams. I didn't believe in myself and it was easier to quit than to dare to be Spiderman or Superman. I want to say I put up a really brave fight and went down heroically. But that wouldn't be true.

The line between Kevin the child and Kevin the man was too thin. There should have been a chasm there but the two were still intertwined. I wasn't grown up enough to stand up to the beating. I hadn't as a child and I couldn't as an adult.

Could I have won that fight? Yes. What hurts so much is the knowledge I didn't give it my all. I could have been a world champion, I so nearly was but instead I embraced defeat.

Later, Colin said: "You done your best, Kev, but only you know what your best was."

And he left it at that because he knew.

PART EIGHT: CAREER'S END

Chapter Thirty-Nine
FINDING THE HERO

I WENT BACK TO LONDON AND INSTEAD OF BEING treated like a loser, was surprised to hear everyone saying how close I'd gone. "You knocked him down, Kev, you put down one the best fighters in the world, you nearly had him. You could have been the champ, man." It was a relief to hear that; it had been my Henry Cooper/Muhammad Ali moment. "But why didn't you finish him off?"

How long you got?

I certainly hadn't lost my appetite for boxing and desperately wanted to defend my British title so I could physically keep my prized Lonsdale belt for ever. Frank Warren lined up Geoff McCreesh, the fighter I was scheduled to face immediately after winning the title but the British board wouldn't sanction the fight. We'd be on Prince Naseem Hamed's bill at Wembley Arena.

Then tragedy struck: McCreesh's parents were involved in a fatal car crash: his mother died and his father was seriously injured. I was asked to show compassion and allow the fight to be delayed for another six weeks. For one split-second I went soft and said: "Yes." That was a massive mistake. I should have said no: he would have had to relinquish the fight.

Then I made another catastrophic mistake: I changed my diet and started using the controversial muscle supplement, Creatine. It was entirely legal but I had absolutely no understanding of the side effects. Everyone was dabbling with it in sport – even Arsenal footballers. It was meant to increase your stamina, muscle tone, energy levels – a fast-track way to being ripped and healthy in a spoonful of powder sprinkled in a drink. But I didn't realise it retained water in your system, which makes you look bigger and more muscular. That's fine if you're looking to put on weight but I wasn't. My struggle was to contain my weight.

Inevitably, I started piling on pounds but couldn't understand why. Foolishly, I didn't make the connection to the Creatine. I was so stupid: but I kept seeing people I knew in the gym with bulging muscles where they'd never had them before. Creatine was clearly working for them.

It was seriously debilitating: I was so desperate I stopped eating properly and even ditched my jacket potato with tuna in the evenings. It was suicidal: I was starving myself, yearning for food all the time and enduring severe stomach cramps. But I didn't work any of this out until after the fight when I stopped taking it – and immediately dropped five pounds.

I'm not being disrespectful: McCreesh should have been a fighter I could deal with. But when I climbed into the ring that night I was already dead inside. A welterweight with the strength of a light-weight. And I was facing an opponent who was empowered, who was fighting for the memory of his mother, whose father was there with him, who was ready to rise to a level he had never attained before.

It turned into a ten-round gladiatorial war and was undoubtedly the hardest fight of my entire career. The first punch McCreesh threw in the first round told me he'd come to rip my head off – and he was doing it for the memory of his mum. I could feel his courage in that single blow. I was dropped twice, my drained body inca-pable of finding the strength to absorb punches it would normally have repelled. He hit me more times in that fight then I was ever hit before.

He threw one right hand and the shudder shot immediately from my cheekbone and soared like an electric current through my entire body and soul. *What the hell, that was harder than Trinidad.* I was just hanging on, fighting to stay alive, fighting for redemption after Trinidad; fighting to restore my pride, fighting for my bloody belt.

I wasn't prepared to lose like a loser again.

My war with McCreesh was the last time Kevin truly *fought* in a boxing ring. Every punch McCreesh threw hurt and hurt deeply. My shots, my retaliations, kept bouncing off him but at least I was battling. I managed to cut him: it only made him stronger. His supporters had come on a journey with him through the hell of his family loss and it felt like they were all shoulder to shoulder with him in that ring, savagely slaying until they could embrace what he'd come for: closure.

I was losing going into the tenth, although I'd rallied in the previous three rounds and the fight was still on a knife-edge. If I won the remaining rounds, I could still do it. Physically I was standing but that was only camouflaging the reality: inside, I was totally spent. We both fought savagely and brutally -- punches, headbutts, elbows, low blows, pushing, shoving: a raw, bruising anything-that-hurts-goes conflict. It was titanic and it sucked any scraps of strength out of me. McCreesh launched a crunching combination of punches into my wilting body and I collapsed.

I lay flat out on the canvas for a few seconds – alone, cold and drained – thinking: *What shall I do?* My body tried to answer and dragged itself up. My eyes latched on to Jackie and I saw her screaming: "Get up, get up, Kev." I somehow got to my knees and heard the ref saying: "Walk forward Kevin, walk forward." I managed to stagger towards him – he could have stopped it then, but this was a title fight, I was the defending champion and he was trying to let me fight until the end. "Box on."

I looked and saw a Greyhound train ploughing towards me at 200mph and instinctively put my feeble hands up as though they would somehow buffer this runaway express. But it was unstoppable: McCreesh hit me, hit me, hit me more, I was crushed back on the ropes, helpless, refusing to fall but unable to respond, just vertically crumbling until the ref suddenly jumped in and cuddled me. "That's it Kev, that's enough, no more, it's over now."

Afterwards, Colin pressed his head against mine and tried to mend me. "Kev, you could have quit in the fifth, the sixth, the seventh – you didn't have to put yourself through all that." But I did: this time I had lost like a champion. The ten year-old within me hadn't thrown in the towel; I'd gone down nobly, trying to fight for my beloved belt. I'd given it my all.

After seventeen years boxing, after winning titles and beating bigger and better opponents, I'd finally found the hero within me – in a moment of defeat. I was badly beat up, bruised, battered, broken – I even had a fractured jaw and needed stitches under my chin – but I'd restored my self-esteem.

I then watched McCreesh's dad climb in the ring and I saw them embrace each other, I saw their love and devotion and their bond in the face of an awful family tragedy and I watched as McCreesh mouthed the words: *"I did this for you, Dad."*

Chapter Forty

SAVIOUR STELLA

I TOLD ROGER WHAT HAPPENED THE NEXT DAY. "RIGHT, that's it Kevin. Your future is here in America, you're coming back over and this time you're going to stay. I'll find a house for you, bring Jackie and April, and we'll make this your home."

It was to be my salvation in a way I could have never imagined.

Jackie agreed, and before we left told me she was pregnant again. It was a surprise and I didn't sense it was a remedy for our relationship. But when we went for the scan and discovered she was expecting a boy, my spirits soared. A son and heir. Someone to continue the Lueshing family name. I'd have history.

The only downside was I knew Colin wouldn't come with us. "Good luck to you, son, you'll learn a lot out there." That was tough but I felt my career had nowhere else to go in the UK. Roger found us a dreamy Colonial-style cottage in Nyack, a picture-postcard commuter village on the banks of the Hudson river, full of sleepy shops selling antiques and designer clothes for wealthy New Yorkers.

Among them was a spiritual shop, brimming with oils, potions, herbs, alternative medicines, tarot cards and strange scents. I was intrigued: it was slightly ramshackle, like a relic from the hippy era and, unable to contain my curiosity, I walked in to have a snoop. As I opened the wooden door a little bell rang. Inside was a jumble of mysterious-looking bottles and boxes with mystical Eastern-looking labels, piled high on whitewashed wooden tables and shelves. As I looked around I noticed a little old woman coming down some stairs.

"Can I help you?" she enquired, politely.

"No, thanks, I'm just looking," but I noticed that she carried on staring at me intensely, deeply, likely she was trying to investigate something within me that troubled her.

I left, feeling slightly spooked by her gaze, like she had over-stepped a boundary and peered into my soul. It was a weird feeling and it stayed with me for the next few days – so much so, that I decided to go back. Jackie and I had rowed again and I wanted to get out of the house – plus I had a backache and was willing to give some massage oils a try. I walked back in and she re-appeared down the same stairs. She instantly recognised me and said: "I'm really sorry about the way I stared at you the other day, it was very rude of me. But when you came in, I sensed something strong straight away. You're a fire sign, aren't you?"

I smiled. I knew what she was talking about. "Yes, I'm Aries; how did you know that?"

"You're a bit of a loner, too, aren't you?" And we started chatting, there was a connection and it felt easy to talk to her. Her name was Stella, she was about 65 years old, and she was still attractive in an older, graceful way. Her nails were immaculate and despite her age she'd kept her figure; she was elegantly dressed with stylish, grey hair and soft, gentle brown eyes. She wore a pair of glasses that dangled over her breasts from a cord around her neck.

She spoke gently and she spoke with wisdom, like she *under-stood* and like she knew the answers. I felt at ease with her, soothed by her calmness, and instinctively asked her whether she did therapy sessions – whether she did counselling?

"Why?" she enquired.

"Because I have nobody to talk to and I feel I want to talk to someone."

She agreed. "But you must be honest Kevin when I ask ques-tions. And if I ask you about your childhood, I do not want you to be over-awed by it because everything you tell me, I have been through myself. I have been there. That's why I spotted you."

She knows.

And she continued: "Because, when I look at you, I see abuse. I see damage, I see pain, I see destruction.

"Kevin, I see sexual abuse."

I was dumbfounded, hypnotised, utterly spellbound. I had not breathed a word to her about Derek – or George – up to this point. All I'd told her was I was a fighter over from England.

She went on: "What made you want to be a boxer?"

"Because I just liked boxing," I replied, unconvincingly.

"No, what made you want to *hurt* someone, Kevin?"

"Well, I suppose I was very aggressive when I was a kid."

"Why, Kevin?"

"Because my dad used to beat us."

"Why did he beat you?" Everything she said at this stage was a "why?", a question. I had never, ever spoken like this to anyone. I had never welcomed such questions and I had never been willing to give any answers. It was though I'd been waiting all my life for this moment; for this woman, who had a way of coaxing out the poisons that were embedded deep within me.

She talked about Derek. "Who was this man, what did he look like, how did he talk, what did he say, how did he say it, what words did he use, what did he give you?" I told her and before I'd even start a sentence, she'd say: "He did this, didn't he?"; "He said this, didn't he?"

How does she know?

"How did you feel?"

"Dirty," I replied.

"Kevin, that wasn't your fault." And she took me back – "How old were you" – and I would re-live it all to her as though I was ten years old all over again. I even spoke to her in a childish voice, like I really was Kevin, or Stan.

Talking about Derek and George so explicitly was difficult; re-living what they did was tough. Stella would make me confront it, though, like she was peeling back an onion layer by layer.

I broke down many times, in floods of tears. I'd go back home after some sessions and sob; deep, deep convulsions in the middle of the night. But I couldn't talk to Jackie about it like I was talking to Stella. I couldn't re-live it with her all over again; I never told her what was really going on.

It was emotionally draining: one time I was with Stella and I started throwing up in front of her from the sheer physical exertion of racking my body with so many evil memories. "Get it all out Kevin," she responded as she handed me a bucket. "Get it out, son."

Slowly, patiently, kindly, expertly, she led me to a place where I could talk about everything without feeling dirty, guilty or ashamed. Without fearing that I may have even enjoyed some of the experiences.

When I spoke to her about the paedophile, she didn't hold back her own feelings. I told her about the day that haunted me the most, the day I went back to Derek and touched him on the doorstep. "Kevin, that was not your fault, you were only a child.

"That bastard, he knew what he was doing. I want to skin that motherfucker. I want to kick the shit out of him.

"I don't blame you Kevin. I would have taken the comics as well. You were just a fuckin' child."

"But I went back."

"NO. You didn't go back like that. What did you go back for? You went back for the attention, for the hug; you went back for what you weren't getting back home. You had nothing to compare it to; you had no experience of what it should have been like. You didn't know Derek's hug wasn't the right sort of hug because no-one had ever shown you anything different. That's what your mum and dad should have been there for – but they weren't. It wasn't your fault Kevin."

I paid her forty bucks for the first three or four sessions but then she said: "I don't want you to pay any more, Kevin. We've gone way past that point now, you and I."

From then on, I would see her four or five hours a week, often behind Jackie's back. We'd meet at her apartment, round the corner from her shop; or we'd meet in a nearby park.

"How did you feel when your dad was beating you? You must talk about this Kevin, you must go back to it, you must re-live it and let it all come out."

Stella was so street she'd offer me a roll-up to calm me down when the conversations became too emotional. She'd have one with me and she'd even find ways of making me laugh about my abuse. "You must have humour, Kevin."

She was unburdening me, gently taking my hand and leading me through it so I would ultimately get to the other side. "We must laugh about these things because there will be times when your mind will say: "Do I really want to rake all this up?" But this isn't about how long it takes, Kevin, this is simply about getting there."

I'd been dying to talk like this to someone all my life; dying to say it to my mum, my dad, my brothers and sisters, Jackie, Roger, anyone. Dying to say: "Help me." Instead, I'd blocked everything out, buried it and pretended it'd never happened.

Stella led me through the stages and the people in my life one by one: the beatings, the paedophile, my bullying, being bullied by teachers, the violence and the boxing, stealing, dealing drugs, Jackie, being a father and being unfaithful, Roger, seeking my father in prison.

"That anxiety, Kevin, the heavy panicky breathing, the moments you stare at yourself in the mirror and talk to yourself in a ghostly voice, all those things, Kevin, that's your dad.

"Now, imagine yourself as a third person Kevin, and think about all those vile things happening to your child."

"I can't."

"Exactly! Of course you can't, and that's the natural response every parent should give. It's a father's duty to protect and shelter their children – but you never got that."

"I'll never leave my kids, Stella."

"I know that, Kevin. I know."

One day we were sat together on a bench in the park and she said: "Let's talk about Jackie. What star sign is she, honey?"

"Virgo," I replied.

"That's earth, Kevin, you're fire and that means your signs aren't compatible!" Then she started telling me the characteristics of a typical Virgo. "Does she argue?"

"Yes."

"Does she always want to win?"

"Yes."

"Honey," she continued. "You are never going to stay with that one. You are too much a free spirit and you will not be able to live with the endless arguing. She needs attention – you don't want to give it; she needs lots of time – you haven't got it; she needs to be number one – you *are* the number one."

We loved Pink Floyd and some evenings we'd sit on her balcony and watch the sun set over the Hudson together, listening to 'Dark Side of the Moon', smoking weed. Me and my 65-year-old angel.

Chapter Forty-One

GOODBYE

STELLA SAVED ME EVERY TIME SHE SPOKE BUT I TOOK her mortality for granted. One day, many months into our relationship, I spotted a 'For Sale' sign outside her shop and I asked her what was going on.

"You know what, Kevin," she replied. "I ain't going to be around for a long time, honey. I've enjoyed my life, I really have, I wasn't going to tell you but it's time for me to sell up."

"Why, Stella?" Suddenly it was my turn to ask the questions. She paused and I saw the flicker of a tear in her kind eyes as she replied, softly: "I've got the Big C, honey."

She laughed, in the same way she'd encouraged me to laugh in the face of evil, and I tried to ask her an avalanche of questions. But she didn't want to answer and I wasn't as good as coaxing it out of her as she had been with me. "No, no, no: this isn't about Stella, this is about you, Kevin," she said. She didn't want my sympathy.

But I sensed this was the beginning of the end in lots of different ways. Jackie and I had lived the American dream – our own little house on the prairie, the birth of our son Louie, April in private school. Roger had even got me a Grand Cherokee Jeep and was paying me 3,000 bucks a month into my own account. He'd started giving back the money he owed me from J-D Weld's sponsorship, too.

The downside was the boxing. Roger had found me a trainer, Don, who had helped Lennox Lewis early in his career. But he was an old man now, supplementing his pension and I was effectively getting paid just to train, not fight.

There was even a moment when Roger was banged in jail for four days as lawyers tried to extradite him back to Britain over his fraud allegations. He survived and finally fixed a fight for me, against an American – Benji Singleton. Following my Creatine disaster, I moved up a weight to light-middle, 10 stones 14 pounds. Physically I was still in good condition but my boxing skills had deteriorated. I was training on memory – *what would Colin have done?* – because I was getting nothing out of the old man. But Singleton had practically been told to lose; I barely touched him yet he gave up after four rounds. I was far from convincing: Roger noticed it and so did some of the heavyweight backers he had brought along.

Professionally, I was bored and frustrated – even though I was living the life, the lack of boxing was needling away at me. I flew back on my own to England to see Frank Warren; if I returned to the UK, he said, he could get me a light-middleweight title fight inside six months.

I returned to Nyack and told Roger. He was fine about it and I realised my departure would signal the end of our relationship.

I wanted Jackie to leave before me so I could say goodbye to Stella and Roger on my own – but she wasn't keen. We argued; April cried at seeing Mum and Dad fight; little Louie was too young to understand but looked frightened as he watched and heard the anger and the insults and the tortured beginnings of a break up.

At one point Jackie said: "I want a divorce, it's over." It was the first time I'd ever heard her say those words. I took her to the airport five days before I was due to leave, kissed April and Louie, and genuinely feared I might never see them again.

I drove round to Roger's home to say my first farewell. It felt like the last supper. He'd paid me everything I was owed, sorted out my flight home, completely honoured everything he ever said he'd do for me. That was not the Roger Levitt I had read about in the newspapers. He shook my hand and said: "You go back and you do what you need to do, Kevin." I knew this was a proper goodbye: he had other projects on the horizon and they were all much bigger than Kevin Lueshing.

Then I went to see Stella and spent the next three days with her. It was summer: the days were dazzlingly blue, the evenings aglow with blazing red sunsets, and we'd just get slowly stoned together, or she'd make me dinner and we'd sit and talk and reflect.

I told her about my row with Jackie and she said: "You will never stay together, Kevin, you don't mix and it will never work."

Then she'd go back over what I'd said about Derek, and she kept reassuring me that it had never been my fault. And I'd hug her and hold her like she was my mum, like I couldn't bear to let go of this woman and the lifeline she had selflessly given me.

We were sat in her apartment one evening and there was some music playing on a radio in the background. "Come on," she said. "Howsabout you and I have a little dance?"

God only knows what we must have looked like: our unequal bodies pressed together – but not in a vulgar way. It was the purest embrace of my life: our arms around each other like a couple at a wedding disco when the slow songs come on at the end.

We fell silent and I started listening to the lyrics of 'Stand by Me' as we swayed gently from side to side.

I knew she was dying and, as I stood so close to her, I noticed her grey hair had thinned out, losing its tangle with chemotherapy. I didn't say a word.

I went back the following evening – my last in America – but she didn't want to see me. 'I know you're in there," I yelled. I stood on one side of the closed door, she on the other, and she explained that more of her hair had fallen out and she couldn't face seeing me. "I don't want you to feel sorry for me, though," she said.

Tears rolled down my cheeks as she spoke. And I understood then that as much as she had saved me, I had helped her in a small way, too. I had helped distract her for a while, helped her focus her mind off the incurable pain she was carrying.

"You're off tomorrow but you will write to me, won't you?"

My tears betrayed me and I sobbed back: "Of course I'll write."

"Don't you start crying Kevin Lueshing. Now get off and let me sit here in peace and watch the sunset."

That was our last conversation. I walked slowly back home, yearning to take care of her, desperate to pulverise the cancer inside her – just like she'd destroyed the cancer inside me.

I tried ringing her a few times when I returned to the UK but each time the phone went straight on to message. 'Hi, Stella, it's Kevin, how are you? Please give me a call." But she never rang back. Two years later I went back to Nyack to see where she was buried but I couldn't find her. I spoke to the person running the shop. "That old woman? Yeah, she passed over a year ago. There was a big parade for her, everyone turned up."

That old woman was my saviour.

Chapter Forty-Two

FAILING A BRAIN SCAN

I RETURNED TO WESTERHAM AND A DOMESTIC ROUTINE, my row with Jackie papered over. April went to a private school and Jackie was back with her girlfriends from the village – I dubbed them the Cappuccino Crew. I didn't like them: they were white middle-class women, every other word was 'darling' but underneath their make-up and plastic smiles they were all trying to out-do one another. "What car have you got? What school's your daughter at? Where do you get you jewellery from? We're going to the south of France this year – howsabout you?" I was just a Homeboy.

I'd come home from training some days and there'd be about six of them, nattering and bitchin' in our front room. Jackie would be trying to keep up with them: "Ooh, we're about to do a photoshoot for *OK Magazine*, aren't we Kevin."

Frank Warren had lined up a fight with Nicky Thurbin and even though I was back with Colin, something was wrong in my training, too. He'd got me to do a tough three-minute routine of non-stop, rapid-fire punching and I just didn't want it; it all felt like a colossal effort. I hadn't experienced that sensation before. I'd tasted the good life in America and suddenly didn't like the idea of sweating for it.

I went for my mandatory medical in Harley Street as usual, and about a week before the fight headed to the Sky TV studios for an interview. It was a Friday, the interview was just about to start when I had to take a phone call from the British Boxing Board of Control. "Kevin," said a voice on the line, "I'm sorry to inform you that your medical has revealed a discrepancy on your brain scan. The fight is off. There is absolutely nothing to worry about – at this stage – but we will need you to have another scan on Monday."

Apparently the scan had spotted a possible area of damage that wasn't repairing itself as it should normally do.

I was panic-stricken: it was like my career was over there and then and in the darkest recesses of my mind I wondered whether I was going to end up with some serious disorder. Straight away I thought about what happened to the boxer Michael Watson – and to Muhammad Ali – and to all the fighters who had been reduced to shadows of themselves after a lifetime of taking violent blows to the head. I re-lived some of the blows I'd taken, and the war I'd just had with McCreesh, and the memories alone sent a shudder that felt just as violent as the punches themselves. Yes, I had felt lethargic in training but I had absolutely no pain, no strange twitches or slurred speech – absolutely nothing to indicate something might be wrong.

I went back to the studio, my mind utterly scrambled and, live on air, revealed to the TV audience: "I can't give away too many details but I've just received a phone call telling me I've failed a brain scan and the fight's off."

I went back for a second scan on the Monday, after spending the entire weekend paralysed with fear, and the next day took another phone call – this time telling me I was fine and the fight could still go ahead. *What the hell?* Apparently the first scan had shown something vague but the second had confirmed it was nothing to worry about. That was about as technical as it got: but the entire drama had sown further doubts in my mind. *Do I want this anymore?* While I felt infinitely relieved, I remained psychologically scarred: there was no way I would go to war in my next fight. Indeed the Thurbin fight was an absolute bore – the first time I ever went the distance, and the first fight where I spent most of the time hugging my opponent so he couldn't throw any punches. I had no venom but did just enough to clinch a majority decision over 12 tedious rounds; I was surprised the judges had even hung around until the end, it was so dull.

Chapter Forty-Three

THROW THE FIGHT

FOR THE FIRST TIME IN MY FIGHT CAREER, I WAS offered money to deliberately lose a fight – £300,000 to fall in the third round.

Beating Thurbin meant I was now the number one challenger for another world title – this time the World Boxing Organisation's Super-Welterweight belt – against a big, bruising beast of a fighter, Harry Simon, from Africa. I still wasn't in the right frame of mind – the brain scan had left a mark; I liked the good life and suspected there were easier ways to make a living; I was sick of Jackie's new circle of friends; and training remained a chore. I kept dwelling on something Nigel Benn had said: "The more a boxer earns, the more the punches hurt."

The Simon fight was dubbed "The Last Chance" but it was one too many for Colin, who had booked a holiday with his wife to Tenerife that week – and wouldn't cancel it. That told me what he thought. I even confessed to Jackie that I didn't want to fight any more.

Nigel Benn recommended one of his old trainers, Kevin Saunders, and he did his best to bully me into shape. He was a hard, brutal, sergeant-major type and I knew he'd get me fit, which to be fair, he did. Physically he got me ready for war; mentally I was still on a verandah with my 65-year-old saviour, slowly getting stoned and reflecting on my life.

I went to training camp in Peterborough, where I lived for six weeks – the coldest, toughest, loneliest, bleakest period of my boxing career. I was so bored, I craved to see Stella again for one last chance to talk to her and pour out my heart. I hooked up with a local girl and took her to the cinema one night. I held her hand and she looked at me and said: "What do you want from me,

Kevin? You've got it all; you're a famous boxer, you're on TV, you've got money, a fancy home, lovely kids and a wife. What you doing with me?" She was about nineteen years old.

I was training like an animal but I hated it and I didn't care about beating Simon. I was in it purely for the money – about 75 grand – and nothing else. In the past I'd have fought for a world title for 50 pence.

Then I got a call from a mate who was a hardcore, full-time gambler. "How you feeling about this fight, Kev?" he asked.

I knew him well enough to tell him the truth, which I did, and he replied: "If you fall in the third round, we'll give you £300,000. But listen, Kev. If you say you'll do this, then you must do it. You can't have a Rocky moment and turn it all round because you suddenly feel heroic and noble going into the third. If you did that, you would have to pay us all back what we would have won. These people are serious, they're not to be mugged and they'll come for you if you betray them. Have a think about it, Kevin: this is about the rest of your life. If you're looking for a way out of boxing, then you might as well get paid extra for it. It's a real offer: £300,000 to lose a fight you are prepared to lose in any case. Nobody will ever know, nobody will suspect anything. But there's no turning back if you say 'yes'. Understand?"

And I genuinely did think about it. I was getting £75,000 for the fight and knew it would be my last. Now I could walk off with £375,000: plenty to set me up for the rest of my life. It was tempting and I stayed tempted for the next two days as I went through the figures in my head.

I kept thinking: *"How could anyone ever prove it, how could they find out? Nobody has seen me speaking to my mate, nobody knows he's made the offer. I'll never tell anyone, it could never go public."*

But at some point my pride kicked in. I'd been training harder than ever – what was the point of that if I was going to take a fall deliberately? Yes, I believed this fight would be my last but I hadn't thought about ending it like a cheat. I planned to go down fighting with a bit of honour. I didn't want money to be a reason to lose.

I thought about the precious moment I'd won the Lonsdale belt, and how I'd open the case and marvel at the framed picture of Lord Lonsdale and what that belt represented. Yes, fighters are butchers and violent. But there is honour, too, and that belt represented that as much as it represented triumph and glory. Fighters want to pulverise each other inside a ring, but once their war is over, the comradeship is strong and real; the hugs and handshakes you see on the TV run deep and there is a genuine bond.

We are all governed by the Queensbury rules, a code of conduct inside and outside the ring that is like a ring of steel separating boxing from thuggery. Deliberately throwing a fight to be part of a betting sting would cut right to the heart of those sacred principles: principles that had served boxing proud for 132 years until then. I didn't want to sell my soul and risk besmirching a sport I believed in.

Then I thought about turning to my children one day and trying to explain to them what I'd done if, somehow, the truth crept out. *April, Louie, I've got something to tell you: your dad was a fraud who deliberately threw his last fight for money.*

I phoned my mate the next day and told him 'no'.

"No worries, Kev. I'll still have a bet on you to fall in the third, though."

The fight was at the Crystal Palace sports stadium, my home turf, and it attracted a huge crowd – just about anyone who'd ever known or supported me. Even celebrity chef Gordon Ramsay was at ringside, sat next to Frank Warren. He'd seen the Trinidad fight, he was a heavyweight boxing fan and a few weeks later he cooked a meal for Jackie and me at his restaurant in Chelsea and chatted with us at our table.

Crystal Palace had been chosen precisely for that reason: it would sell out with my local fans. I couldn't think of a worse place to lose. My changing room was next to Simon's and I shuddered when he started warming up: I could hear the ferociousness of his grunting as he tore into the pads. It sounded like a scene from the film *Zulu*. Slaughter.

I was terrified.

But I won the first round comfortably – Simon simply couldn't cope with my speed and jabbing. He was throwing bombs, missing, and I was counter punching with ease. We had a little exchange in the second – slugging into each other, like two gun fighters waiting to see who falls first. I threw a huge punch, it connected, his arms flailed out limply and his legs buckled. *Shit, I might win this.* And I waded in, just like I'd waded in against Trinidad: no co-ordination, no thought, no artistry, just a desperate lunge of wild punches. He weathered the storm.

Then the third: the round the betting syndicate wanted me to fall in; the round that, psychologically, always seemed to be significant. The round I beat Smyth and Saunders in; the round I lost to Trinidad in – and now? Simon came out and connected with a body shot that crippled me; I fell and on the way down stared first at Gordon Ramsay and then Frank Warren next to him. And I could see Frank had spotted something he'd seen before in many fighters: *Lueshing doesn't really want this anymore.*

I clambered up but Simon clipped me solidly on the head and I went straight back down. Fight over. Career over. I was interviewed ringside almost immediately and said live on air: "That's it – that's my last fight. You won't see me fighting again."

Inside I felt humiliated, this wasn't really how I'd wanted it to end, especially in front of so many people that I knew and who had stuck by me for so many years. I felt deflated, like I'd let them all down. And of all the rounds, it had to be the third – although I genuinely had no regrets about not taking the gambling money.

I had to go to an after party and sat with my brothers and sisters in a private room, too ashamed to mix with the hangers-on. But Errol was in no mood for small talk. He walked straight up to me and said: "You quit."

The next day, Jackie went out with the Cappuccino Crew and I sat alone in my cellar back home. The memories started gushing back and the consequence of what I'd done started to dawn: I was history. I'd converted the cellar into a little office and I brought out all my old boxing photographs: as soon as I held a picture of me, aged eleven, holding a trophy after winning my first fight, I broke down inconsolably and wept like the child I was in that photograph.

What had Stella said?

Let it all out Kevin, you have to let it go.

I stared and stared at it through my tears and saw a boy on the verge of a dream, with a nervous smile that camouflaged a paedophile's evil abuse and the cruelty he was enduring at home; a boy who'd tasted his first hint of adulation, who'd enjoyed the adrenalin-fuelled thrill of hitting an opponent and getting praised for it; a child who couldn't quite believe he'd been treated to real Pepsi Cola and crisps afterwards. Then I dragged out more pictures; my meeting with Maloney, beating Kirkland, holding the Lonsdale belt, turning towards the corner seconds after knocking down Trinidad. It was my entire career being played out in my hands – only now it was finished. I must have sat there for three hours re-living the highs and lows.

I felt utterly alone: the only people I could ever talk to had gone – Roger, Colin and most especially, Stella. I needed one of them to say: "Don't worry, it'll work out fine." Deep down I knew I'd retired too early. I was only 29 and I still wanted to be Kevin 'The Look' Lueshing – but I didn't want the pain that came with it. I'd taken the easy way out and not worried about leaving a shadow over my legacy. A stain that suggested there was a quitter within me.

Ultimately, I could never conquer my overwhelming anxiety, the stomach-churning panic attacks and my crushing sense of dread – exactly the same crippling emotions I'd felt throughout my childhood. The fear of walking home towards a beating, like being in a long tunnel heading towards something sinister and not being able to turn back. I felt like that every time I walked towards a ring: each agonising step dragging me towards something satanic and torturous. Mike Tyson apparently experienced similar mental tortures but he managed to channel the negativity and turn it into something ferocious. I never worked out how to do that.

My tears flowed and only stopped when April and Louie came down to the cellar. She put her arms round me and said: "I'll kiss it better for you Daddy. Where's it hurting? Come on, Louie, let's make Daddy better." She kissed my eyes, bless her, and she was soft and gentle and she gave me in that innocent moment the love I had craved for 29 years.

That's what it's all about, Kevin.

PART NINE:
LIFE AFTER BOXING

Chapter Forty-Four

GETTING STONED WITH MIKE TYSON

I SUPPLIED MARIJUANA TO MIKE TYSON WHEN HE CAME to Britain on a controversial question-and-answer tour.

Controversial because a lot of people felt a convicted rapist shouldn't be allowed in the country to make money. He was based in a suite at London's swanky Grosvenor Hotel and I suddenly got a panicky phone call from one of the event organisers, who knew me – and knew the people I was connected with. "Kevin, it's urgent, we need your help. Can you get us some decent weed for Mike Tyson? We need it right now."

So I jumped in my car, sped over to Brixton where I knew a supplier, and headed back to the Grosvenor with the best-quality marijuana I could find. Tyson was doing an interview with Sky when I arrived, he was dressed in jeans and a white T-shirt and he looked ragged, overweight and weary – like he'd just stepped off a long-haul flight. I had to hang around until that was over, feeling increasingly intimidated by the prospect of handing over a packet of weed to one of the most volatile, intimidating and unpredictable humans on the planet. Suddenly the camera crews started moving out, Tyson looked over, stared *into* me, and said: "Are you the guy with my stuff?"

"Yes, champ."

"Cool – let's go roll some up."

He led me through another door, into his bedroom, and made it clear he expected me to prepare two joints. I did a small one for me and then panicked. *How much weed do you give Mike Tyson?* I decided he wouldn't be interested in anything small, so I rolled up a monstrous king-sized joint. By my standards it was a whopper.

The pair of us then sat side by side on his bed and I watched, transfixed, as he lifted the roll-up to his mouth, sucked on it heavily and inhaled deeply, like he was taking in life-saving oxygen. Then he pulled it away and looked at quizzically, inspecting the size, structure and quality. "It's OK, it's OK," he proclaimed, although his judgement sounded worryingly unconvincing. I breathed a nervous sigh of relief; he seemed calm and started talking away like we'd known each other for years, telling me about what he was doing, what he'd done. I remember thinking: *Shit, I'm sitting on a bed getting stoned with Mike Tyson.*

"Man", he continued, "I'm so fucked up, sometimes I wake up in hotels and I don't even know what country I'm in or what I'm meant to be doing. I don't even know who I am sometimes."

He'd already sucked any remaining life out of his roll-up by now and I offered to do him another. "No man, you don't make them big enough," he replied and then made one for himself. "This is how you do it." That joint must have been six times bigger than anything I'd ever seen.

Then he started talking about the last time he came to Britain, to fight Julius Francis, and the well-publicised bust-up he had with Frank Warren over who should pay for some jewellery he had bought in London.

Tyson told me his version of events and then took another long look at his joint, put it back to his mouth and inhaled deeply again, like he was finding the strength to continue with his story.

I couldn't believe what I was hearing and witnessing. Then he started asking me about my life and who I was. He'd never heard of Kevin Lueshing. I remember thinking I needed to find a common ground and reckoned he must know Felix Trinidad. So I told him I'd knocked Trinidad down in the second round of a world title fight.

"No way, man!" he said, genuinely impressed. "You had Felix Trinidad on the floor? You look way too pretty to be a fighter, you look more like someone out of *Baywatch* or something. So… what happened?"

"Well, that's when reality kicked in, didn't it?" I replied, smiling. He thought that was hilarious and started laughing. He leant towards me and put his arm round my shoulders, like a great big cuddly bear. "You're all right kid," he said. I even began to warm to him.

It was clear the joints were having their effect, though, and he was getting stoned. He started looking around the room, in a fidgety and agitated way, and then made a series of phone calls as we chatted. By the tone of his voice, he was talking to girls; about 30 minutes later two walked into the room and sat with us, giggling and flirting.

Then Tyson turned to me, looked at his joint and declared: "This stuff ain't great. In fact, it's shit, man. This really the best you can do? Can't you get me anything stronger?"

I had a decision to make and I had to make it quickly. Did I really want to be Mike Tyson's drugs mule? I hadn't minded coming to the rescue this once – but did I want to get roped into something that could get a bit too heavy for comfort?

"Sorry, champ," I stuttered, "that's really the best stuff I can get." Suddenly I didn't feel so chilled or confident about my new best pal.

Suddenly it was like I'd turned off all the lights and plunged the room into darkness. He switched: coldly, ruthlessly and menacingly. "What do you mean, man?" he snapped, his eyes drilling into me.

The room felt chillingly familiar – like a boxing ring – hostile and tense; all my old feelings of dread and anxiety and fear came cascading back and I was face to face again with a monster who wanted to rip me apart. *Christ, I thought I'd escaped all this.*

I shivered and then Tyson broke the icy silence. "Well, Kevin, I'm afraid you can't hang around with us no more. You gotta go." I looked at the girls, and their faces were plunged downwards, their eyes fixed to the floor not daring to take a look.

I put my joint down, got up and walked out, my eyes too timid to make contact with anyone or anything other than the carpet. Incredibly, Tyson held out his arm as I walked past, and we shook hands – but it wasn't friendly, his grip was too aggressive as though he were deliberately trying to squeeze the life out of me. It was a real Jekyll and Hyde moment; where there had been laughter seconds earlier, there was now menace and danger.

He wasn't putting on an act for the girls' sakes, either. The following evening I attended his Q-&-A session because I had arranged for Frank Bruno to be on the top table alongside Tyson. I escorted

Bruno's wife to the event and as we walked into the main function room, Tyson clocked me almost immediately and even though he must have been 200 yards away, he fixed me with the same terrifying stare that had crushed me 24 hours earlier. Bruno's wife turned to me and said: "Kevin, what on earth's up? You look like you've just seen a ghost." I was so terrified I pretended I needed to visit the gents, turned round and hid in the bar area before the lights went down in the main arena and I could creep back in.

Later that night I bumped into one of his entourage, who grabbed me by the shoulder and said: "Heh, man, what the hell did you do to Tyson the other day? He told me he never wanted to see you again – and he didn't even want to see me talking to you, either."

The following day I had to go back to Tyson's suite because I needed to see the tour organiser about a potential business deal. I went up in a private lift, absolutely dreading the thought of seeing him, and crept slowly past his bedroom door, which was slightly open. I noticed a couple of girls inside and then suddenly I heard Tyson yelling, ferociously: "I don't want this fuckin' shit, man. I ain't fuckin' going and none of you is going to make me."

I gulped, petrified he might see me. The man I was due to meet came out into the corridor, spotted me and whispered frantically: "Get the fuck out of here, quick, Kevin. For fuck's sake, don't let him see you."

I saw some emergency-exit stairs and thought *screw the lift*. I have never run so quickly down a staircase in my life.

Chapter Forty-Five

NIGEL BENN AND MY DIVORCE

NIGEL BENN GOT ME THROUGH MY DIVORCE – JUST NINE months after my boxing career ended.

The Dark Destroyer, as he was known, was one of boxing's most-ferocious fighters and we become close pals after I retired. I was doing some PR and realised I could put a lot of work Nigel's way. He was interested: I arranged a nationwide Q-&-A tour, similar to Tyson's, and there was a stampede for tickets and signed photographs. We were pulling in serious money. I was hustling and enjoying it; he was enjoying the spotlight and attention.

This was also the start of the celebrity/reality TV era and I got Nigel on *I'm a Celebrity, Get Me Out of Here*, which took him to a different level of super-stardom and riches. Then came *Gladiators*, when he went head to head for a series of endurance challenges with his old boxing adversary, Chris Eubank. That sparked plenty of publicity in the papers.

Our families got to know each other and we even went on holidays together. We were all in Majorca together once when Jackie and I had a thunderous row. It really kicked off and Nigel said to me: "Kevin, I can only see you two splitting. There's too much aggression between you."

He was right, of course, but I threw myself into my PR work rather than confront the issue. Deep down I knew everything Stella had said was coming true.

Then Jackie arranged to go to Greece for a holiday with the kids, while I stayed at home working. I spoke to her over the phone when they arrived and she said: "Kevin, I've posted a letter to you. Make sure you read it."

"Letter? What do you mean, Jacks? What you talking about?" But she refused to say any more.

The letter came a few days later: I opened the envelope and there were three pages inside. I looked at the top of the first sheet and instantly saw the words 'I want a divorce." I ripped the three pages to shreds straight away: I didn't want Jackie to have the pleasure of thinking I'd read it.

But I was devastated. *How often would I see my kids?* It felt like my entire universe was about to end. April and Louie had given me a family, a unit – a structure I'd never experienced as a child myself but had come to cherish as an adult, despite my problems with Jackie.

I went round to see Nigel: I remember knocking on his big mansion door at 11 o'clock at night, sobbing. I told him everything as I bawled my eyes out. "I knew this was coming, my friend," he said. "But don't worry, this is the best thing for all of you. It will be hard but we are here for you."

Nigel and his wife Caroline insisted I moved in with them while I sorted myself out. I was terrified of losing access to my kids but knew I somehow had to reach an amicable agreement. I didn't blame Jackie; I hadn't been a good husband and I'd had it coming for a long while. Nigel was pragmatic. "If that relationship was worth fighting for, Kevin, I'd help you, I promise. But it ain't. Let it go my friend.

"You must remember what you've done to that woman. You've hurt her, you've betrayed her, you abandoned her. You weren't there when she needed you, were you?"

"True."

"So this is what you must do. You must be man enough to tell her it wasn't her fault. You owe her that."

I did what he said. I called her and said: "Jackie, I'm sorry. I am so sorry for all the pain and everything I did. If anything I respect you for having the courage to end this. I really do."

It was the first time I had talked properly to her about our relationship. I'd needed Nigel's help and support but the more I spoke, the more I realised it was a long-overdue conversation.

Jackie and I reached an agreement and we divorced on the grounds of my unreasonable behaviour. How could I argue with that? I got to see the kids every Wednesday – and look after them every other weekend. I could also have them at Easter and in the summer holidays as well. I'd spoil them, of course, and we'd go on wonderful holidays together to places like Disney world and Barbados. I'd even met another woman by then, Fenella, and sometimes she'd come with us. She had the looks of a Page 3 blonde but she was classy and educated. Fenella was recently divorced and I found it easy to talk to her. We didn't row, either.

Our relationship snowballed and I proposed to her on a skiing holiday in Canada. We got engaged, bought a house together in the country near Leeds Castle and everything seemed rosy. She had a little boy from a previous relationship but the more she saw of April and Louie, the more something inside gnawed at me. Fenella was loving towards her own son, kind and considerate, but she struggled to be inclusive or bond with mine. Ultimately, that drove us apart. I loved her then – but I loved my children more.

Jackie remarried and had twins and in the end it suited everyone for Louie, who was nine at the time, to permanently live with me. I can't pretend I was a perfect father but if there's one thing George did teach me, it was how *not* to raise a child. There have been times when Louie has exasperated me and tested my patience to the limit, but only in a normal teenage way. I will always love him and I will protect and defend him. The same goes for April, too. I have instilled in both of them that they must never lie, and if they're in trouble they must always tell me – no matter how bad.

That formula seems to have worked pretty well so far.

And no, I've never struck them like my father struck me.

Chapter Forty-Six

MERCY FOR McCLELLAN

ON FEBRUARY 25, 1995, THIRTEEN MILLION TELEVISION viewers in the UK witnessed a fight that would remain in the DNA of British boxing for ever: Nigel Benn's tragic battle with Gerald McClellan. It wasn't a fight, it was a brutal war that nearly killed McClellan and left him with devastating injuries: blind in both eyes, paralysed, his hearing and short-term memory severely limited and his speech impaired.

While nobody could ever forget that night, boxing forgot about McClellan. Years after the fight I watched a YouTube clip that revealed he was practically penniless, with only the love of his sisters keeping him alive. The contrast with Nigel couldn't have been sharper – he was at the height of his new-found celebrity status, we were coining it, and yet there was the fighter who had challenged him for a world super-middleweight title, abandoned and broken in a wheelchair.

I've mentioned the Queensbury rules before: looking after your own is part of boxing's culture. The sport had dropped its guard and needed to be reminded about its duty to McClellan.

My plan was to raise funds by organising a glittering charity auction night for 1,100 guests at the Grosvenor Hotel. I had to shell out £25,000 of my own money and borrow another £10 grand off a close pal of mine, Simon Fellows, to reserve the venue. But I reckoned fight fans would pay for the privilege of witnessing the two fighters meet for the first time since that catastrophic night.

Nigel was willing to do it and willing to do everything he could to help sell it. The fight had haunted him for many years and was one of the reasons he became a born-again Christian. But neither of us knew how McClellan would react. So, I phoned his sister, Lisa, in

Freeport, Illinois. 'Hi, my name is Kevin Lueshing, I represent Nigel Benn." *Will she slam the phone down?*

"I don't wanna talk to you," she snapped. But I stopped her hanging up and kept on talking. I cut to the bottom line: I was offering her an opportunity to make serious money that would help support her brother.

"I don't trust you motherfuckers," she replied.

I kept whittling away. "Lisa, fight fans in England have never forgotten how brave he was. They'll want to help him." I told her Nigel was a born-again Christian.

"I dunno, I just dunno," she said. "How do I know you won't screw me over?"

I promised her that would never happen, I promised her I'd pay for all their flights and hotel accommodation and I promised I'd lay on everything they needed. "All you have to do is get on the plane," I added.

She thought about it and said: "OK, get it sorted and let me know when everything is in place."

I went into overdrive, selling tickets at £250 each, doing deals. The sports editor of the *News of the World* agreed to pay £10,000 for the first picture of Nigel and McClellan together; celebrities agreed to donate items for the auction – Nigel donated his number plate 'BENN1'; Prince Naseem Hamed even put up a treasured world title belt.

I called the event 'A Night of Champions for a Champion' – guaranteeing there'd be a champion boxer sat at every table. Tickets sold – but with one week to go, I still had 500 left and was starting to panic. I'd break even – but that wasn't the point.

Then I got a call from Lisa McClellan – just before they were about to fly over. "Kevin, we've got fuckin' problems, man," she said. "They won't let Gerald out of the country because he hasn't kept up his child maintenance payments."

Oh Christ. In a flash I could see the entire event collapsing. 'How much does he owe?", I stuttered.

"Twenty-five thousand bucks," she replied. I fell silent. It had already cost me £12,000 just to pre-book the flights and £25,000 to reserve the Grosvenor. Was she having me over? I didn't know, she sounded sincere, but I had no choice. So I arranged for the $25,000 to be wired over there and then. I didn't sleep again until it was confirmed they were on the plane.

But good things happened, too. That same night I turned on the television to watch a big Amir Khan fight and watched in disbelief – and joy – when a little feature about the Grosvenor night came on and my ticket hotline number flashed on to the screen. It was free publicity beyond my wildest dreams and it worked. The phones immediately started and we sold out that night.

The event was planned for Thursday, February 24, 2007 – twelve years since that fateful night. The McClellans landed on the Monday morning and I waited with a limo at the airport for Lisa, her two sisters – Sandra and Stacey – and Gerald. I hugged them as they came through, and held Gerald's hand while he sat in a wheel-chair. This was a man who'd been in a coma for two months after emergency brain surgery to remove a clot; it was sad and tragic to see his crumpled body and to hear him struggling to speak. He'd been a ferocious warrior – he'd nearly won the fight himself, knock-ing Nigel down twice. But neither of them would quit that night.

I never had that courage.

Nigel met Lisa on her own two days before the event. The two sat together in a room, and although they never spoke a word, they quietly held hands. Their eyes never looked up from the floor but their silence sounded like twelve years of conversation, twelve years of shared anguish and guilt and despair and sadness. It was electrifying. I'd arranged for a camera crew to film everything – ITV were paying to make a documentary – but I stopped them getting anywhere near that moment. It was too personal for the world to see. Then Nigel said: "I'm sorry, I'm so sorry."

"No, you don't have to apologise," she replied, and they hugged. "We have no bitterness towards you, Nigel, I want you to know that. We have come here for closure and we appreciate what you are doing. Thank you." I left the room at that point, uncomforta-ble on the sidelines of such a private and emotional moment. This wasn't my business.

I arranged for Nigel to meet Gerald the next day. Nigel was incredibly nervous, pacing around, mumbling to himself: "What do I say to him?" He looked and sounded like me before a big fight. Again, it was in a private room but this time filmed. Gerald came in on his wheelchair, his body shaking. Lisa went over to him and said: "Gerald, Nigel Benn is here and he wants to say something to you."

Nigel got down on one knee in front of the wheelchair and took hold of his hand. "Lisa," Gerald said. "This motherfucker nearly took my life." And then he laughed. "Don't worry, man, I know it wasn't your fault. I know you didn't mean it."

And then he continued: "Lisa, is he crying? Is he showing any emotion? Tell me true, Lisa."

He didn't need to ask: tears were rolling heavily and unashamedly down Nigel's cheeks. Everyone could see them – but not Gerald's deadened eyes. "Yes, Gerald, he is very upset." It was too much for Nigel, he got up and turned to leave the room. But Lisa stopped him, cuddled him and he stood there, sobbing inconsolably on her shoulder.

The following night was a dream come true: the Grosvenor was packed with celebrities and famous faces. The room plunged into silence the moment Gerald appeared, wheeled out by Nigel. Every single person stood up and started a slow handclap as the pair made their way to the top table. That triggered Nigel again and his tears rolled.

Then came the auction and people started bidding crazy money: £30,000 for Prince Naz's belt. One young city banker paid £25,000 just to meet Gerald privately afterwards. Don King donated 25,000 dollars via a phone link – so Frank Warren stood up and donated £25,000 to out-do him! Others simply walked up to me and gave me money, saying; "Please give that to Gerald."

I went home with a bin liner stashed full of notes. We made £120,000 for him – more than he'd ever earned in his career.

I was proud to have been a boxer that night.

Chapter Forty-Seven

SEEING DEREK

THERE WERE TIMES, AS I WENT THROUGH MY TEENAGE years, when I saw Derek again, either in the park, or strolling down the street – always walking his dog but always away in the distance, on the other side. In fact I'd look out for his dog rather than him. Where one was, the other would be. We never made eye contact, and although I knew he was there – and maybe he sensed I was, I don't know – we never spoke or acknowledged each other.

One night I was jogging down the street, training, and I actually ran past him. I'd seen him some way off, heading towards me and I clocked the lopsided walk, the stoop, the seediness. My eyes fell to the pavement, my heart pounding excessively but not from the running. I momentarily thought about crossing to the other side but didn't, I just kept going, refusing to look up. *Derek's getting closer, closer.* I could hear his uneven stomp on the pavement, *louder*, then his breathing, heavy from lack of exercise and too many roll ups. We physically passed and as we did, I caught it. Powerful, nauseating, suffocating.

Old Spice.

I often thought about him after that and whether I should go back to his grey house and kill him. Knock him out, beat him to a pulp until he cried and whimpered and begged for mercy as I kicked the last few perverted breaths out of his pulverised body. Yes, I definitely thought about that, it wasn't difficult.

I didn't because I was still racked with guilt and shame. I still thought it had all been my fault. I was the dirty one. Not Derek.

And I kept my filthy secret buried while I was a boxer because I was worried it would soil my career. People might pity me, but who would fear a sexually-abused boxer?

Then one night a gang of mates heard there was a paedophile ring operating from a house in Beckenham, about half a mile from Derek's home. It was the talk of the neighbourhood, and they decided to go and cause trouble. I tagged along. We got there, like a bunch of vigilantes sniffing for blood, and started shouting and screaming – "Come out you fuckin' perverts" – and then hurled bricks and stones at the windows. Suddenly a back door opened and I watched, frozen, as Derek hobbled out of the back door with a younger man and dragged himself down the street as fast as he could. I wanted to scream: "There he is, there's the bastard." But I didn't.

That would have meant explaining how I knew him.

I still occasionally see the younger guy hanging around Bromley. I don't know who he is, and I can't say for sure he's a paedophile. He just looks like one.

I never saw Derek again and I convinced myself he must be dead.

But I carry his face in my mind for ever. I've tried to turn it into a grotesque, ugly face but deep down, I know, it wasn't. There was nothing threatening in his face; his eyes were, cruelly, kind and gentle – even though they were covered by magnifying-glass lenses, their heavy black frames cracked and held together by peeling clumps of old sellotape.

I can see his seediness, though. There's no disguising that. I see his grey dirty jacket, his grubby jeans and a straining belt that has two extra holes punched in it to navigate his sagging stomach. I see his nylon shirt, the sort that never needs ironing but does really, and I see a wide, brown tie that's skewed and stained and shorn of decency.

I see the worn out laces in his worn out shoes – one heel higher than the other. I see his scaly skin, the angry blotches of eczema, his yellowing fingers. Then I see the grey: the grey Y-fronts, the grey semen, the grey walls on the outside of his house. I hear his footsteps as he follows me up the stairs, his breath heavy but his voice whispering so the invalid lady downstairs won't hear: "That's it, my little buddy, that door straight ahead. In you go."

When I drift into those images, which sometimes I still do, I realise that I've started rocking, involuntarily, and I can hear my breathing getting disturbed and anxious.

I've never gone back to his house, not even to stand outside. I've never walked down that road, walked up the drive-way, stood outside the door and pressed the buzzer. But I can still hear its ring: the melody you hear when an ice cream van comes down the road. That sounded inviting when I was ten.

If he was still alive today – he could be – and I had the chance to speak to him, I would say: "I forgive you." I have to say that because my faith in God has made me accept it is the only thing to say. Otherwise I'd turn angry and dark and vicious. I don't want that anger and bitterness inside me ever again.

But if I didn't have that faith, then I would say this: "I want you arrested, you bastard."

And I would scream and yell and swear and curse and call him every filthy name under the sun. I wouldn't care if he was in a wheelchair and maybe his son was pushing him down the road. I'd want him to hear my pain and I'd want his family, and the entire world, to know how he destroyed me. "You stole my childhood, you filthy pervert. You stripped my innocence, you stole it and you polluted it."

I'd certainly say all that.

And I would definitely, definitely go to the police and even if he was decrepit and dying and over 100 years old and full of sorrow, I'd drag him through the courts and I'd tell the judge and jury what he'd done to me and I wouldn't stop until he was left to die in a prison cell. That's what I'd do.

If I hadn't found God.

Chapter Forty-Eight

DAD DYING

I STARTED SEEING SLIGHTLY MORE OF GEORGE AS THE years passed. He came back to England once he'd served his prison sentence in Jamaica, and my brothers and sisters would invite him to birthday parties, or have him round for Christmas. We'd be in the same room together, and maybe he'd chat to Louie and April or his other grandchildren – he was always kind to them – but he and I would very rarely talk.

He even came to the McClellan night and I was glad of the chance to show him how far I'd come. I was dressed for the occasion and rubbing shoulders with celebrities. At the end of the evening, the Master of Ceremonies quietened the room and said: "Ladies and gentlemen could you please show your appreciation to Kevin Lueshing for making this incredible night possible." I spotted George staring at me. I'm sure he looked proud.

But he wasn't the same man any more, physically or mentally. My mother had left him; his body was thinner, shrunken and still carried the scars from the shooting in Jamaica. He looked withered and if I felt anything at all for him, it was only pity. He'd had his chances to say sorry in the past and never taken them. Maybe my animosity had waned but I still wanted to keep him at arm's length. I expected nothing from him, and in return he had to expect nothing from me. I couldn't even remember the date of his birthday.

Over the next couple of years, though, my brothers and sisters let me know he'd been for various tests in hospital, and the words 'prostate cancer' were banded around. I heard them, but I paid little attention. Then I got a call from Lorna's grown daughter, Sherise. "Uncle Kevin, grand-dad's not well. He's in Lewisham hospital."

245

"What's wrong with him?" I asked, half-heartedly.

"He's got cancer."

I felt immune, like I didn't even know the man. I was no more sad or concerned than I would have been if it had been a neighbour. I'd get updates, he'd come out of hospital, then he'd be back in, but I never went to see him and I never tried to find out for myself how he was. I'd just be told now and again.

Then I got another call from Sherise. "Uncle Kevin, you really should go and see your dad."

"Why? Is he about to die?"

"Mum says he's got three or four days left."

And I replied: "Don't muck me about. I'll see him if he's genuinely about to go. But I'm not sitting at his bedside for weeks on end holding his hand."

Sherise was shocked by the coldness of my response but added: "He's been asking to see you. He keeps saying , 'Is Kevin coming?'"

The next day I even got a text from him. "Hi, son, are you coming to see me?" Not Kevin, not boy. *Son.*

Reluctantly, I agreed to go. I didn't really want to be exposed to emotions and conversations, although I did wonder whether he might want to say something he should have said years ago.

I felt no sense of rush or panic or distress as I drove to the hospital the next day. Visiting hours finished at 6pm – I got there about 5.15pm. I wouldn't be staying long. I walked into his ward: there was a curtain drawn around his bed. Lorna and Sherise were with him, and also a pastor, which I hadn't expected. My dad wasn't a church goer, but my sister believed.

George didn't see me at first. I noticed how shallow his eyes appeared; they were staring into the distance, haunted and fearful, maybe studying a distant place that was dark and sinister and evil. He looked emaciated, his skin a dirty yellow, his cheeks sunken, his mouth hanging open, no teeth left inside. But my arrival broke his stupor, he turned and his eyes suddenly flicked back on, like he'd just found an oasis in the middle of a desert. He smiled and whispered: "All right, champ?"

"All right, *Dad.*"

He was clearly elated to see me. "You come, you come, I knew you would, I believed it," he said. It was though he had been waiting a long while for this moment. He'd been slowly dying for six months and I was the only one left who hadn't visited.

We said all the usual stuff, small talk, dancing around what needed to be said:

"You OK?"

"As well as can be expected, everyone's fussing too much."

"They looking after you in here?"

"Can't complain – how's the kids?"

"They're all doing fine."

It was a conversation going nowhere, with no substance or meaning and it kept getting interrupted by nurses and staff popping their heads around the curtain. In the end, I turned and said: "Would you mind if I just had a few minutes on my own please with my dad?" Everyone left.

I looked at him, at the father I'd never had, at the man who, when he was full of life, had used his strength and vitality to destroy my childhood. I looked at him now, at his hollow human remains, and heard myself saying: "I forgive you, Dad."

And I added: "You don't have to worry ."

I hadn't rehearsed those words, they just came out and they felt right. Then, in the faintest, barely-audible whisper, he replied: "I'm so sorry, my son. I'm so sorry. I knew it was wrong. You were a good boy and I loved you."

I sat next to him, and could barely believe what I was hearing as he told me how he'd watched me fight Felix Trinidad while he was in prison. "I was so proud of you, son, you so nearly had him. I always knew you had a left hook."

His breathing became heavier and more erratic, like every word was an effort, or maybe his last. I tried to calm him – "It's OK, Dad, don't worry, it's passed" – but he continued:

"I'm sorry I never treated you right. But I loved you, you know."

He then slowly stretched out his hand and opened the top drawer on his bedside cabinet. Inside was the gold ring he'd worn all his life, too big now for his emaciated fingers. "I want you to have this, Kevin," he said, as though it was his dying wish.

"No, I don't want it, I don't need it," I protested.

"Please, son, I want you to have it. I want you to keep it."

I kept saying no, but he found the strength to grab my hand and he thrust the ring on to my palm. "I won't be here much longer, please, take it, it's for you." His hand, in my hand, felt so fragile.

George and Kevin holding hands. Like a father and son. Like it should have been 35 years earlier but now the tables had turned. Now he could go to sleep, or go to wherever he was heading, having felt some compassion and maybe some love within those hands. I'd never felt that when I was a child.

Then he added: "I know I wasn't there for you but I always thought about you.

"I didn't need to beat you like I did, it was wrong, it was cruel, son. I know that. But I always knew there was something in you. You had the determination inside." His voice was trailing, getting weaker, but he kept repeating the words 'wrong' and 'sorry' like he was making his last confession.

I felt proud – and I felt cynical. Proud because he was finally admitting his guilt and praising me for what I had achieved without him. Cynical because he knew his time was up. Shame he never found the courage to be so apologetic and doting when I was younger. Shame he left it until the very end, when it was too late for us to start again, to find a father-and-son bond. *Why didn't you say all this earlier, George? We might have been mates.*

I was there for about 25 minutes. I hadn't known what to expect but when he said the word 'wrong' I realised just how much I'd needed to hear that. 'Wrong' meant that none of the beatings and cruelty and violence had been my fault. He was accepting the blame. 'Wrong' meant more than 'sorry'. Anyone could say 'sorry'.

I mumbled something about needing to get back to see the kids, and he held my hand again. "All right, son. You take care of yourself, you take care of your kids as well. Alright?"

"Yeah, Dad."

"Alright, son, love you. Bye."

As I walked out of the ward I knew I'd never see him alive again.

I got back to my car and drove off, my mind re-living the conversation and trying to decide whether he'd been sincere. I decided that he had genuinely wanted to see me, that seeing all six of his kids had mattered to him on his deathbed. I was the last, I was the hardest to persuade. I was the unfinished business. I was the one most like him.

But I didn't drive away full of new-found love. He was still a man called George. I went home and told Louie that grand-dad was about to die. He just said: "Oh." Like me, he didn't know the man.

George died two days later – Lorna sent me a text at 7am: "Dad's gone, RIP." My brothers later told me they'd emptied a little silver suitcase he always took with him whenever he worked abroad. Inside were badges from all the countries he'd ever visited – and newspaper clippings of my fights.

I went to his funeral in Elmer's End and helped carry the coffin in with my brothers. I was staggered by how many people turned up, including my mum. I never realised he had been so well known. All my brothers and sisters made a speech or read a psalm and I realised I had to do so as well, although I had nothing prepared.

So I stood in front of the congregation and said: "I don't need to tell you about the history between Dad and me but I would like to say that, on his deathbed, we made our peace and I'm glad he's gone knowing that. I'm just sad he didn't stay long enough for us to start again."

I looked at all the faces staring at me, plunged into silence, so many sad people, and I broke down in tears.

As I drove away from the funeral, I put my hand into my jacket pocket and my fingers suddenly latched on to the gold ring he'd insisted I kept. It was heavy and chunky and it reminded me of my childhood; not because he wore it on the hand that constantly beat me but because he would regularly ask me to keep it polished for him.

I kept driving, my eyes on the ring more than the road. Did that ring symbolise anything? Was its circle the beginning and the end of our relationship? It was tarnished – was that important, was it significant? Why had it mattered so much to him that I kept it? Was this just another way of proving to me how sorry he was? How 'wrong' he'd been? If I hadn't accepted it, who else would have got it? It was pretty much the only valuable item he had left in the world. Was he trying to give everything he possessed to me, to prove his sincerity?

It was solid and genuine and it was probably worth something. But how much? And to whom? Did it have a sentimental value that money could never hope to measure? How could you put a value on something that the cruellest man I had ever known gave me on his deathbed?

I knew in flash what I had to do. I carried on driving until I reached Lewisham High Street. I headed for a pawn shop my mate ran and I pawned the bloody thing and used the money to buy a PS3 for my son.

That was how much it was worth.

Chapter Forty-Nine

BELIEF AND FINDING MY SOULMATE

I DIDN'T FIND GOD THE NIGHT MY FATHER BEAT ME RAW but, Lord knows, I prayed. I prayed and prayed that my dad would find a job soon that would take him away from the house for a long, long time.

I didn't find God, either, when I ran from Derek for the last time, although I prayed again that night. I prayed nobody would ever find out what had been happening.

But I did find God the night I was handcuffed, strip-searched and flung into a police cell. I prayed extremely hard that night – only this time my prayer was heard and my life changed for ever.

I have always been intrigued by danger and seediness: I have found the temptation to be somewhere bad irresistible. When I was in New York, and working out ways to deal drugs, I became friendly with a gang of Puerto Ricans who even started calling me 'Champ' and admired the fact I had fought against their hero, Felix Trinidad.

One night I went to one of their apartments above some run-down shops, deep in the Bronx. There was about six of them inside, all smoking weed – and, something I hadn't witnessed before, cleaning guns.

I stood transfixed and terrified in equal measure as they chucked the guns to one another like they were toys, laughing and joking and taking mock aim at one another – even though they were loaded.

I shouldn't have been there but at the same time the adrenalin was pumping and there was a course thrill searing through me. "Don't worry, man, it's only a .22, it's only got half a magazine," they mocked, as they laughed at the look on my face.

I prayed silently to myself at that moment. I'm not sure whether God answered but nobody got shot.

I had no idea then about the concepts of Christianity or forgiveness; I just had vague notions about good and bad. By and large, I was attracted to the bad. I didn't believe in God then, but I did pray a few times, that's for sure. It was usually a last resort, when all hope had gone.

Strangely, I never prayed before a fight, although I often saw other fighters do it. I just didn't believe it would make any difference.

I started to question and look for answers when I met Nigel Benn. He'd done so much wrong in his life he was practically the devil incarnate. But he'd started going to church with his wife and, out of curiosity, I went along with them. We'd drive to a large Pentecostal church in New Cross, where – much to my amazement – I felt instantly at home. Like I belonged.

I was spellbound by the gospel singing, in particular. It left me in goosebumps and I'd eagerly and enthusiastically sing along myself. I felt very comfortable amongst it all, and felt nobody was judging me. I imagined it must have been like going to a meeting of Alcoholics Anonymous. As soon as you walked in, everyone seemed to be equals.

One day, I was walking casually past a much smaller church in Bromley when I suddenly heard a powerful blast of gospel music coming from inside. It was so strong it stopped me in my tracks and I thought: "I've got to go in there."

The building inside was plain, simple but somehow overwhelmingly holy. I sang along for nearly half an hour and went back the following Sunday. I've been going to that church now for the last six years.

I have changed, considerably, as a result. I'm far less angry with the world, I don't swear so much, and I've stopped resenting people.

But it was that night in the police cells that really rooted my Christianity.

I was selling tickets at the time for concerts at the O2: I'd picked up four on eBay and then sold them on to a woman for a nice little profit. But on the night of the concert, I suddenly got a call from her. She was hysterical: the tickets were forged and she'd been refused entry. "Don't worry," I said. "I'll drive over right now and give you your money back. I'm really sorry, I had no idea."

My son was living with me full-time then and I said: "I've just got to drive over to the O2, don't worry, I won't be long." It was his birthday the next morning, when he'd be fifteen.

Off I went, wearing tracksuit bottoms, flip-flops and a jacket over a T-shirt. I quickly spotted the woman outside and gave her the money back straight away. But within seconds I was surrounded by security guards, who accused me of selling fake tickets. They'd already alerted the police; I was arrested there and then, hand-cuffed on the concourse outside the main entrance, and forced to walk in shame to the car park.

I didn't look like The Look; I looked like a tramp.

There were still plenty of people milling around, as well. Some of them recognised me and started shouting: "You alright, champ, what's going on, why you in cuffs, what've you been doing then?"

It was humiliating and one of the lowest points in my life. I felt desperate and broken. I was driven what felt like miles and miles to a police station somewhere in central London and all I could think of was Louie back home, on his own, on the eve of his birthday, probably worrying why on earth I hadn't come back yet.

But my humiliation wasn't over. At the police station I was finger printed and had to pose for one of those mugshots that always make you look like a criminal. A swab was taken from inside my mouth and then I was strip-searched. I started begging for permission to call my son but the police wouldn't let me: they were still thinking about searching my house and didn't want Louie moving anything.

It was utterly crushing and I broke down, in floods of tears. Inconsolable sobs because I felt so utterly ashamed and lost and I couldn't shake off the image of Louie all on his own, wondering where his dad was.

I felt utterly weak, pathetic, vulnerable and helpless; the strip search simply added to my total humiliation. Naked on the outside; naked on the inside.

Just like Stan.

I was given a prison number – I was reduced to that – and put in a cell. It was squalid and ugly inside and I felt like a terrified kid all over again. *What am I going to tell Mum? George will beat me to a pulp when he finds out.* I even scratched my name on the wall: "Kevin was here."

Besides the sheer desperation, there was also a violence inside me that wanted to punch the walls and unleash some aggression. Instead, I slid on to my knees and prayed. It was impulsive; it felt like the only thing left in the world I could do.

I prayed to be forgiven, even though I didn't really know what I'd done wrong. After all, I'd actually returned the money: I wasn't deliberately trying to sell dodgy tickets. But somehow it seemed I was in the cell for all the other stuff I'd got away with over the years. I protested my innocence as I prayed but I also added: "Help me, I'm begging you. Please make sure Louie is safe."

I clambered back on the bench and sat, in silence, waiting. Then, after a couple of hours that felt like an eternity, I heard a noise outside my cell door and a little spyhole suddenly opened up. Next, some fingers poked through and a voice said: "Kevin Lueshing... what on earth are you doing in there, mate? Don't worry, I'll have you out in a minute."

Sure enough, the door opened and in walked a kid I used to hang around with at primary school! I called him 'Ginge' then; he was bald now but I recognised him instantly.

He was now a senior detective with the police but he'd followed my boxing career closely. "I've checked your files, champ," he said. "I can't help thinking you shouldn't be here, especially as you gave the money back."

I was out five minutes later, and even got a lift back to my car, which was still outside the O2 arena.

I knew as I drove home that my prayer had been answered that night. I had reached out and asked for help. Yes, I was desperate, but attending my little church every Sunday had left me with something I'd never had in my life before: belief.

My prayers were answered again soon after when I met the only woman I have ever been faithful to in body and soul; the only woman I have ever *wanted* to marry: Zoe Floyd.

I met Zoe via a dating website. I'd given up on ever finding a soul mate, someone I could truly feel connected with. But it was instantly clear Zoe and I had so much in common. I don't mean superficial stuff like favourite films or music; I mean something far deeper – something that affects you spiritually and emotionally.

We met for the first time on May 23, 2013: I'll always remember this date because I had it tattooed on my wrist. I was ridiculously nervous driving to her home in East Sussex but as soon as I saw her, and spoke to her, I knew she was the one. There was kindness in her voice, she sounded honest, and she looked stunningly beautiful, with soft blue eyes and gorgeous thick, long hair which she'd dyed a striking red colour back then. I liked that a lot; it told me she had confidence.

It felt so easy to be natural with her – I never felt she was judging me as we chatted away. There was no falseness, arrogance or competitiveness. She had a cheeky smile which would light up her face each time I tried to be funny. We sat together in a local pub for a couple of hours and it felt like we'd known each other for ever.

We discovered some incredible coincidences between us. Tragically, she'd lost her first child, Mitchell, who had been born on the same day my April was born. Her mum's name was also Barbara and, incredibly, Zoe was in a bad car accident when she was eleven – the same age I was when I had mine.

It was astonishing to unravel all this but what was even more astonishing was how comfortable I felt alongside her. It was so natural talking to Zoe that, after a couple of months, I told her absolutely everything about me: the abuse, the affairs, everything. It felt like talking to Stella all over again.

Zoe trusted me and she believed in me. I couldn't lie to her, I didn't want to lie to her. I instinctively wanted to grow old with her, even though she made me feel 20 years old all over again.

After eighteen months together, I knew I had to propose, so I started agonising over how to do it and what could make the moment extra special.

Valentine's Day was on the horizon, and I'd noticed Lionel Richie was doing a concert on the night in Vienna. I'm a big fan of the old black and white movie *The Third Man*, so I phoned the amusement park in Vienna where the giant Ferris Wheel in the film still works. It's like an old-fashioned version of the London Eye, except you sit in original tram carriages instead of modern pods. I asked whether I could book an entire carriage purely for myself, and have a table set in the middle with champagne – ideally, just when the sun was starting to go down!

To my delight, they agreed, so I went out and searched for the best possible diamond I could find. It took me a month to find the right stone – graded one below flawless. Even though I was so well prepared, I was still incredibly nervous when we landed in Vienna; Zoe had absolutely no idea what was coming.

We checked into our hotel and then headed straight off to the Ferris Wheel, where there was a huge queue of people. But we were ushered right to the front: our carriage was waiting, with a table and champagne exactly as I'd wanted. We went inside and straight away the wheel started turning, stopping only to let people into the other carriages. Higher and higher it went until it reached the top – and stopped, dead still.

I was nervous and excited, just like I used to be before a fight. I turned away from the stunning view of Vienna outside and stammered: "Zoe."

"What?!"

Suddenly I realised the famous theme tune to *The Third Man* was playing gently through speakers inside the carriage. I dropped on to one knee, said: "Will you marry me?" and showed her the diamond ring, still sparkling in its little box.

My heart felt like it was about to explode as I waited for her response. I started to say, "Zoe, what's your answer?" when she suddenly silenced me.

"Oh my God, Kevin! Yes… yes… I will marry you."

And with those ten words, my faith in marriage was restored. For the first time in my life, I would be married because I – *Kevin Lueshing* – wanted to get married. This time, it would be for the only reason that matters: I loved someone so much I couldn't bear to be without her for the rest of my life.

Maybe my proposal was a bit cheesy but it felt truly romantic. We could see people in the other carriages, clapping, smiling and waving at us and some of them were even taking photographs. Then it was straight off to see Lionel Richie, who played all his biggest, slushiest hits. It was the icing on the cake.

I had prayed to find someone like Zoe, and once again my prayer was answered. But as I've reflected on my life, I've come to realise there were other occasions where just maybe someone was looking after me.

For example: I somehow cheated death when I was labouring on a building site. I was working on a high-rise block, and had to walk along those builders' planks that wrap around the outside of new buildings while they're being built. I was many floors off the ground and turned to go left – but for some inexplicable reason stopped, turned and went off towards the right instead. Seconds later the board I'd been on collapsed and plummeted. I would have died instantly had I still been on it.

When I was badly injured in my mother's car crash, and went flying through the windscreen, I should have been killed on the spot. Instead, I was left with stitches.

I've even thought long and hard about the biggest test of my belief: the night George beat me raw. That night I curled up in bed and prayed furiously: "Please let my dad get offered a job abroad."

God hadn't spared me diabolical pain that night but I never got a beating as ferocious as that from George ever again. Something inside him changed and although he couldn't find love, he found some degree of restraint.

I've even tried to square my religion with Derek and, in particular, what I would do if he was stood in front of me right now. God would expect me to forgive him, I know that, and that's what I would do, otherwise I can't be a Christian. That doesn't mean he shouldn't be punished for what he did: I'd want him to be humiliated, like I was. I'd want him to be imprisoned and to know he'd lost all his power.

But I can still forgive him and be comfortable with that concept.

Chapter Fifty

THE RIGHT TO BE A CHILD

TELLING MY STORY LIKE THIS HAS MADE ME SCRUTINIZE my life, especially what passed for my childhood and how my experiences moulded my character and shaped the human being – and the dad – I've become.

I have to accept the little boy being abused was me. I can no longer delude myself into believing it happened to two characters called Kevin and Stan.

They were me…

I was The Belt Boy.

I risk being judged, but I have reached a point in my life where I never want to hear of another child on this planet suffering what I went through. *That is my motivation for writing this book.*

Sometimes it worries me that I seem to enjoy being with children more than adults. Don't misinterpret this: it is said with innocence, purity and love. It's not a dark side of me I am struggling to suppress because of my history.

It is entirely because I didn't have a childhood myself. I look at children today of all ages – from the very young to moody teenagers – and I see happiness, hope, wonderment, potential, joy, love. And I have come to understand these must never be luxuries, they must be rights. Like breathing air, or being free to live as you please.

Basic, human rights. *The right to be a child.*

After all I endured between the age of ten and fourteen, I have little doubt I should be sprawled under sheets of cardboard under a motorway flyover right now, jacking up, wasted, drinking whatever passes for alcohol. I know of other boys who endured the same hell as me and they've ended up this way.

In the end, boxing saved me and whether God engineered it that way, I'll never know although as I get older I like to think He did. *Belief.*

Boxing triggered within me a talent I was blessed with. That may sound corny and clichéd but it's true, it's how I climbed out of the cesspit. The only place where I felt some sense of sanctuary was in the gym, hitting a punch-bag – or even in the ring, hitting an opponent.

There were many times I wanted to tell my parents about Derek but the fear of George saying "What were you doing in that white man's house?" stopped me in my tracks. Kids should never be so frightened of their parents that they can't tell them they need help, or they're afraid, or something bad might be happening that they don't understand.

Parents must understand this. Parents must keep the communication between themselves and their children open at all times. *If a child can't talk to Mum or Dad, then Mum or Dad are to blame.*

I remember saying to my daughter April when she was old enough to understand: "April, you must never, ever, lie to me because I will die for you. I don't care how bad the problem, I just have to know what it is you've done or what's wrong."

It worked. She's never lied to me to this day.

But with my dad, I was too scared to tell him anything. George would have pulled Derek apart limb by limb – but he would have done the same to me, too.

Sometimes people ask me whether God would have approved of me being a boxer – and even would I allow my son to become a boxer? The answer is yes to both questions.

Boxing is a sport: it is violent, of course, but it's not violence. Boxers are serious, trained, sportsmen who understand there are rules of conduct. We fight inside a ring, not out on the streets; there is a world of difference between the two.

I've already seen Louie box and I can see it's in his blood: I see bits of me in the way he hits the pads: he throws a very hard punch and I can see he has the talent. He also has the anger and the aggression I had – boxing can give him the discipline to control that. He goes to the gym all the time and he knows how to fight. That's what I've taught him.

I still love boxing and I enjoy the coaching sessions I run with local kids. I take them through the basic skills – no other sport requires so much psychological and physical discipline. I still watch fights on TV, and I know most of the current boxers.

I fought in a truly golden period for boxing when every bout seemed to be between household names and millions would stay up late to watch fights on the TV.

The future looks just as exciting now: as I write this, Britain has eleven legitimate world champions at differing weights – all of them proper, recognised belts. Boxing excels when its champions are exciting to watch and fighters like James DeGale, Anthony Joshua and Tyson Fury are genuinely entertaining. Who on earth would have predicted Fury beating Wladimir Klitschko? That was one of the biggest upsets boxing has ever seen and shocks like that are what continue to make the sport such a massive box-office attraction. I feel just as good about where boxing is now as where it was when I was fighting.

I still look after myself physically, too; I carefully watch what I eat and drink and I can still throw a punch.

Yep, I can still bang – you wouldn't want to mix with me in the ring…

AFTERWORD

SOMETIMES I HAVE A DREAM, AND IT HAUNTS ME.

A little boy, ten years old, is in a dark room, possibly a cellar, definitely somewhere black, bleak and wretched.

It's extremely dark in the room but there's something clearly wrong with the child. He has raw, bloody scars across the palms of his hands and he is whimpering: a low-pitched wail of anguish that seems too quiet for the pain he is suffering. The boy is desperate to howl out, to let the world hear his agony – but he is too scared to scream and yell and holler. He doesn't dare let anyone hear the pain he's in, not even his parents.

There's a telephone in the room and in my dream I'm screaming at the boy to pick it up and call for help.

"Pick it up, pick it up," I plead, but of course he can't hear me. I know he's seen the phone, though; I see him looking at it. The problem is, he doesn't know who to call: he trusts nobody anymore – not his family, not his school teachers. Nobody. He is utterly alone and frightened and I keep seeing his frail body trembling.

But *I* know who he should call and I scream a number at him, always the same one: 0808 800 5000.

It is like the combination number to a safe. Dial it and it will open a door to safety, security and salvation. Dial it and the child's pain will start to subside and the wounds heal.

"Trust me," I plead. "I know this number, I know who will answer and I trust them – so you must trust them, too."

But still the boy can't hear and my nightmare slowly begins to fade.

That dream, which still recurs to this day, was one of the reasons I became involved with the National Society for the Prevention of Cruelty to Children; the number in my dream is their helpline.

It is there for every tortured and abused and abandoned child to call when they no longer trust anyone else in the world.

And it is there for anyone who suspects they know a child in desperate need of help.

I was a professional boxer for eight years but the only fight that truly meant anything to me was the one against child cruelty.

I had the initials NSPCC sewn on to my boxing shorts and wore them with pride as I became the British welterweight champion and knocked down one of the world's most famous fighters in a world title bout.

Such was my belief and commitment to this wonderful organisation I even agreed to talk on their behalf to 120 MPs in the Houses of Parliament.

The story you have just read is what I told them.